LEARNING HOW TO LEARN

The Ultimate Learning and Memory Instruction

JERRY LUCAS – DR. MEMORY™

Learning That Lasts™

Lucas Educational Systems, Inc. – Dallas, Texas
www.doctormemory.com

Published by:

LUCAS EDUCATIONAL SYSTEMS, INC.
Post Office Box 794747
Dallas, Texas 75248 U.S.A.

Printed in the United States of America

Library of Congress Card Number: 00-104326
ISBN: 1-930853-02-5

Lucas, Jerry
Learning How to Learn

Dedication

To all people everywhere who have struggled trying to learn.

Acknowledgements

I wish to express my gratitude to all of the people over the years who have helped me. Bill Murray, who has been my right arm for twenty years; Rolland Dingman, Mike Webster, Tony Price and Jon McIntosh who have brought the pictures in my mind to life in so many projects; Robert Wiley, who assisted me in so many ways; and my wife, Cheri, who has always believed in me and with me.

Contents

About the Author

As a boy with a very active mind, NBA legend Jerry Lucas challenged himself by inventing mental games to test his memory. At an early age, Jerry realized that being a successful student in school took knowing not only HOW to learn but also HOW TO RETAIN that learned information. He became determined to develop ways to make the learning process EASY, FUN and LONG-LASTING.

Like a farmer who plants small seeds in the soil and carefully tends them so that they grow, Jerry has devoted his life to cultivating ideas and methods for fun and easy memory-retention methods. The resulting methods are now known as **The Lucas Learning System**™ and have earned him the title of **Doctor Memory**™.

Jerry graduated Phi Beta Kappa from Ohio State University. Not only a scholastic achiever, he excelled as an athlete as well. Jerry became the only basketball player in collegiate history to lead the nation in field goal percentage and rebounding for three years, thus becoming the only three-time recipient of the Big Ten player-of-the-year award. This achievement still has not been duplicated or surpassed. Chosen seven times as an All-Pro during his professional basketball career, Jerry was named one of the 50 most outstanding NBA players of all time. Being inducted into the NBA Hall of Fame in 1979 was perhaps his crowning achievement as an athlete.

Recently, Jerry was chosen as one of the five most outstanding college basketball players of the twentieth century by *Sports Illustrated* in its article entitled "Team of the Ages," which appeared in the November, 1999 College Basketball preview issue.

Although Mr. Lucas initially achieved fame and success by his impressive basketball accomplishments, he continues to score off the court as well. Through the years, Jerry has taught his memory-retention system to millions of people either in seminars or through sales of his books. Not only did he co-author the *New York Times* best-seller *The Memory Book*, he also has entertained countless television viewers with guest appearances on TV talk shows during which he dazzled large numbers of studio audience members by demonstrating his ability to meet and remember all of their names.

In total, Jerry Lucas has authored more than sixty books in the field of memory training and learning systems. **Doctor Memory**™ is now widely known and respected as an expert in developing the many methods that encompass his concept known as **Learning That Lasts**™.

Foreword

Everyone is attracted to what is enjoyable and rewarding in his or her life. The contention and the conclusion I believe you will reach after reading and applying the principles and learning systems taught in this book is that we can and will change one of the most difficult and discouraging dilemmas facing the population today. We can make learning fun and rewarding. We can change young lives and give them hope instead of despair. We can teach students how to face, attack and solve learning problems effectively and efficiently.

Many of us approach every learning problem, even after years of school, by having to use repetition. This boring, rote-type process dulls the senses and defeats the user. Unfortunately, your basic ability to learn and your knowledge of how to learn has not changed much since you entered school. Yes, you have slugged it out with repetition over the years, but you are still using the Stone Age tool of repetition to try to learn. You have a very limited mental toolbox. Fortunately, there are legitimate tools of learning to select for various learning problems, much like an auto mechanic selects the proper tool from his tool box for his various needs. These learning tools enable the user to analyze, attack and solve any learning problem effectively, efficiently and with confidence. Most importantly, the user will experience rewarding, satisfying results as he or she selects the appropriate tool from a complete array of tools in his or her mental toolbox. My goal with this book is to make you a Master Mind Mechanic who knows how to analyze, attack and solve any learning problem, not with the Stone Age tool of repetition, but with sophisticated, modern, high-tech learning tools. It is time for a change, a much needed, refreshing and life-changing transformation. It is time for you to acquire a full set of tools for your mental toolbox by using the learning methods available with The Lucas Learning System™. I am excited and overjoyed to reveal in this book what I have worked on and developed over my lifetime. I have a drive to create learning tools and systems for educational needs. The Lucas Learning System™ will profoundly change the way we learn forever.

CHAPTER 1

Introduction

When a child enters school the child is often very excited and full of anticipation for this new "learning" experience. However, far too quickly students begin to make comments like, "I don't like this," or "This is no fun." Unfortunately, a young mind full of unlimited imagination and potential begins to turn off and tune out. Worst of all, students spend a disproportionate amount of their time agonizing over the rote memorization of facts and figures. Learning **How to Learn**, even though that is the proposed reason for going to school in the first place, is not the focus of their studies. Since a student is not taught **How to Learn**, the student often has to rely on boring repetition to try to remember the necessary information to pass tests and become educated.

It doesn't have to be that way – **Learning really can be fun**. Learning and laughing at the same time, or even laughing during the process of learning are not unnatural. It will happen more often in schools, homes, churches and places of business when the systems taught in this book are applied.

There are only three steps in the educational process. They are:

1)   Getting information.

2)   Learning the information.

3)   Using the learned information.

Unfortunately, there is a great chasm or abyss in our present day educational system between steps 1 and 3. **Getting information** is no problem. It is given to us through textbooks, other printed material and the Internet. **Learning the information**, if we are not taught how to learn, becomes the boring, repetitive, non-productive process that we have become all too familiar with. The rote process may enable us to remember the information long enough to pass a test, but it leaves our minds in short order, and we can't really **use the information**, because it hasn't really been learned. Unfortunately, students try to learn and relearn and relearn the same information because no real learning has taken place. Not only do they forget most of it shortly after taking a test, but they graduate from high school, having forgotten or lost most of it. Students

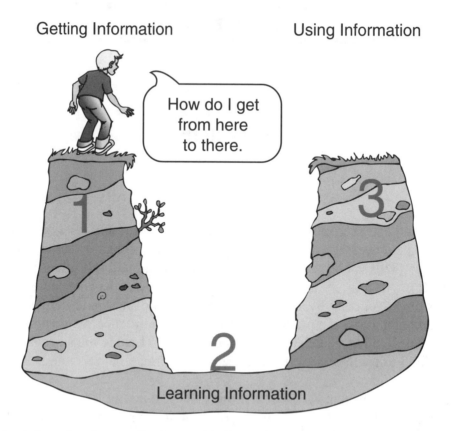

keep falling back into the chasm of unlearned information as shown in the above drawing. After a period of time and repeated failures, many of them simply give up and mentally drop out. When that happens the results are often disastrous. Our prisons and welfare rolls are testaments to our failure in this area. If they don't give up but keep fighting this uphill battle, they take this inability to learn into their adult life and job. Industry then spends billions of dollars trying to teach what was already covered in school. Unfortunately, when the same repetitive processes are continued in industry, the results with the adult students continue to be less than satisfactory.

Everyone is attracted to what is enjoyable and rewarding in his or her life. It is my contention, and the conclusion I believe you will reach after reading and applying the principles and learning systems taught in this book, that we can and will change one of the most difficult and discouraging dilemmas facing America today. We can make learning fun and rewarding. We can change young lives and give them hope instead of despair. We can teach students how to face, attack and solve learning problems more effectively and efficiently than in the past.

If you have a mechanical problem with your automobile, you need to take it to a qualified mechanic who possesses the knowledge and has the proper tools with which to find and repair problems in your car. One problem may require a simple tool like a screwdriver or a wrench. Other problems may require much more sophisticated and perhaps even electronic tools. The correct tool or tools are selected from his toolbox to solve or repair each problem. You will feel much more at ease if you can find a **master mechanic**, because he certainly will not only have the tools for the job, but he will possess extraordinary skill with which to use them.

In education, there are varieties of learning problems that need solving or fixing like mechanical problems in a car. They include learning how to read and write, how to spell, grammar and punctuation rules, English and foreign vocabulary, definitions, formulas, the periodic table in chemistry, lists, numbers, muscle location, graphs, speeches, magazines or manuals and much more. Of course, the list goes on and on. Which learning tool did you use to learn definitions? Which learning tool did you use to learn formulas? Which learning tool did you use to learn vocabulary? The **tool** used for every learning problem is **a Stone Age tool** at best. It is **repetition**. If we were **auto mechanics** we would be out of business if we had only Stone Age tools, because we wouldn't possess the up-to-date tools to correct problems, being able to compete with more qualified mechanics, especially **Master Mechanics**. We approach every learning problem even after years of school by having to use repetition. This boring, rote-type process dulls the senses and defeats the user. Unfortunately, your basic ability to learn and your knowledge of how to learn has not changed much since you entered school. Yes, you have slugged it out with repetition over the years, but you are still using the Stone Age tool of repetition to try to learn. You have a very limited **mental toolbox**. Fortunately, there are **legitimate tools of learning** to select for various learning problems much like an auto mechanic selects the proper tool from his tool box for his various needs. These **learning tools** enable the user to analyze, attack and solve any learning problem effectively, efficiently and with confidence. Most importantly, the user will experience rewarding, satisfying results as he or she selects the appropriate tool from a complete array of tools in his or her **mental toolbox**. My goal with this book is to make you a **Master Mind Mechanic** who knows how to analyze, attack and solve any learning problem, not with the **Stone Age tool of repetition** but with **sophisticated, modern, high-tech learning tools**. It is time for a change, a much needed, refreshing and life-changing transformation. It is time for you to acquire a full set of tools for your **mental toolbox**.

In reality, we are still in the Stone Age as far as learning is concerned. So many incredible advances have occurred in aviation, electronics and many other areas, but we still attempt to learn with repetition. Yes, we do have better repetition equipment like computers, but they still haven't changed the basic problem. It is time to **get out of the Stone Age** as far as learning is concerned, and move into **high tech, up-to-date learning** methods available with **The Lucas Learning System**™.

I admire America's teachers. They are interested in the youth of America, wield considerable influence on their lives, and most of them are highly dedicated, underpaid in my opinion, and do the best job possible under the circumstances. However, they cannot teach what they have not been taught. Teachers, like the rest of us, were not taught learning systems when they were in school. They had to use the Stone Age tool of repetition to pass tests like everyone else. A teacher cannot teach what he or she has not been taught. Teachers are more or less reduced to the roles of drill sergeants making comments like, "Just go over it or say it repeatedly until you know it." Such attempted learning is no fun and becomes stressful for the teacher, the student and the parent who tries to help. This process develops a lack of confidence, a lack of self-esteem and causes people to grow into adulthood making statements like, "I can't seem to remember anything," or "I have a terrible memory." People do not have bad memories, just untrained ones. I am excited and overjoyed to reveal in this book what I have worked on and developed over my lifetime. I have a drive to create learning tools and systems for educational needs. **The Lucas**

Learning System™ will profoundly change the way we learn forever.

This book will teach you in-depth general applications that go way beyond what was taught in *The Memory Book* that can be used for everyday learning problems in your social or business life. It will also teach students how to use tools to solve their learning problems. In addition, it will present examples of full curricula that I have written to show you how to solve various learning problems in the future.

I developed specific aids for my children, so they would enjoy the learning process at an early age. I began to teach these methods to them at the earliest possible age, so they could attack and solve learning problems by themselves. I taught them my sophisticated learning systems only when they needed them. For instance, there was no need for them to learn a system for location problems until they needed to locate and name muscles in anatomy or countries in geography, for example.

How It All Began for Me

As a boy, I had a very active mind like most children, but the release of my mental energies began to be a slight bit different than most people. I began to invent mental games to keep me occupied when I was bored, especially during long automobile trips. On one particular long vacation trip with nothing to do, I saw a word on a billboard and got an idea. I wondered what the word would look like if I mentally rearranged the letters in the word and put them in alphabetical order. Therefore, with my little grade school mind, I mentally began to rearrange the letters in alphabetical order. I did it, then saw another word on a billboard and rearranged the letters alphabetically in that word as well. I continued with this process using other words that I saw the rest of the trip. It was something to do to relieve boredom. Some words were too long and complicated for me to attempt at first, but I was hooked after that day. I continued to do it every day of my life without anyone knowing it. Neither my parents nor my brother knew I was doing it. It was something to do to relieve boredom. That mental game lead to many others in time. Suffice it to say my mind was always active with some mental game or activity. My mind was very active and looking for activity to keep it occupied.

I began to realize that memory and learning were becoming more and more important to me as a student in grade school. I also began to realize that I was not being taught **How to Learn**. My teachers were not saying things like, "Here is what you have to learn for your next test and here is how to learn it." They were saying things like, "Here is what you have to learn for your next test. The test will be on Friday." No further help was forthcoming except maybe some repetitive drills in class. Learning the material became my responsibility. What did that mean? Repetition - repetition - repetition. I didn't like it and neither did my classmates, but what could we possibly do? I didn't know, but I was not happy with what I needed to do to pass my tests. I was doing well on tests because I was diligent, but eventually I said to myself, "There has to be an easier, more fun and long lasting way of learning than repetition." So began one of the great adventures of my life.

I was determined to think of ways to make the learning process easy, fun and long lasting. That meant experimentation through trial and error. Now my active mind had a real adventure to explore, a real challenge. That simple beginning, that small seed has grown into **The Lucas**

Learning System™.

At first, since I was so good at alphabetical spelling, I began to put the first letters of words in lists in alphabetical order. I was able to remember the alphabetical list, and this memory aid helped lead me to the actual list, because the alphabetized letters triggered the information in the list. I did not realize until years later that I was using a very basic **anagram** device. An **anagram** learning device is a word or phrase developed by rearranging the beginning letters of a word, phrase or list. I will discuss this technique in detail later, but as a young boy I began to use that idea without realizing what it was. Since this concept was limited in its application, I began to experiment with other ideas, be involved in trial and error and eventually began to research memory training. Through the years, **The Lucas Learning System**™ began to take form and become reality. Several people have taught general applications using memory aids of one kind or another which have been helpful, but I believe my contribution not only solves learning problems but also specific educational needs. I have written several detailed curricula for education which you will learn about during your study of the systems taught in this book.

I am going to take you back to the place where all of the trouble really began — when you first entered school. You had no real learning problems before then, because your parents, your first and best teachers to date, were using the best method of learning — your photographic mind. Like I stated before, you were instructed to **see**, **recognize**, **register** and **retrieve** pictures as has already been discussed. You also had a great imagination as a child. You invented playmates and situations to keep your mind and your time occupied. As children, we get bored very easily and develop all kinds of make-believe situations to stay active and occupied. School, unfortunately, dulls that great imagination. We don't like what we have to do and subconsciously turn off our imaginations and similar skills while trying to find something more enjoyable and fascinating to tune into. Unfortunately, this leads to far too much television, video games and passive instead of active involvement. What differed in my development was that I didn't turn off the imagination. I turned up the imaginative and creative juices even more by trying to develop tools of learning. As a result, Dr. Richard Watson, a good friend of mine who has tested some of my learning curriculum, has said to me, "Jerry, you're different from the rest of us teachers because you think like a child." I consider that to be one of the greatest compliments I have ever received, and he meant it that way. You need to start thinking once again as you did when you were a child. I will teach you how to stoke the childish fires of your imagination and how to have the wide-eyed anticipation you once had toward learning before school altered it.

A Beginning for You

There are several points I want to discuss and have you understand before actually beginning to teach you. It is vitally important that you understand the principles behind **The Lucas Learning System**™ before any instruction starts.

The very best way to begin is with a test. Isn't that wonderful? I will be able to predict how you will do on this short test. All I want you to do is put a check mark on the yes line if you feel you can answer the following questions, or place a check on the no line if you cannot answer the question. Here they are:

1) _____ Yes _____ No   Can you describe what a giraffe looks like?

2) _____ Yes _____ No   Can you name 12 of the 23 uses of a hyphen in grammar and punctuation? You might be thinking, "I had no idea there were 23 uses of a hyphen." I find that even English teachers make that comment.

3 _____ Yes _____ No   Can you list the furniture in your living room in order from left to right around the room without being in the room?

4) _____ Yes _____ No   Can you name 30 of the 48 rules of capitalization from grammar and punctuation? You might be thinking the same kind of thoughts you did when I asked you about the uses of a hyphen, "I had no idea there were 48 rules of capitalization." In my research when writing curriculum for grammar and punctuation, I found that many rules are grouped together instead of separated for clarity and better understanding.

5) _____ Yes _____ No   Can you name the basic parts of the outside of an automobile from front to back? This does not mean that you would have to name any working parts in the engine or drive chain.

6) _____ Yes _____ No   Can you write the formula for the quadratic equation?

7) _____ Yes _____ No   Can you describe the appearances of most of the houses on the street where you live?

8) _____ Yes _____ No   Can you list the rules for using an apostrophe?

9) _____ Yes _____ No   Can you describe the contents and location of the items in your chest of drawers?

10) _____ Yes _____ No   Can you name elements number 10, 30, 9, 41, 16 and 5 from the periodic table in chemistry?

I would say that you answered a yes to questions 1, 3, 5, 7 and 9. Why am I so sure? Because those were all items that you have seen with your eyes in a tangible manner. They are not intangibles that conjure up no picture in your mind. To understand the importance of that last statement, I must talk about the learning process of a young child.

When a child reaches the age when he or she is able to communicate with his or her parents, the first learning experiences begin. Parents are normally very eager to begin teaching their children and, in fact, become the first and best teachers the child ever has. You will understand why I believe parents are the best teachers a child ever has as this discussion continues. A parent begins to teach a child the only normal and natural way they can. Since the child can't read and doesn't know numbers, printed material certainly can't be used. All a parent can do is point to and identify tangible objects in the home and environment. In this process, the following is typical. A parent will point to an object, perhaps a chair and say, "This is a chair. Look at it. This is a chair. Say chair." The child then looks at the chair, says what it is and the parent rewards the child with a hug, smile or similar pleasantry. The child may not actually learn what a chair is with this initial exposure, but after a few other exposures and similar incidents the child will learn what a chair is. How does this learning take place? The following sequence explains what actually happens. The child **sees** the chair, **recognizes** what it is and **registers** a picture of it in his or her mind. A miracle has just occurred, but the greatest miracle is yet to happen. What is really exciting is that the next time and every time that child ever thinks of a chair again, a picture of a chair automatically appears in the child's mind. The child **retrieves** a mental picture of a chair effortlessly and automatically. The knowledge of a chair locks forever in that child's mind. It can never be lost or forgotten for the rest of the child's life. The information has become **knowledge**, which is **the goal of all education**. This is the first and most important miracle of learning. It will be repeated thousands and thousands of times during that child's life.

I want to lead you through a typical sequential learning experience in the life of a child and its parent or parents. A parent will typically do the following when beginning to teach a child to recognize animals, for instance. The parent could point to a picture of a cow and say something like this, "This animal is called a cow. Look at this picture. This is a cow. This animal has four legs. Do you see the four legs? We get milk from cows. Do you see this? This is where milk comes out of a cow. It is called an udder. Say cow. Look at this picture again and say cow again. What is this animal called? Cow, that is correct. Look at the picture and say cow one more time." This procedure will continue until the child learns what a cow is. What happens during this process? Once again the child must **see** the cow and **recognize** the cow, so he or she can **register** a picture of a cow in his or her mind. Once the picture registers in the mind, the child can **retrieve** a mental picture of a cow by just thinking of it, because now the child knows what it looks like. Another miracle has taken place. The cow has become **knowledge** that the child can use. The bold words are **see**, **recognize**, **register**, **retrieve** and **knowledge**. We will discuss these five in detail throughout this book.

In the next learning session, the teaching might continue like this. The parent might say, "Look at this picture again. You will remember that this is a cow, and we get milk from a cow." Let's assume that the parent then shows the child a picture of a horse. I think we would agree that the child would call a horse a cow if asked to identify the animal without any explanation, because the child has never seen a horse before. The only animal the child knows is a cow. It is the only animal the child has **seen**. The parent could then point to the picture of the horse and say something like this, "This animal is called a horse. Look at this picture. This is not a cow but it is a horse. This animal also has four legs like a cow, but it is different from a cow, as I will **show** you. We don't get milk from a horse. There is no udder to give milk like the cow has. I also want you to see that a horse has a longer neck and a different shaped head and tail. People ride on horses to get from one place to another. They were used to get from one place to another before we had cars. Say horse. Look at this picture again and say horse again. What is this animal called? Horse, that is correct. Look at the picture and say horse one more time." The parent will probably point to each animal one at a time and ask the child to identify it. When the parent is assured that the child has recognized the difference between a cow and a horse, the lesson will probably end. Once again the child must **see** the horse and **recognize** it, so he or she can **register** a picture of a horse in his or her mind. Once the picture registers in the mind, the child can **retrieve** a mental picture of a horse by just thinking of it, because now the child knows what it looks like. Another miracle has taken place. The horse has now become **additional knowledge** that the child can use. Now the child knows the difference between a cow and a horse, because he or she has **seen** the difference and **registered** the differences in his or her mind.

I want to go through another potential lesson in this series. I will assume that the parent will teach the child what a giraffe is next. The parent would point to a picture of the giraffe. If the parent asked the child what the animal was, he or she would most likely say a horse, of course, because it looks like that animal he or she has already learned. At that time, the mental retrieval storage mechanism, the mind, only has two animals stored in it to call upon to compare with the giraffe. The parent would probably say, "This animal is called a giraffe. It is not a horse. Look at this picture, and I will **show** you the differences. This animal also has four legs like a cow and a horse, but it is different from both of them, as you will **see**. We don't get milk from a horse or a giraffe, only from a cow. There is no udder to give milk like the cow has. I also want you to see that a giraffe has a much longer neck and a different shaped head and tail." The parent would probably point out other differences that the child could **see**. The parent then might say, "Look at this picture again and say giraffe. What is this animal called? A giraffe, that is correct. Look at the picture and say giraffe one more time." The parent will probably point to each animal one at a time and ask the child to identify it. When the parent is assured that the child has recognized the differences between a cow, a horse and a giraffe, this lesson may end. Once again the child must **see** the giraffe and **recognize** it, so he or she can **register** a picture of a giraffe in his or her mind. Once the picture registers in the mind, the child can **retrieve** a mental picture of a giraffe by just thinking of it, because now the child knows what it looks like. Another miracle has taken place. The giraffe has now become **additional knowledge** that the child can use. Now the child knows the difference between a cow, a horse and a giraffe, because he or she has **seen** the differences and **registered** the differences in his or her mind. The mental retrieval storage mechanism has added another picture to **retrieve** at any time. The **knowledge** that the child possesses has grown by one more picturable item. There is no limit to the amount of information that can be registered in the mind with pictures. Each tangible item is different from other tangible items, and each item has this identity when thought about. It should be very comforting to realize that there is no limit to the amount of information that can be registered in the mind using your **photographic mind**. The only limit is the amount of time you are willing to spend developing and inputting information. You will be very excited when you learn how easy it is to learn when using your **photographic mind** for all intangible information.

What does this mean? It means that God has blessed us with the ability to see pictures in our minds, and it is the only way for us to learn as children. As children, we learn by the already mentioned procedure. We **see**, **recognize**, **register** and **retrieve** information that becomes usable **knowledge** by **storing pictures in our mind**. We all have what I call a **photographic mind**.

Notice that I didn't say a photographic memory but a photographic mind. My definition of a **photographic mind** is simply the innate ability that we all possess to store and retrieve pictures of tangible items we have seen, recognized and registered in our minds. We actually possess an **automatic photographic mind**, because the retrieval mechanism works automatically. Once a tangible item has been learned, a picture of that item automatically appears on the **mental screen** in our mind when we think of it. Even blind people see pictures in their minds. My first blind student had been blind from birth, and I told him that I didn't think my systems would help him, because **The Lucas Learning System**™ was dependent on our innate ability to see pictures in our minds. His reply was, "I don't have any problem seeing pictures in my mind. When I think of an elephant, I may not see exactly the same thing in my mind as you do, but I know what an elephant looks like from having one described to me and having felt a statue of an elephant. I have no difficulty seeing pictures and distinguishing one thing from another in my mind." I was pleasantly surprised, and he turned out to be an exceptional student.

Your photographic mind will enable you to learn faster and better than you ever dreamed possible. This is the only way to learn as a child, and it is, and always will be, the best way of learning anything. That is why our parents are our best teachers, in my opinion, because they teach us by using our very best learning gift. In addition, what they teach us in this photographic style is never lost or forgotten. It becomes **knowledge** that we can use throughout our lifetime. I will teach you how to use your photographic mind in all learning problems. Be encouraged; you have far more ability to learn than you ever imagined.

I haven't yet discussed the definition of a photographic memory. The two words define themselves. They mean to photograph and remember. Someone with a pure photographic memory would have the ability to photograph and remember everything the eyes saw. For instance, that person could look at page after page of printed material, photograph the information on the pages on his or her mind, and be able to retrieve that information by reproducing it on the mental screen in his or her mind. I don't believe anyone has that ability. I know I don't, but I am closer and closer to having that ability by learning how to use my photographic mind. Now it's your turn.

Getting Started

Before teaching you the **tools of learning**, this warrants some further explanatory discussion. Observation is very important in learning. The dictionary defines observation as the act of noting, perceiving or seeing. It is my contention that there is much more to true observation than this dictionary definition. I think information must register in the mind before it is truly observed. Let me prove it by taking you through a few of the observation drills that I use in my seminars.

You may be wearing a watch. If so, don't look at it until after I ask you a question and ask you to look at it. Since you own the watch, you have seen it hundreds or even thousands of times. Try to answer this question about the number six on your watch without looking at it. Do you think the number six on your watch is a Roman numeral or the regular Arabic number six that we use in our number system? Please don't cop out and say, "I'm not really sure." If you aren't sure, guess. After you have decided which of the two you believe the number six to be, look at your watch to see if you were correct. Typically, about 20% of you will have missed. The people who miss realize for the first time that they don't even have a number six on their watch but just a dot, dash or some type of mark in the place where the number six would be. You may have been one of them. Certainly, the people who miss knowing this have seen their watches many times, but true observation didn't occur, because they didn't remember. **The information didn't register on their minds**.

I also ask people in my seminars to try to remember who is pictured on the five, ten and twenty dollar bills. When I ask the audience to respond in unison by calling out the last names of the men pictured on those bills, the names that are called out are amazing. However, I do ask everyone to participate in the drill by calling out a name even if they aren't sure. I ask them to at least guess "Smith" if no other name comes to mind. You may not know whose picture is on these three bills. Certainly, the people in my seminars have seen a myriad of these bills before, but many cannot remember because the information didn't register on their minds. The excuse is normally, "I haven't seen enough money to be sure. I guess I need to see a lot more." A greedy excuse at best.

Let me ask you about a phone dial as I do the students in my seminars. Please don't look at a phone dial if one is near you. I want you to try to remember which letters are on the number one on a phone dial. In my seminars, I ask for a show of hands of the people who think the letters A, B and C are on the number one, and about two-thirds of the hands go up. Do you agree with them? If you do, you and they are wrong, because there are no letters on the number one of a phone dial. The letters begin on the number two. There are also no letters on the zero, and two letters are missing. Do you know which ones? Most people can't answer these questions even though they see and use a phone almost daily. True observation doesn't really take place, and the information isn't remembered. Are you beginning to agree that there is more to observation than the act of noting, perceiving or seeing?

One more observation should suffice to drive home my point. In a moment, I want you to read the few large bold words at the bottom of this page. Here are my instructions before doing that. When you read the large, bold words, don't speed read them and don't drag through them slowly. Just read them at a normal rate of speed to yourself. Don't read them out loud. Then after you read the words only once, I want you to turn back to this spot and continue reading. Do it now. How many of the word "the" did you read? Almost 100% of the people in my seminars answer one "the," but they are wrong. I would imagine that you had the same answer.

PARIS
IN THE
THE
SPRING

Now look at the words again, and you will notice that there are actually two "the's" among those few words. What happened? Yes, you saw both "the's" with your eyes, because you looked at the words, but one of them didn't register in your mind. True observation didn't take place. To learn, information must register in your mind. You already possess the necessary talent to have that happen. Your photographic mind will allow you to accomplish that task, but you need the proper **learning tools** to be able to become a **Master Mind Mechanic**.

You became an **Apprentice Mind Mechanic** when you began to read this book. When you are finished learning the systems in this book and finished learning how to use the tools developed by those systems, you will become a **Master Mind Mechanic**. That is my goal for you, and it should be your goal for yourself as well. A **master** always needs to teach an **apprentice** how to apply his trade. Therefore, you will get many practice opportunities throughout this book, and I will make many application suggestions to improve your skills.

What Is Learning

Before discussing the learning tools, I want to spend a little time discussing the actual process of learning. Learning is simply the process of connecting items of information together. Most learning requires the connection of **one** piece of information to **one** other piece of information such as a state to its capital, a product to its price, a name to a face, a word to its definition, a number in the periodic table to the element at that number, or an English word to its foreign equivalent when learning languages. I call this **One-On-One Learning**. I played basketball for many years at all levels of competition and played the well known **One-On-One** game countless times when practicing. That simply means **that one player plays against one other player**, and the most accomplished player wins the game. It would be far more difficult for a player to win if he or she had to play **Two-On-One**, **Three-On-One**, **Four-On-One** or even **Five-On-One**. When I was young, I used to be the One in Two-On-One and even Three-On-One games. I felt I would have to work harder and improve faster if I had to play against two or even three players at a time. You will face similar kinds of what seems like overwhelming odds in certain learning situations, but be of good cheer. You can win in seemingly highly disadvantageous learning situations that require a Five-On-One or perhaps even a Twenty-On-One disadvantage. Imagine trying to learn a magazine. The various pages would present many seemingly difficult situations. One page might have four pictures, three or four stories and ten or fifteen detailed facts or pieces of information on it. On various pages, you may face a Seventeen-On-One or a Twenty-On-One situation. You would also have to keep all of the pages from becoming confused with one another. It seems and sounds hopeless, especially when there may be 100 pages in the magazine. You certainly may not believe me at this point, but you can solve even these complex learning problems with **The Lucas Learning System™**.

My goal is to make you a fully qualified **Master Mind Mechanic**. I was an All-American and All-Pro basketball player, but I am also an All-Pro **Master Mind Mechanic**. I became an All-American and All-Pro, because I was able to apply the tools of my trade. I was able to run, jump, shoot, rebound and apply the other physical tools required to perform with excellence. You cannot be an All-American or All-Pro **Master Mind Mechanic** without the proper **mental tools of the trade**.

I always ask a couple of questions in my seminars before beginning my instruction. First I ask, "Let's suppose I called out 30 or 40 items one at a time fairly quickly and you didn't write them down. How many of you think you could repeat that list of items backwards in order without leaving any of them out?" Instead of seeing a show of hands, I began to hear giggles and negative comments about a lack of ability. I respond by saying, "You all seem to have the same disease. I have come to call it the 'I can't' disease. All of you will be doing that very soon. I want you to know that I have a lot more confidence in every one of you than you have in yourselves. I know you can do it easily. It's not that you cannot do it. You have simply not been taught how to do it." Next I say, "What if I gave each of you a 100 page magazine and gave you six hours to learn the basics from every page. I would come back in six hours and ask questions like these. Tell me what is on page 47. Tell me what is on page 22. Fully describe page 76 to me. There is an ad for a Cadillac automobile in the magazine. Tell me on which page it appears. Now tell me the license plate number of the car. Now tell me the 800 number to call for information." The laughter and doubt displayed at this point is overwhelming. I respond by saying, "Now I know the kind of disease you have. I call it the 'I know I can't disease.' Believe it or not, I could teach every one of you how to do that." The laughter continues, because everybody truly believes it is beyond his or her capabilities. You probably believe the same thing at this point, but I want you to know that I also have a lot more confidence in your ability than you do. You are getting ready to embark on one of the great adventures of your life. Before you know it, you will be accomplishing what may have caused you to laugh in disbelief throughout your life. Enjoy the ride.

CHAPTER 2

The Tools of Learning

There are **eight basic tools of learning**. Some of them have adaptations or variations that the **Master Mind Mechanic** must understand and have at his disposal in his **mental toolbox**. He must also know which tool or tools to select for which problem or problems. First, I just want to list the various tools with a brief explanation for their use to acquaint you with them. Most likely, you have never heard of them though you have been asked to learn throughout your whole life. I have taught conventions of hundreds of Ph.D.'s who do not know anything about these tools either. They passed their tests and obtained their degrees using repetition like everyone else. Your **mental toolbox** will start to be filled with these tools shortly.

The eight systems or tools of learning are:

1) **The Link System** - This tool is used to remember information in order. It has a few variations or adaptations. They are:

    A) **The Pure Link System** - This tool connects the items in a list to one another like the links in a chain to remember them in order.

    B) **The Associate Link System** - This tool connects or associates information to something else that you are familiar with. This adaptation to the **Pure Link System** can be used to remember very simple or very complex information in order or in any arrangement you may require. There are many, many possibilities for using this tool.

    C) **The Directional Link System** - This tool is used to connect information in a predetermined direction. The pre-planned direction determines the order in which the information is learned. This adaptation is especially helpful with maps and other visual information.

    D) **Sub Link** - This isn't really a separate tool, but I am listing it separately to emphasize it. A **Sub Link** is simply a **Pure Link** that is used within another **Pure Link** or within another tool to allow you to learn more detail at a particular point in the overall information you are learning.

2)   **The Anagram System** - The dictionary defines an anagram as a word or phrase formed by rearranging the letters of another word, phrase or list of information. You will learn several applications of this most useful tool. One of them is called the **Directional Anagram**.

3)   **The Sound-Alike Word System** - This tool is used to make intangible words tangible, so they can be pictured. Most of what we are asked to learn is in word form, so this is an indispensable tool. I have already briefly discussed this tool.

4)   **The Consonant Number System** - This tool is used to make numbers tangible. When words and numbers are tangible, the major task of learning is made easier. This tool is very important, because it is the basic building block of several other tools. This system also has a few variations or adaptations. They are:

A)   **The One Sound Method** - I can't tell you any more about this until you learn **The Consonant Number System** other than to say it is one way to picture and remember numbers.

B)   **The One Word Method** - It only makes sense that I can't tell you any more about this method either until you learn **The Consonant Number System** other than to say it is another way to picture and remember numbers.

C)   **The Combination Method** - This tool is an application that combines the   principles of "A" and "B" above. I can't tell you any more about this method either until you learn **The Consonant Number System** other than to say it is yet another way to picture and remember numbers.

D)   **The Adjective Peg Word Method** - This application will be taught when I teach you how to learn long digit numbers. It obviously has to do with the application of adjectives along with numbers. I can't tell you any more about this method either until you learn **The Consonant Number System** other than to say it is yet another way to picture and remember numbers.

5)   **The Peg Word System** - This tool is used primarily to remember information in and out of order by number. It is based on the principles taught in **The Consonant Number System**.

6)   **The 200 Word Locator** - This tool is used primarily to remember specific location problems such as locating and naming a muscle in anatomy or a city, country or river on a map. It is also based on the principles taught in **The Consonant Number System**.

7)   **The Look-Alike System** - This tool is used to make symbols in math, chemistry, the

appearance of rocks in geology and many more items tangible.

8) **The Substitute System** - This tool substitutes or changes one item or thing for another item or thing so it can be pictured. A specific and specialized pattern is normally developed for this application.

    As an **Apprentice Mind Mechanic**, you must learn how to use these tools efficiently and effectively. The basic purpose of all of these tools is to make the intangible tangible so it can be seen and easily registered in the mind. It is very important for you to know which tool to use to solve the particular learning problem facing you. You will be taught how to analyze, attack and solve a learning problem like a highly trained automobile mechanic does with a mechanical problem. Some tools are very simple; others are more complex because the information to be learned is more complex. I discussed that when mentioning the One-On-One and other challenges. These tools work well whether you need to learn a short shopping list, a list of dates in history, foreign languages, the periodic table or complex business procedures. A **Master Mind Mechanic** can solve any learning problem. When you learn how to use all of these tools, you will have a full complement of tools in your **mental toolbox**, and you will be able to solve any learning problem quickly and confidently.

    A Master Mind Mechanic should also be an ODD person. I became a very **ODD** person. What do I mean by that? That means that I was very Organized, Disciplined and Diligent. The three letters in the word **ODD** stand for Organized, Disciplined and Diligent. I will talk about organization, discipline and diligence throughout this book. A student, for instance, should return to his or her residence after a lecture and briefly organize lecture notes and class instruction to determine what needs to be learned. As a college student I was **organized** and **disciplined** because, being an athlete in a major sport, I didn't have as much time as other students had. I was also **diligent** to review the learning aids I had developed. I always arranged for interviews with my professors to learn how they conducted their classes. I asked if they tested from lectures or the text. If he or she said, "I test from my lectures only," I wouldn't even buy a textbook. I simply made sure I attended every class, took good notes and **organize**d my notes on a regular basis. Therefore I was a straight "A" student my freshman year at Ohio State. You will learn later how I did this as you learn the application of my systems. The important thing for me was to be **disciplined** to do a little each day so I wouldn't get behind and have to stay up long hours when mid-term and final tests were given. I was also **diligent** to review on weekends. A businessperson must do the same thing. Lost notes, memos or correspondence not only can be embarrassing, but can lead to business failure. I'm not talking about something that requires hours of application on a daily basis. I'm just talking about a little here and a little there on a regular basis. On a regular basis is the most important point. Don't let things pile up so you get way behind and find yourself caught in the trap of not enough time. Learn to be an **ODD** person.

Making Memory Aids More Memorable

    It is a well known fact that unusual or out-of-the-ordinary things are easier to remember than normal or run-of-the-mill things, so to make memory aids more memorable the pictures created should be unusual, out of the ordinary or, in some cases, just plain silly or ridiculous.

How many times have you said or heard someone say, "Oh, yeah, that reminds me"? What happened in that situation? Something that was seen or heard jogged the memory and reminded you of something else. That is actually what learning is all about. When connecting the pieces of information, one of the pieces will remind you of the other and vice versa. The problem in learning without systems is that these connections take place subconsciously, and the person doesn't really know what is happening. The person doesn't really control the connection since repetition is used. They may think they know the information, but no conscious, purposeful connection was made, and the information can't easily be recalled. There is no tangible mental image to return to. The information just seems to float away into space, never to be retrieved again. By consciously controlling this connection process and knowingly developing it, the **Master Mind Mechanic** can learn anything and will have a conscious file of ample "Oh, yeah, that reminds me's" to file away and be able to retrieve.

Five methods that can be used to make your learning connection pictures more memorable. They are:

1) **A**ction - Action always causes the mind to be more aware of input information.
2) **D**istortion - By distorting items in your pictures they can be made more memorable. You can see items bent, twisted or out of shape in some way.
3) **E**xaggeration - When this method is employed, an exaggerated number of items are seen in your pictures. Perhaps you see millions of something instead of just one.
4) **O**ut of Proportion - To use this method you see items larger than life or very tiny. They can be seen as giant or minuscule.
5) **S**ubstitution - With this method one item is used in place of or substituted for another item.

If you examine the beginning bold letters in that list of five suggestions, you will notice that the letters are **ADEOS**. These letters remind me of the misspelled Spanish word ADIOS. When you think of this misspelled Spanish word, you will remember the five methods.

A	=	Action
D	=	Distortion
E	=	Exaggeration
O	=	Out of Proportion
S	=	Substitution

I use Action and Substitution much more than the other suggestions. They seem to work better for me. They are also represented by the first and last letters in the misspelled Spanish word **ADEOS**. You should think of this misspelled Spanish word and what it suggests when you practice forming pictures later.

CHAPTER 3

The Pure Link

It is time to begin - enough theory! As was stated earlier when the seven basic tools of learning were mentioned, **The Pure Link System** connects the items in a list to one another to remember them in order. This tool is called **The Pure Link System** because its use reminds one of the links of a chain. The first link of a chain is joined or connected to the second link, the second link is joined or connected to the third link, the third link is joined or connected to the fourth link and so on until the last two links in the chain are joined or connected. The links of a chain are connected to one another, and the first link automatically leads to the second link, the second link automatically leads to the third link, etc. **The Pure Link System** employs that same principle to remember lists of information **in order only**. Each piece of information connects to the next piece of information like so many links in a chain. Many bits of information need to be remembered in order. A simple list is the prime example of information that needs to be learned in order or sequentially. A formula is an orderly arrangement of symbols. A shopping list is a practical list that can be remembered in order. A speech is a list of thoughts that a person wants to deliver to a group of people in order. A simple link can be used to remember a speech, but you will learn other methods as well.

I am going to teach you a simple ten-item made-up list to begin your **apprenticeship**. Any learning **apprentice** must learn the tools of the trade and their applications before becoming a **Master Mind Mechanic**. Normally a link is begun by picturing the purpose or use of the list and connecting it to the first item in the list, but this is only a made-up list. When doing a practice list it is best to see yourself associated to the first item in the list. The first item in the list will be a submarine. In the picture at the top of the next page imagine yourself as the person being dragged behind the **submarine**. Later when you are asked what was dragging you, you will easily see this picture in your mind and know it was a **submarine**. See this picture clearly before continuing. Look up from reading right now and imagine that you see a submarine floating across the room. Vividly imagine that you actually see the **submarine**.

The next item in the list is a **horse**, so we have to connect a horse to the submarine to start our linking process. Here is where the **ADEOS** rules come into play. We want to connect a submarine and a horse in an unusual way to make our mind focus on the two items that are connecting together in a unique way. It's almost like we want our mind to say, "Well would you look at that! I don't think I've ever seen anything like that before." That kind of picture will force the registration that is necessary for the learning process to occur. Look at this picture.

You see a picture of a submarine that looks like a horse. Imagine that it walked out of the water on horse's legs while wearing a saddle. Look at that very unusual picture. It connects or links a submarine and a horse. The Substitution Rule of **ADEOS** was used in this instance. A submarine was substituted for a horse.

The next item in the list is a **watermelon**. When you look at the picture below you will see that a watermelon is riding a horse. The two items have been connected or linked together in this silly picture. Never in my life have I seen a watermelon ride a horse except in this picture. The unusual has occurred, and you mind will take notice.

The next item in the list is a **key**. When you look at the picture below you will see that a watermelon is being used as a key. The two items have been connected or linked together in this silly picture. The silliness of the picture causes your mind to take special notice.

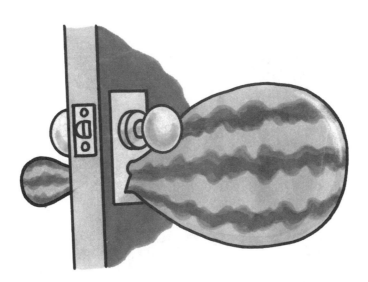

The next item in the list is a **tennis racket**. When you look at the picture below you will see that a large key is being used as a tennis racket. The two items have been connected or linked together in this silly picture.

The next item in the list is a **shoe**. When you look at the picture below you will see that after playing tennis the person used tennis rackets as shoes. The two items have been connected or linked together in this silly picture.

The next item in the list is a **cigar**. As you can see in the picture, the man took his shoe off, lit it and smoked it like a cigar. He turned his shoe into a cigar. The unusual nature of the picture causes registration on the mind.

The next item in the list is a **telephone**. As you can see in the picture, the man added a mouthpiece, an earpiece and a telephone cord to his cigar. He turned his cigar into a telephone. The unusual nature of the picture causes registration on the mind.

The next item in the list is an **airplane**. As you see in the picture, a telephone sprouted wings and became an airplane. You might call that Dial-A-Flight. Simply dial a plane reservation on the phone, watch the phone sprout wings and fly where you dialed. See the picture clearly.

The last item in the list is **soap**. As you see in the picture, an airplane is using a bar of soap after a long hard flight. Don't all airplanes soap down after a hard day? The silly picture causes your mind to take special notice. See the picture clearly.

Since soap is the last item in this particular list, I want you to imagine yourself as the person in the picture below. Imagine that you are the person who is slipping on the soap. Later when I ask you what you slipped on you will see this picture in your mind and will know you slipped on soap. By seeing yourself associated to the last item in a list you know you have come to the end of the list. See this picture clearly before proceeding to a test.

In almost every case, the Substitution and/or Action Rules of **ADEOS** were used when developing these pictures. As I said before, substitution and action are my most used applications when developing pictures.

It's time to be tested. Without looking back at the pictures, answer the following questions. After a question is asked, do not proceed before answering it, because I must mention the next item to continue the test. You will have no problem remembering this list anyway. This is effortless and non-repetitive learning at its best. You were taught to **see** the items, **recognize** them and **register** them in your mind in pictures, so you can now **retrieve** them. Look up from this book across the room. What did you imagine was floating there? Again, since this list is just a made-up list, it is not connected to anything to establish a use for it.

What was dragging you? That is the first item in the list. When the submarine walked out of the water, what did it look like? A _____ was riding the horse? The watermelon was then used as a _____. The key was then used as a _____ _____. The tennis rackets were later used as _____? The man jerked his shoe off and turned it into a _____. The man added some things to his cigar and turned it into a _____? Right in front of your eyes you saw the telephone turn into an _____. The airplane was using _____. Who slipped on the soap? Since you will remember that you slipped on the soap, you will know you have reached the end of the list.

Are you surprised that you remembered the list so easily? A better test now will be for you to close the book, look across the room and recreate the list by yourself. When you look across the room, just think of what is floating there and see each item as one item leads you to the next like the links of a chain.

Why was that so easy? For a couple of reasons primarily. The first is that you were finally taught a simple system for remembering a list of items. I don't know how many years you attended school, but I think it is safe to say that you were never taught a simple little idea like this no matter how many years you attended school at what levels. Another reason that it was so easy to learn is that every item in the list was tangible and thus, easily stored in your photographic mind. There were no intangibles to struggle with. As you learn other techniques and tools, you will find that all information will be made as tangible as this list of ten items. Then you will be able to link lists of intangible items as well as tangible ones.

I'm not an artist and never drew pictures for my own learning needs. Mental pictures can work as well as tangible pictures in most cases. I created tangible pictures and had artists draw them later for educational needs for my children. Two times two will always be four. The sounds made by the letters in our alphabet don't change, and the capitals of our states don't change. Since this kind of information doesn't change, I began to develop definitive pictures of almost every fundamental that my children had to learn, and then have them drawn. Then they could see them, recognize them, register them in their minds and retrieve them when necessary. My goal was to make learning fun and easy for them, so they wouldn't rebel and turn off and tune out like almost everyone else does. I had the same goal for them that I have for you, to make them and you a **Master Mind Mechanic**.

Picture Connection Practice

It may have been a long time since you tried to imagine silly little pictures. Perhaps it was as far back as when you entered school, so you probably need a little practice with your imagination. This is simply a little drill that will cause you to think of unique ways to connect two items together. Use the **ADEOS** rules when making these connections. This is not a Pure Link practice. You will not be connecting a list of items together. You will simply be practicing connecting one individual item to another individual item to begin to stimulate your imagination. Write your connection pictures on the blank lines following each pairing. Be silly; you don't want these pictures to be logical. This practice will help you add a more experienced tool to your **mental toolbox**.

Elephant to Kite	Fan to Gas Pump
Bread to Arrow	Candle to Snake
Umbrella to Monkey	Luggage to Window
Chair to Feather	Chewing Gum to Bed
Ocean to Toothpaste	Toaster to Fish

Pure Link Practice

Shortly I will provide several made up lists for you to learn in order using the Pure Link Method of learning lists. Simply begin the list with the top item in the list and connect or link the first item to the second item with a mental picture connection between the two items. See the picture clearly, and then see another mental connection between the second and the third item. Continue to link each subsequent item to the last item until the list is finished. Only do one list a day for the next three days for practice. The lists vary in length, but you will be able to remember any length of list with this application. Remember to apply one or more of the **ADEOS** rules to each picture connection.

You should always take the time to do the practice drills I suggest. If you want to grow from an **apprentice** to become a **Master Mind Mechanic**, you certainly need experience to reach your goal, so please for you own sake, don't pass up these practice sessions when I assign them. They are vitally important for your growth and improvement. This practice will help you add a more experienced tool to your **mental toolbox**. I will repeat this same statement often throughout this book.

List 1	List 2	List 3
Spoon	Grass	Soap
Watch	Motorboat	Bear
Tree	Ham	Gum
Table	Ticket	Nail
Bird	Fish	Rocket
Car	Snow	Balloon
Mouse	Hammer	Teeth
Dam	Airport	Flag
Hen	Bed	Razor Blade
Bullet	Ears	Typewrite
	Match	Cake
	Rabbit	Bathtub
	Book	Moon
	Ski	Jail
	Needle	Horseshoe
		Hat
		Gate
		Lamp
		Ice
		Guitar

Simple Errands, Appointments and Shopping Lists

The **Pure Link System** can be used to help you remember simple errands, appointments and shopping lists. Although you will learn ways to remember these needs in more sophisticated and detailed fashion later, you can apply what you have just learned to help you in the meantime. You don't need a more sophisticated system to remember these simple applications anyway. You will only need the more sophisticated applications for more complicated and detailed errands, appointments and shopping lists.

My suggestion is simple. In the evening, begin to think of what errands, appointments and shopping needs you have for the next day. As you think of them, simply link them together in your mind with silly little pictures. Let's assume you need to make a bank deposit the next day. I always like to begin my simple reminder lists like these by imagining myself employed where I need to go. In this case, I would think that I was a bank employee. I might see myself going straight to the bank the first thing in the morning to count several million dollars in the bank vault. To practice with this list, imagine that you are going to do the same things I am about to describe. See yourself preparing to go to a bank vault to count money the first thing in the morning.

Next, let's assume that you need to remember to mail some letters tomorrow. What you would need to do now is associate letters to the bank in some silly way. You will remember that the principle of the pure link is to connect the items to be learned or remembered to each other one at a time. You won't use any outside associations of any kind with the pure link. To continue the link, imagine that you place thousands of dollars in several letters and address them to yourself as you are counting the money in the vault. As I said, these need to be silly pictures. You wouldn't last very long as a bank employee under those circumstances.

Let's also assume you have to remember an appointment with the fire commissioner. To continue the link, you would need to form a connection between letters and the fire commissioner. Imagine that you see the letters burn up as you place them in a mailbox. See that picture clearly right now. The fire will remind you of the fire commissioner. I guess the letters should burn up anyway since you increased your pay as a bank employee beyond all decency.

Next, you may realize that you need to pick up some clothes that you left at the cleaners. You would then need to make a mental connection between the fire commissioner, something to do with fire or the fire department and the cleaners. Imagine that the fire commissioner drove you to the cleaners in a large fire truck with sirens sounding. Imagine that event right now.

Perhaps you realize you need to pick up some shoes at a repair shop the next day. You would need to connect the cleaners to the shoes. Let's assume that you examined the clothes at the cleaners and saw dirty shoe prints all over them. See that picture right now. That would easily remind you that you needed to pick up the shoes.

Perhaps you also need to buy a saw tomorrow. A silly connection between the shoes and a saw would be required. Imagine that you pick up the shoes from the repair shop and saw them in half with a saw. Imagine that vivid picture right now.

Here is the simple list one more time:

Bank - Letters - Fire Commissioner - Cleaners - Shoes - Saw

Look at the list one more time and think of the silly associations that were made between each of the items. To apply this idea you would go over the link in your mind just before going to bed. You would think of it again in the morning before leaving for the day. Your errands for the day would be fresh in your mind and you would be reminded to take any items you needed for the day's activities. In this case, you would be reminded to take the letters you need to mail. These errands and appointments don't necessarily have to be accomplished in the order of the link. During the day when you have some spare time, review the link and you will be reminded to do what you haven't already accomplished. If during the day you are reminded of something else you need to do, just add it on to the end of the link and make up a silly association. I always review my simple errand pictures one more time before going home. That way I can make sure to accomplish what I haven't already done before going home.

This idea will save you a lot of time. You should begin to do it for practice purposes just to become more familiar with the systems anyway. As I stated earlier, you will be taught more sophisticated ways of learning and remembering more complicated and specific errands and appointments later, even by exact day and hour, but you should apply what you know when you learn it. Simple needs only require simple solutions.

CHAPTER 4

The Sound-Alike Word System

The **Sound-Alike Word System** is a **tool** that is used to make intangible words tangible, so they can be pictured in the mind. Most of what we are asked to learn is in word form, so this tool is exceptionally important. Of course, many words are already tangible and automatically conjure up a picture in the mind. Those are the types of words that your parents and others began to teach you before entering school. Our problem is not with these words because they can be seen in our mind. Our problem is with intangible words. They are abstract or intangible and don't conjure up a comfortable picture in the mind. If you think of an elephant you can easily see an image of an elephant in your mind, but what about a pronoun? If a pronoun came to your front door do you think you would say, "Well, there's a pronoun. I haven't seen one of those things in a couple of days." I would think it is safe to say you have never seen a pronoun and wouldn't know how to go about seeing one. That is why it was so difficult to learn that kind of intangible information in school. You had no idea what a pronoun was or looked like, so you attempted to repeat the words that defined a pronoun until hopefully you learned it. A pronoun isn't a particularly hard problem, because it is defined with such a few words. When you had twenty or thirty rules in grammar to learn and had nothing to look at but intangible words, frustration set in quickly, and the joy of learning vanished in a hurry. The **Sound-Alike Word System** will give you the ability to make intangible words like a pronoun picturable, so they will be easier to learn.

The idea behind this system is to develop a new word that will be tangible in place of the original word that can't be pictured. We know what a squirrel or a fox looks like. Each has its individual identifiable picture, so we can't confuse it with anything else. We can do the same thing with a **pronoun** or any other intangible word using the **Sound-Alike Word System**. We simply say the original word slowly and think of something that it sounds like that can be pictured, thus the **Sound-Alike Word System**. It doesn't have to necessarily sound exactly like the original word, but the closer we can come to the actual pronunciation the better. Look at the picture at the top of the next page.

You see an obvious picture of a nun. She is swinging a golf club. She is a very good golfer. In fact, she is a pro golfer. That makes her a **pro-nun** or a **pronoun**. Now you have seen your first pronoun, but it won't be your last. I promise you that. That picture does not teach us what a pronoun is. It is not intended to. It is simply intended to show us what a pronoun looks like. If you saw a nun walking toward you swinging a golf club you could now point to her and say, "There is a pronoun. I have seen one of those things before."

When my children were young, as I have already stated, I wanted to make the learning process fun for them, so I developed a learning picture for the basics that they had to learn in school. I changed what was previously intangible to tangible pictures and had artists draw the learning connections, so my children could **see, recognize, register** and **retrieve** the information from their minds. The ultimate goal was to make learning so much fun that they would be eager to learn more. They were, and in time I began to teach them my sophisticated learning systems and tools so they could become **Master Mind Mechanics** themselves. When they needed to learn the states and capitals, I developed and showed them pictures of the states and capitals that connected a state to its capital in a tangible picture. They were learning that each state and capital had its own identifiable picture like a cow, horse or giraffe.

Let's begin to apply this idea by learning a state and its capital. Look at this picture.

  You see a picture of an **ark**, like Noah's ark, with a **can** in front of it. The ark is holding a **saw**. The **ark**, the **can** and the **saw** identify this as the state of **Arkansas**. It is now tangible and has its own individual identity. We haven't learned anything until we connect the capital to the state. Remember that learning is the process of connecting pieces of information together. A state and a capital are a simple **One-On-One** learning situation. Look at the picture again, and you will see that the ark is using the can as a holding place to saw a **little rock** in half. Now a picture for the capital, **Little Rock**, is connected to the picture of the state. Look at the picture again. You have just seen your first Arkansas, but I guarantee you it won't be your last. Now that you have **seen**, **recognized** and **registered** an Arkansas in your mind, just the thought of Arkansas in the future will enable you to **retrieve** the picture, because you have now identified and registered a picture of an Arkansas. It is almost like you are back on your parent's knee again, and your parent has just identified an Arkansas to you like so many other things when you were a child. I told you it was necessary to go back to the very beginning to build a proper and lasting learning foundation.

  I developed pictures like this for all of the states and capitals to make it easy for my children to learn all of the states and capitals. Other parents asked me to help their children learn the states and capitals with the same pictures, so I eventually published a book of the states and capitals myself so others could learn them as quickly and efficiently as my children had. Something that once was such a problem in the past had become fun to learn.

  Why shouldn't every child have the same opportunity to learn with fun aids like this one?

Yes, I developed it myself, but later and gradually, I would begin to teach my children how to develop pictures themselves; and, as I said before, these pictures don't need to be drawn by an artist. In most cases mental pictures work just as well, as you will learn.

I must get on a soapbox at this point. If I had the attention of a million grade school children by satellite hookup and asked this question, "How many of you know what a tiger is? Raise your hand if you know." What do you think the response would be? I don't think there is any doubt that every child would raise his or her hand, because they all would know what a tiger was. What if I asked this question, "How many of you know the capital of the state of Arkansas? Raise your hand if you know." What percentage of the hands do you think would rise in response to that question? It is anybody's guess, but I think we could agree that the response probably would be very low. Certainly not 100% like the tiger question. Why? Because every child had seen and learned what a tiger was, but none of them had seen and learned what the capital of Arkansas was. Their photographic minds easily retrieved a tiger, but their photographic minds had never even seen an Arkansas.

Let's assume that the following lesson then took place, and I taught them all as follows by saying, "I want to show you a picture that will teach you the capital of the state of Arkansas. Look at this picture. You see a picture of an **ark**, like Noah's ark, with a **can** in front of it. The ark is holding a **saw**. The **ark**, the **can** and the **saw** identify this as the state of **Arkansas**. Now you can see an Arkansas. Look at the picture again and you will see that the ark is using the can as a holding place to saw a **little rock** in half. Now a picture for the capital, **Little Rock**, has been connected to the picture of the state. Look at the picture again." I would then talk about the picture a little while longer to make sure they understood it fully. It is exciting to see how well children respond to these pictures when I give demonstrations in schools. They get excited, laugh and have fun with the process. The key words here are "laugh" and "fun." There is too little of that type of response in our schools today.

Let's make another assumption. If I had the same satellite hookup with the same one million children one week later and again asked this question, "How many of you know what a tiger is? Raise your hand if you know." As the week before, I think that every child would raise his or her hand, because they all would still know what a tiger was. What if I asked this question again, "How many of you know the capital of the state of Arkansas? Raise your hand if you know." I think that we could probably agree that practically all of the children would raise their hands, because they had the opportunity to **see**, **recognize**, **register** and now **retrieve** a picture of an Arkansas. What a difference a picture makes! You have heard the cliché, "A picture is worth a thousand words." It certainly is when it comes to learning. It is my contention that every child in every school should have the opportunity to learn with these kinds of pictures. They would have more fun, look forward to the process more eagerly and certainly have more confidence and self-esteem. The long-term goal would be to teach them to use learning systems to be able to create their own learning aids and become **Master Mind Mechanics** themselves. What if we fell somewhat short of that goal with every child? Motivation enters each life and its activity. At least they would learn the basics of what have become known as the three R's. They would learn how to read, write and use many other skills by pictures. They could become a functioning member of society instead of a ward of society who ends up in prison or on welfare, due to not learning basic skills in school in order to become gainfully employed. This is not a pipe dream. You will see samples of curriculum I have developed to make this dream a reality. It is what has consumed me for the last twenty years. Enough soap boxing, back to the job at hand.

The idea we have been discussing is quite simple. You need to change an intangible word to a tangible picture so it has its own identity. Then you can make the proper connections according to which tool will best solve the learning problem. I will give you some words and their phonetic pronunciations a little later, so you can begin to practice developing sound-alike words yourself. Before doing that though, I want to show you a couple more learning problems I solved with The **Sound-Alike Word System** to make learning fun and easy for my children.

My son, J. J., came to me one day and said, "Dad, I have to learn the names of the presidents of the United States in order. Will you develop a picture to make it easy?" This was not a simple One-On-One learning situation, because there had been 40 presidents up to that time. It was a Forty-On-One problem. The One in the Forty-On-One was the presidents. The Forty in the Forty-On-One was the names of the presidents. I was always eager to help my children learn, so naturally, I agreed to do it. The list of sound-alike words that I developed for the first ten presidents are below. The whole idea, of course, was to make the names tangible, in order to see them.

Washington - **Washing** a **ton** of clothes
Adams - An **Adam's** apple
Jefferson - A **chef** who is h**er son**
Madison - **Mad at** a **sun**
Monroe - **Man row** (A man rowing a boat)
Adams - An **Adam's** apple
Jackson - A toy **jack** and a **sun**
Van Buren - A moving **van** with a **bur**eau (Chest of drawers) **in** it
Harrison - A **hairy sun**
Tyler - A **tiler** (One who tiles floors)

After I developed the sound-alike words, I needed to arrange them in order so they could be seen and learned in sequence. You can see the picture that I developed below. I will lead you through it and teach it to you as I did him. First, you see a lady **press**ing **dents** out of the bumper of that car. Since she is **press**ing the **dents**, the picture is identified as teaching the **presidents**. I told you earlier when teaching you the made-up link that each list should start with a picture of what the information is, and the rest of the information should be linked to that beginning picture. The lady pressing the dents is a perfect example of that principle. After learning the picture, just the thought of the presidents would get my son into the correct picture because of this sound-alike word and picture for the presidents.

With her other hand the lady is **washing** a **ton** of clothes. Because of this part of the picture, you can see that the name of the first president is **Washington**. The lady who brought her the ton of clothes in the wheelbarrow has a large **Adam's** apple which tells you that the next president is named **Adams**. The lady with the large Adam's apple turned around, and her Adam's apple pointed at a **chef** who is h**er son**. This tells you, and more importantly, shows you that the next president's name is **Jefferson**. The chef is cooking over a hot grill, and a hot sun is beating down on him. He is so hot that he lifts his fist and shakes it at the sun. It is so hot that he is **mad at** the **sun**. This tells you and shows you that the name of the next president is **Madison**. Below the sun you see a man in a boat looking up at the sun. He is perspiring like the chef. It is so hot that he wants to get away from the sun. That **man row**s a boat to get away from the hot sun. **Man-row** will tell you and show you that the name of the next president is **Monroe**. Notice that the man rowing the boat also has a large **Adam's** apple. That will tell you that the name of the next president is **Adams**. This is our second president named Adams. As you can see, he rows his boat into a toy **jack** that is perched on a **sun**. This tells you, and more importantly, shows you that the next president's name is **Jackson**. You will notice that the jack fell out of a moving **van** with a **bur**eau **in** it. Again, you have a picture that tells you and shows you that the next president's name is **Van Buren**. Painted on the side of the van is a sun growing hair. It is a **hairy sun**. With this picture you can see that the next president's name is **Harrison**. This must be the Harrison Moving Company. The hairy sun hands a stack of tiles to a man so he can go to work. He makes his living by laying tiles on floors. He is a **tiler**. By seeing this part of the picture we learn that the name of the next president is **Tyler**.

This picture teaches the names of the first ten presidents in order. When we think of the **presidents** we will see the lady **press**ing **dents** out of the bumper of the car. Then all we have to do is see what happens in the rest of the picture.

To make sure you know this information well, go back up to the place where I began to teach this picture and go over the picture again. In school a teacher could review this picture as many times as necessary. To know the information, the picture must register in the mind. Some will register it faster than others will, but all can do it.

Now that you have reviewed the picture, answer these questions. When you think of the presidents in your mind, you see a lady who is _____ the _____ out of a bumper of a car. That will get you into the correct picture, the one that teaches the **presidents**. With her other hand the lady was _____ a _____ of clothes. The lady who brought her the clothes in the wheelbarrow has a very large _____. When she turned around her Adam's apple pointed to a _____ who is her _____. The chef is cooking over a hot grill. It is so hot that he raises his fist and shakes it, because he is _____ at the _____. Down below the sun a man is looking up and wants to get away from the hot sun. To get away the _____ begins to _____ a boat. The man rowing the boat also has a very large _____. His boat crashes into a toy _____ that is perched on a _____. The jack fell out of a _____ with a _____ in it. A _____ is painted on the side of the van. The hairy sun handed a stack of _____ to a man, so he could go to work. That man lays _____ on floors to make a living, so he is a _____. By answering these questions, you were able to **retrieve** the names of the presidents in order with no problem.

The next step is for you to be able to recreate the picture in your mind and name the presidents without my questions. Try that now. When you are able to do that you will have learned the picture and the presidents. As I stated earlier, some will register the picture faster than others, and some will require more review of the picture than others, but all can learn the picture a whole lot quicker and keep the information a whole lot longer than with repetition. It is understood that this process is a whole lot more fun.

To learn the rest of the presidents, the pictures simply continue. For instance, in the next picture the tiler dumps his tiles into a **polk**a dotted **poke**. This is slang for a bag or sack. There are actually two sound-alike words for President Polk. I won't continue with the rest of the pictures, but that is how the process continues.

This picture of the first ten presidents is certainly more complicated than the picture for Arkansas and Little Rock. Arkansas and Little Rock were a simple One-On-One learning problem that required a simple One-On-One picture. The ten presidents were a Ten-On-One learning problem that became a Forty-On-One problem for my son when he learned what was, at that time, our forty presidents. This obviously means that a more detailed picture is required for the presidents than a state and its capital, but although it takes a little longer, it works just the same. More information will require more effort and more time whether you try to learn it with the Stone Age tool of repetition or with the high tech picture method.

A mental picture would work just as well for someone with experience, but J. J. was just beginning to learn, and it was important to make the process as easy and fun as possible. For me I could have simply used a simple pure link for the presidents. By connecting the sound-alike word for each president together like the links of a chain, I could have accomplished the same thing. It would have been important in that circumstance for me to keep a record of the pictures that would have been developed for future use.

I began to get exciting results with my children when they used the pictures I developed and had drawn to help them learn. They didn't get bored and rebel, because they were having fun and were being rewarded with results from their efforts. My other children used the same picture when they needed to know the presidents. I began to create more and more pictures that became standards for our family. Because of this fun process, I was easily able to begin to teach my children how to develop their own pictures for their own learning problems. As a matter of fact, they looked forward to learning how to do it by themselves. Naturally, I had them begin with simple One-On-One learning problems like a word and its definition or a foreign word and its meaning. During this process, they were learning how to do what I could do. When the need arose, I began to teach them my sophisticated systems that would solve more complicated learning problems. They were on their way to becoming **Master Mind Mechanics**.

Before having you begin to practice developing sound-alike words yourself and teaching you other tools, I want to show you another picture I developed for my son J. J. He came to me one day and said, "Dad, I have to learn the rules of capitalization. Will you develop a picture for me?" This would be my first venture into developing pictures to learn grammar and punctuation but certainly not my last, because I have developed pictures to learn all of grammar and punctuation. I believe you will agree with me after learning parts of this next picture that these pictures should be used in all of our schools to learn this most difficult material.

J. J., his classmates and his teacher were in the same difficult position that millions of people had faced for hundreds of years. They had to learn many rules of capitalization that were just intangible words. There was nothing to see, no aids, just the anticipation of another battle with the boring process of repetition. However, it wasn't to be in this case for J. J. For the first time, a child was about to learn the rules of capitalization by seeing them.

I began to develop the picture by thinking of a sound-alike word for **capitalize**. Look at this picture.

I thought of a **cap** with **tall eyes**. You can see the baseball cap with tall eyes on the front of it. Say **cap-i-tall-eyes**. It sure sounds like **capitalize**, doesn't it? I had a beginning point. Now I had to think of a few other things. Some of the things I had in mind were that I wanted to try to develop a way to keep as many rules as possible in the same place, whatever that place might turn out to be, so they would have a lodging place or their own address. I had no idea at the time how many rules J. J. had to learn. Later research would show me that there were actually 48 rules of capitalization, but the most I could find in any textbook in later research were 21. Most textbooks grouped rules together. I felt they would be much easier to understand, if they had stood on their own. Eventually I did that when developing pictures to teach all of the rules of capitalization. By the way, I found that to be the case for almost all of the rules of grammar and punctuation.

Since I decided to use a baseball cap, I began to think of how I could use a baseball team to teach what to capitalize. I knew that kids liked games, especially baseball, so I felt a learning aid built around the game of baseball would be fun. The idea came to me, "Why not use sound-alike words to picture the words in a rule and make the subsequent picture a player on the baseball team." That way I could develop my own special Capitalize All Star baseball team and teach my son what to capitalize by playing a baseball game with him. It sounded like it could have a lot of merit. On the next page you can see the picture that resulted from that idea. Turn the page and notice that every player is wearing a cap with tall eyes on the front of it. That means you capitalize every one of them.

I want to teach you a few of the players to show you how well this idea and picture worked. You will have to look back and forth from my instruction to the picture of the baseball team occasionally. My son was about to become the first child to ever learn what to capitalize by playing baseball. Look at the first baseman. I told J. J. that all he needed to do was listen to me and learn who played each position. When he could recreate the picture in his mind without looking at it, he would know what to capitalize. Look at the first baseman. She is a nun who is swinging a golf club. You already know what she is. She is a **pro-nun** or a **pronoun**. J. J. had learned what a pronoun was earlier when I taught him the eight parts of speech with pictures. Notice that she is not hitting a golf ball with her golf club but is hitting an **eye**ball. I said to J. J., "The **pro-noun** at first base is hitting an **eye**ball instead of a golf ball. That will tell you that the first baseman is the **pronoun I**. Notice that she is wearing a cap with tall eyes to tell you that you capitalize the **pronoun I**. Later when I ask you who plays first base on our Capitalize All-Star team, you will be able to recreate the picture of the first baseman in your mind and say, "I capitalize the **pronoun I**, because she is my first baseman." I made sure he understood the first baseman by going over the picture a few more times. Then I took the picture away from him and asked, "Can you tell me who the first baseman is?" He said, "Sure, she is the **pronoun I**." He had learned who the first baseman was, and as a result he knew to capitalize the **pronoun I**.

It was time to go on to another player. I'm not going to take the time to teach all of these players to you. I just want you to understand how well these kinds of pictures work as we work toward building your skills. I won't go through the dialogue I used with J. J. for the next few players I teach you. I will simply teach you directly. Look at the catcher. He is a soldier with a soldier's uniform. As a matter of fact, he is a foreign legion soldier. The cloth hanging down behind his neck helps us know he is a foreign legion soldier. When I was a boy and saw foreign legion soldiers in the movies, they always seemed to be serving in the desert and the cloth helped protect their necks from the hot sun. The word **legion** is the key word for this rule. The large red letter "S" simply means that the word is a plural word. That leads us to **legions**. Notice that the letters "**RE**" are on the foreign legion soldier. When we put the letters "RE," the word **legion** and the letter "S" together we end up with **re-legion-s**. **Re-legion-s** is the sound-alike word I developed for the word "**religions**." So then, the catcher tells you and shows you that you **capitalize religions**.

Without looking at the picture, do you know who the first baseman is? Sure you do. It is the **pronoun I**, which tells you one of the rules of capitalization. Do you remember who the catcher is? Sure you do, **religions**. You have learned two rules of capitalization for the first time by seeing them.

I want to teach you a couple more rules. Look at the left fielder. The left fielder is a seagull. The key word here is **gull**. Notice that the gull has a speaking bubble above its head and is saying, "**Gee**." The gull is writing on an "**O**-shaped" **graph**. Let's put those words in the proper order. The word "**Gee**" is spoken by a gull that is writing on an "**O**-shaped" **graph**. The **gull** loves playing left field. These words in the proper order are **Gee-O-graph-gull** or **geographical**. The gull is also wearing a **name**tag with a letter "S" on it. This is my picture for the word **names**. Putting the whole thing together, we have **Gee-O-graph-gull names** which tells us and shows us that the rule playing left field is **geographical names**. Look at the picture again and make sure you know who the left fielder is.

I only want to teach you one more player before telling you how J. J. used this picture in test taking and composing. Look at the right fielder. It is a **calendar** obviously, but its **eye**s are very unique. Its eyes are **Tums**, the medicine for your tummy. This tells you and shows you that you capitalize **calendar eye-Tums** or **calendar items**. That includes those items that appear on a calendar such as days of the week and months of the year. So then, your right fielder is **calendar items**.

Let me give you a simple little test before talking about using this picture. Without looking at the picture, do you remember who plays first base? It is the _____ ___. Do you remember who the catcher is? It is _____. The left fielder is the only player who was speaking. Do you remember the left fielder? The left fielder is _____ _____. ___. Do you remember who the right fielder is? The right fielder is _____ _____. I'm sure you remembered all of them.

Let me tell you what happened to J. J. when he took his test in the second grade after learning this complete baseball team. If the question, "Do you capitalize calendar items," was asked, he would simply say to himself, "You sure do, because that is my right fielder." There was no doubt in his mind. Why? He could see the answer. He hadn't studied intangible words that were difficult to learn and difficult to recall; he had studied a picture that was fun to learn and easy to retrieve. If the question, "Do you capitalize geographical names," was asked, he would simply say to himself, "You sure do, because that is my left fielder." Let me ask you, "Do you capitalize religions?" You know that you do, because it is the _____ on our baseball team. "Do you capitalize the pronoun I?" Of course you do. You know that she plays _____ _____.

What is the normal procedure when trying to learn rules like these? The student, with perhaps a parent's help, goes over the rules again and again many times by repetition to try to be able to pass a test. They may have retained the rules for a short enough period to pass the test, but they lose most of the material, if not all of it, shortly thereafter. Since they haven't really learned it, they can't use it. They have fallen back into the black hole or abyss of forgotten material. But the struggle isn't over. That student will be called upon to learn the same rules year after year to pass tests. But year after year he or she will keep falling back into abyss of forgotten material. Yes, some of it will be retained from constant review and use, but most of it is lost from year to year and, unfortunately, that student and countless others will graduate without having learned the most basic rules of grammar and punctuation. Does this sound painfully familiar to you?

Well that didn't happen for the rules of capitalization for my son J. J. After he had learned the complete picture, I became a baseball announcer who would announce fictitious games while we drove places in our family car and had nothing else to do. I might say, "The batter just hit a long fly ball to the right fielder who caught it. Who caught it J. J.?" His reply, of course, would be, "Calendar items." The fictitious game would continue. I made sure as the announcer that all of the players were mentioned several times for these reviews. In a short period of time, J. J. learned the picture solidly and has known it ever since. J. J. got so good at learning and retaining these kinds of pictures that it was amazing. He was so good, no doubt, because he had been practicing it from the time he was about three years old.

I subsequently developed two other pictures to teach the rest of the rules of capitalization. I found so many rules after detailed research that they wouldn't all fit on the positions of a baseball team. If you look back at the baseball picture you will notice there is some information that is also placed in the right, center and left field stands. I used everything I could to clarify the rules. There are a total of twenty rules taught in this picture.

There are some rules specifically stating that you **do not capitalize** them. This normally causes even more problems for the student. It becomes increasingly difficult to remember if they do or do not capitalize that particular rule. I solved this problem by developing a special baseball picture using umpires only with no players. You **do not** capitalize an umpire. All of the umpires are **donut**s and, as a result, you certainly **do not** (**donut**) capitalize them. Students laugh at this application, have fun with it and, more importantly, they learn the rules.

There is one more baseball picture that teaches the rest of the forty-eight rules. This picture has the clean-up crew on the baseball field after the game is over. When the student sees who is cleaning up first base, etc., he or she can easily learn the rest of the rules.

After developing that picture for what to capitalize, I was off and running. I subsequently have developed learning pictures for all of grammar and punctuation. They aren't all published yet, but when they are, learning grammar and punctuation will be more fun, easier to learn and much easier to recall and retrieve. Students might finally be able to move on to using grammar and punctuation properly without falling back into the abyss of forgotten information. What do you think? Do you think this will help America's students, teachers and parents who want to help their children?

I will show examples of various curricula I have developed from time to time as you proceed through this book.

You might think, "I don't have the imagination or creativity to develop pictures like that." Well, neither did I when I first began to learn. I couldn't even be considered an **Apprentice Mind Mechanic** at that time. I didn't know anything about learning systems and developing pictures. I taught myself how to do it, and I want to teach you how to be able to do it as well. You don't have to teach yourself as I did, because I will be your teacher.

Sound-Alike Standards

Before any sound-alike practice drills, I am going to list a few sound-alike standards I have developed to help me create sound-alikes for intangible words. Words or syllables occur repeatedly, and it is a good idea to have a standard for them. I will list them in alphabetical order. Remember that these sounds don't have to be the exact same sound. They only have to be close enough to remind you of the original word. Standards are used over and over, so there won't be a problem if the sound is not precisely the same as the pronunciation of the original word. I have by no means listed all the possibilities for each sound but just a few to stimulate your thinking processes.

about - a boxer - he fights **a bout**
after - a r**after**
all - an **awl** which is a hole punching tool
amaze - **a maze**
any - a hen with a letter "e" on it - I've come to just use a hen or a **henny**

anyone - a hen with a number one (1) on it - **henny one**

appear - **a spear**

are - a letter "**r**," an **ar**k, an **ar**cher or **ar**t

at - an **at**tic or a hat pronounced with an English accent in which the "h" is not spoken

away - **a** scale on which you **weigh** things

ba (buh as in Manitoba) - a **bun**

be - a **bee**

before - **four bee**s or a **bee** with **four** wings

ble - a **bull** - as an example the word "**humble**" would be a **hum**ming **bull**

bring - a **bee** worn as a **ring**

but - a **goat** - it **butt**s

by - waving **bye**-bye

cal (cul as in medical) - a **cul**vert

call - a **telephone** on which you make a **call**

came - a candy **cane**

ceive - a **sleeve**

come - a **kum**quat

con - a **con**vict

could - a cow chewing its **cud**

de - **deep**, a **dee**d or another short word that begins with this sound

dis - a **disc**, a **dish** or to **disc**o

el (elbow) - an **el**evator, an **el**l (the train) or an **el**ephant

else - **Els**ie the cow

ence (unce) - **h**unts pronounced with an English accent in which the "h" is not spoken

er - **er**mine or to stutt**er**

even - a **teeter totter even**ly balanced

for - **four** of something, a **four**some in golf or a golfer yelling "**fore**"

from - a **Fram** oil filter

fy - **fly**

go - a **green traffic light** - it is time to **go**

have - cutting something in half - to **halve** it

he - a **donkey** - it says "**hee**-haw"

him - a **hymn** or a **hymn** book

his - a **hiss**ing snake

I - an **eye**

ing - a w**ing**

ish - an **itch**

let us - **lettuce**

lieve (believe) - a **leaf** or to **leave**

man - a **mann**equin

me - a music staff (do-re-**mi**)

ment - a **mint**, I **mint** leaf or ce**ment**

my - a **my**na bird

new - a **gnu** (an African antelope)

ob - **lob**

on - an **awn**ing

or - an **oar**

per - a **purr**ing cat or a **pur**se

place - a **place**mat

pro - a **pro** golfer or any **pro** athlete

quent - a **quint** (one of five children) or to s**quint**

re - to **re**ad, to **re**ap, a **re**am of paper or to **re**am something

ref - a **ref**eree

said - a **sed**ative or **sed**iment

saw - a **saw** (the tool)

some - a **sum** (2+2 = 4)

stay - a **sitting dog** told to **sta**y or a **sta**ble

ter - a **ter**m paper, a **ter**mite or a **tur**tle

they - a stack of **hay**

them - a **thum**b

tion (shun) - to **shun** something, to **shine** or standing at atten**tion**

us - a map of the **U.S.**

vide - to di**vide** something or something that is very **wide**

way - a one-**way** sign

what - a **light bulb** (it uses **watt**s)

who - an **owl**

Sound-Alike Word Practice

You should always take the time to do the suggested practice drills if you want to grow from an **apprentice** to become a **Master Mind Mechanic**. You certainly need experience to reach your goal; so please, for your own sake, don't pass up these practice sessions when I assign them. They are vitally important for your growth and improvement. This practice will help you add a more experienced tool to your **mental toolbox**. I have developed many sound-alike words already during my teaching as examples. The first was a pro-nun for a pronoun. Therefore, every time you think of a pronoun in the future you will se a pro-nun in your mind. The principle is quite simple, and it must be applied to intangible words before they can be pictured and easily remembered. I also developed sound-alike words for Arkansas, the presidents and what to capitalize. The best way to make up sound-alike words for intangible words is to say the intangible word very slowly and listen for obvious pictures that might come to mind. Many times a picture will come to you almost automatically, but with some words you will have to use your imagination. Sometimes I only use part of a long word and develop a standard to picture it. I have developed a very basic application rule for all of my systems, which I call my **Golden Rule**. It is **use as little as possible to learn as much as possible**. You will begin to develop your own standards as you practice developing sound-alike words.

I will give you a little more instruction before you practice on your own.

Organize - The three syllables in this word are pronounced **oar-guh-nize**. We aren't limited to those exact syllables when developing a sound-alike. I always examine the make-up of the word as well as its pronunciation when developing sound-alike words. If we examine the word **organ**ize, we can see that it starts with the word **organ**. I always look for words within words to make it easier. The rest of the word after organ is pronounced **eyes**, so an obvious sound-alike for this word would be **organ-eyes**. Another possibility would be **oar gun eyes**. These three words don't follow the exact pronunciation of the syllables either. Many times you will have more than one choice for sound-alike words. I choose the one I believe will make the information that goes with the intangible word easier to learn.

Conceive - This word is pronounced **kun-seeve**. Even though the beginning syllable is pronounced **kun**, I use a **con**, or **con**vict, for this syllable. This word begins with the word **con**, so why not. This has become a standard for me. I always picture a convict for the letters con even though they may be pronounced a little differently as in this word. I picture a **sleeve** for the **seeve** or **ceive** sound. I picture a convict ripping sleeves off of himself or someone else to picture this word. It all depends on how it fits with the other information that needs to be learned. If you needed to learn the definition of **conceive** which is **to form or develop in the mind**, you could see a **con**vict ripping his **sleeve**s off, **form**ing them into a ball and forcing them **into** his **mind** to **develop** a picture of them. I mentioned the standards for both syllables in this word in the sound-alike standards listed above.

Reference - This word is pronounced **ref-er-unce**. I want to teach you another little trick that can be used while discussing this word. For the sound **ref**, I always use a **ref**eree. If we followed the exact phonetic pronunciation of the word we would have to picture the syllable "**er**" next, but I don't do that. I repeat the "f" sound before the "er" sound and arrive at "**fer**." I picture a **fur** for this manufactured sound. There are no hard and fast rules when developing sound-alike words. I do whatever works! That is my only rule. So far I have a **ref**eree who will do something with a **fur**. For the sound "**unce**" I use the word "**hunts**" and drop the "h" and pronounce it like an Englishman which would be "**unts**." In the end I have a **ref**eree wearing a **fur** who **hunts** for something, and the word has been made tangible.

An intangible word, its phonetic pronunciation and a space to write a sound-alike word you make up have been listed. My pronunciations may not be the same kind that you will find in a dictionary, but they will represent the exact sounds made by the words. Fill in your choice for a sound-alike on every blank line. This will be good practice for you. Some of the words are actually people's names, but it doesn't matter. Remember to look for words within these words. In addition, look to blend some syllables together to make them one sound.

Demonstrate - dem-un-straight

Existence - egg-zis-tunce

Saskatchewan - sass-ka-chuh-wan

Provide - pro-vide

Territory - tear-i-tore-e

Systematic - sis-teh-ma-tick

Knowledge - gnaw-lidge

Conclusion - kun-clue-zhon

Tiefenbach - tie-fin-back

Quadrant - quad-runt

Subsequent - sub-suh-quint

Tangent - tan-gent

Element - el-i-mint

Conjunction - con-junk-shun

According - uh-cord-ing

Periodic - pier-i-odd-ick

Oblique - oh-bleak

Logarithm - log-uh-rhythm

Obtuse - ob-toose

Be on the lookout for intangible words and practice with them continually. You will only get better and better. You will be amazed at your progress if you just do it. Phone books provide great sound-alike practice. Open a phone book, pronounce names slowly and try to hear what the name sounds like that can be pictured. This is an excellent practice procedure.

CHAPTER 5

The Consonant Number System

Learning numbers has been one of the most difficult learning tasks but, as with everything else, numbers can be made easier to learn by making them tangible. **The Consonant Number System** will enable you to make numbers as tangible as a cow, horse or giraffe. Please don't get in a hurry as you learn this system. This system is the most powerful learning tool of all. Several other tools are based on the knowledge you will learn in this system. Therefore, take your time and make sure you understand every principle and fundamental before going on.

The two key words in this system are **consonant** and **number**. This system develops a very usable learning tool by connecting the **ten consonant sounds** in our alphabet to **the ten digits in our number system**. There are only ten digits in our number system, 1 through 0. There are no more digits. Yes, these ten digits can be arranged to form billions of numbers, but there will never be more than ten digits. Although there are more than ten consonant letters in our alphabet, there are also only **ten hard consonant sounds** that are made by these consonant letters. Different letters can and do make the same consonant phonetic sounds. As an example, say the letter "T" out loud. When you say the letter "T," your tongue puts pressure on the inside of your upper teeth. Say the letter "T" again, and you will see what I mean. Say it a few more times to be more aware of your tongue placement. Now say the letter "D" out loud. When you do you will notice that your tongue puts pressure on the inside of your upper teeth in the very same way the letter "T" does. Say the letter "D" out loud a few more times to notice and feel that the same thing happens as when you say a letter "T." Now say the letters "T" and "D" one after the other a few times and this phenomenon will become apparent to you.

Say the letter "B" out loud a few times and you will notice a puckering motion made by your lips. Say the letter "P" out loud a few times and you will notice the very same puckering motion is made by your lips as when you spoke the letter "B." What does this mean? It means that the letters "B" and "P" make the same hard consonant phonetic sound. Your vocal apparatus does the same thing when you say these two letters.

You will soon learn **that there are only ten hard consonant phonetic sounds in our alphabet.** They are matched up with the ten digits in our number system to provide a remarkable learning tool known as **The Consonant Number System**.

To develop this system, each of the ten consonant sounds is assigned a number value. To begin with, let us discuss the vowels and vowel sounds. Since this is **The Consonant Number System**, vowels and vowel sounds will not be assigned a number value. You will understand this better later. Only consonant sounds will be assigned a number value.

Let's get started. The sounds made by the letters "T" and "D" are assigned the number value of one (1). Since both of these letters make the same basic sound, their sounds will be assigned to only one number. The letters "T" and "D" will equal the number one (1) when they make their normal consonant phonetic sound. I am going to give you memory aids to help you learn these letter, number combinations. I don't think anything should be learned by repetitive, rote-type memory. You can use one (1) finger on each hand to form a letter "T." You see a picture of that below. This will help you remember the first letter sound for the number one (1).

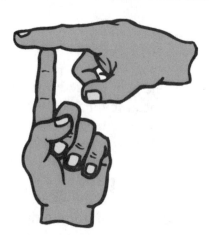

The letters "T" and "D" when put together form the well-known substitute for a TouchDown in football, a "T-D." Since the familiar "T-D" contains the two letters that are connected to the number one, we will use it to our advantage. A football official signals a TouchDown or a "TD" by raising his arms in the air like you see in the picture below.

Notice that the official has **one finger raised on each hand** as if saying, "You have just scored one **T-D**." A team can't score more than one "**T-D**" at a time. This little memory aid will help you remember that the sounds that go with the number one (1) are the sounds made by the letters "**T**" and "**D**." In the future when you review you will recall, when thinking of the number one, that a football official holds up one finger on each hand as he signals a "**T-D**." This little aid will easily remind you that the consonant sounds representing the number one (1) are the sounds made by the letters "**T**" and "**D**." For the rest of your life the letter "**T**" will represent the number one, and the letter "**D**" will represent the number one. The important principle is the sound made by the various consonant letters. Letters can and do make different sounds when used in different situations. Most of them can be relied upon, but not always, as you will find out. For instance, the letter "**T**" makes a sound that is different than its normal sound in some words. The letter "**T**," consequently, is **not totally reliable**. Occasionally it will make different sounds, but for the most part, it is reliable. This phenomenon will be discussed after you learn all ten letter and number combinations.

The sound made by the letter "**N**" is assigned to the number two (2), so there is only one letter sound connected to the number two. The letter "**N**" is a **totally reliable letter**. It always makes the same sound in any usage and always equals the number two. The picture below will help you remember this letter, number combination. As you can see, a letter "**N**" simply fell on its side. When a letter "**N**" falls over, it looks very much like a number two (2); and in reverse, when a number two (2) falls over it looks very much like a letter "**N**." This memory aid will help you learn this letter, number combination. In reality, I should say this **sound, number** combination instead of **letter, number** combination, because the sound made by the letter is what is used instead of the letter itself. But I will continue to use the words "letter, number" combination and not be totally technical.

The sound made by the letter "**M**" is assigned to the number three (3), so there is also only one letter sound connected to the number three. The letter "**M**" is also a **totally reliable letter**. It always makes the same sound in any usage and always equals the number three. The picture below will help you remember this letter, number combination. As you can see a letter "**M**" simply fell on its side. When a letter "**M**" falls over, it looks very much like a number three (3); and in reverse, when a number three (3) falls over, it looks very much like a letter "**M**." This memory aid will help you learn this letter, number combination. Thinking of the well known **3M** Company may also give you an additional memory aid.

The sound made by the letter "**R**" is assigned to the number four (4), so there is also only one letter sound connected to the number four. The letter "**R**" is also a **totally reliable letter**. It always makes the same sound in any usage and always equals the number four. The picture below will help you remember this letter, number combination. As you can see, I have spelled out the number fou**R**, and the letter "**R**" that ends the spelling of the number fou**R** has been made much larger than the other three letters. This will give it special significance in your mind. By the way, the number fou**R** is the only digit that ends in the letter "**R**" when spelled out. To lock this awareness in even more, I want you to pronounce the number fou**R** giving very special and drawn out emphasis to the ending letter. The purpose of this exercise is for you to hear a very prominent and long lasting "**R**" sound when you say the number fou**R** in this fashion. Say the number fou**R** several times in this manner listening for the prominent "**R**" sound. This memory aid will help you learn this letter, number combination.

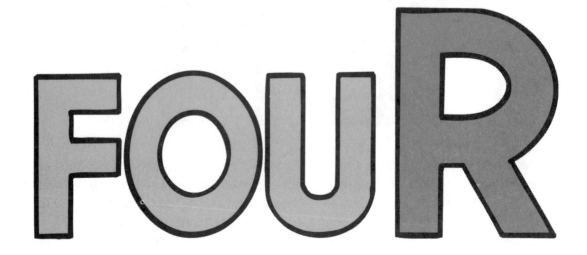

The sound made by the letter "**L**" is assigned to the number five (5), so there is also only one letter connected to the number five. The letter "**L**" is not a totally reliable letter as you might think. In rare occasions, it can and does make another sound. Most likely you will run across that odd sound, so we will consider it a **reliable letter**. The picture below will help you remember this letter, number combination. As you can see, a hand has been drawn. Of the five fingers, four of them have been bunched together while the thumb is extended. Hold your fingers up in the same way. You will notice that a letter "**L**" is formed by your index finger and thumb. The important point is that you used all five fingers to form this letter "**L**." The memory aid is always with you. Simply hold up five fingers to represent the number five, place four fingers together with your thumb extended, and you will form the letter, number combination for the number five. This memory aid will make it easy for you to learn this letter, number combination.

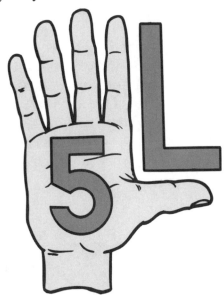

You don't have a clue yet how you are going to use this system, but a review is in order before continuing with the five other letter, number combinations. When you think of the number one (1) the memory aid used to recall the two letter sounds connected to the number one should pop into your mind. Think of a football official. Do you remember the aid and the two letters? The two letters are _____ and _____.

There was only one letter assigned to the number two (2). Remember what letter the number two looks like when it falls down. The letter is _____.

There was only one letter assigned to the number three (3) as well. Remember what letter the number three looks like when it falls down. The letter is _____.

There was also only one letter assigned to the number four (4). Remember what letter is prominent when the number four is pronounced. The letter is _____.

There was only one letter assigned to the number five (5). Remember what letter was formed with your five fingers. The letter is _____.

These letter, number combinations are really very easy to learn. The next five combinations will take a little longer because there are more letter sounds assigned to the numbers, but they are just as fun and easy to learn.

The number six (6) has four letter and/or letter combination sounds assigned to it. Of course, they all make the same sound, or they couldn't be grouped with the same number. The four are the sounds made by the letter "**J**," the letters "**SH**" when used and pronounced together, the letters "**CH**" when used and pronounced together, and the sound made by what is known as a "**Soft G**." I call these four sounds the "CHoo-CHoo" sounds. You will find out why later.

A letter "**J**" and a "**Soft G**" make the same exact sound. Say the words "**Jump**" and "**Giant**," and you will notice that both words begin with the same exact consonant phonetic sound. If the word "**Giant**" were spelled "Jiant" it would sound the same way as the correct spelling of "**Giant**." This proves that the sounds for a letter "**J**" and a "**Soft G**" are the same exact sounds. Now say the words "**SHut**" and "**CHew**." Once again you will notice that they make the same basic sound as the "**J**" and the "**Soft G**." The same thing happens with your vocal apparatus when you say these four sounds.

These four sounds can be grouped together and remembered by thinking of what I call the engine number six (6) "CHoo-CHoo" sounds. You see a picture of it below. Engine number 6 is chugging down the track. As it does, it makes the train sounds of "**Juh**," "**SHuh**," "**CHuh**," "**Guh**." Say "**Juh**," "**SHuh**," "**CHuh**," "**Guh**" several times. Remember that this "**Guh**" sound is a "**Soft G**" sound that is heard at the beginning of the word "**Giant**" when making these engine number 6 sounds. Start slowly and speed the sounds up as you go like the sound engine number 6 would make as it increased its speed. By thinking of engine number 6 later and the sounds it makes, you will remember the four sounds that go with the number six (6).

There are three sounds that are assigned to the number seven (7). These sounds are what I call the back of the throat guttural sounds. They are all formed in the back of the throat and sound somewhat like a clearing the throat sound. The sounds are the basic sound made by the letter "**K**" as in the word "**Kick**," the sound of a "**Hard C**" as in the word "**Cow**," which is the same exact sound that is made by the letter "**K**," and the sound made by a "**Hard G**" as in the word "**Go**." You will remember that a "Soft G" makes the same sound as a letter "J." The "G" sound connected to the number seven is the back of the throat guttural sound, a **hard sound** and **not a soft sound**. I have rearranged these three sounds a little differently in the picture below to help you learn them. You will notice that a number seven (7) looked up at a traffic light. It thought to itself, "When this light turns green, I am going to **Go Kick a Cow**." As you can see, it did just that. It is **hard** to **Go Kick a Cow**. The cow won't want to be kicked. It probably will run away and make it a difficult or hard task. This will help remind you that these are **hard sounds** made by the letters "G" and "C" and not soft sounds. The **hard rocks** in the picture will also help remind you that these are **hard sounds**. When you think of the number seven, see it preparing to **Go Kick a Cow**, and you will remember the three sounds that are assigned to the number seven.

There are only two sounds assigned to the number eight (8). They are the sounds made by the letters "**F**" and "**V**." Say these two letters out loud a few times and you will notice that your vocal apparatus do the same thing when they are pronounced. Your upper teeth touch your lower lip when these two letters are spoken. To remember these two sounds, we will use the word **ate** along with the word **eight**. These two words sound exactly the same. In the picture below you will notice that a number **eight** (8) **ate** some **F**ruit and **V**egetables. The "**F**" in the word **F**ruit, and the "**V**" in the word **V**egetables have been associated to the number **eight** (8) in this picture as a memory aid to help you remember these two sounds. Later when you think of the number **eight** (8), automatically think of the word **ate** and see a mental picture of what the number **eight** (8) **ate**, and you will remember these two sounds. The number eight got thirsty when it ate and it drank some V-8 juice as well. A number 8 and a handwritten letter "f" both have two loops as another aid. These memory aids will make it easier to remember these two sounds.

There are also only two sounds that are assigned to the number nine (9). They are the sounds made by the letters "**P**" and "**B**." Say these two letters out loud a few times and you will notice that your lips pucker in the same way when they are pronounced as was stated earlier. The memory aids pictured below will help you learn that these two sounds go with the number nine (9). First of all you see a number nine (9) that is looking into a mirror. The mirror reversed the number nine to make it look like a letter "**P**." So then, a number nine (**9**) and a letter "**P**" are mirror images of one another. The next part of the picture shows you that two letter "**P**'s" can be used to form a letter "**B**." One of them has to be upside-down and backwards, but it still works. So then, when thinking of a number nine (**9**), imagine it looking into a mirror and you will be reminded of the letter "**P**." Then think of two letter "**P**'s" forming themselves into a letter "**B**," and you will be reminded of the other letter sound.

There are three sounds that are assigned to the digit zero (0). They are the **hissing sounds** made by the letters "**Z**," "**S**" and a "**Soft C**" as heard in the words Cent and City. A "Soft C" sounds exactly like a letter "S." The memory aids pictured below will help you learn these three sounds. When thinking of the digit Zero, you will notice that it begins with the letter "**Z**." You will then notice that a Snake, which begins with the letter "S," has formed itself into the shape of a **Z**ero. I used a Snake because **it "hisses" for these hissing sounds** as well as starting with the letter "S." In the middle of the **Z**ero formed by the Snake, you will notice a "Cent" which starts with a Soft "C." A slang word used to mean zero is the word "**Z**ip." By thinking of "**Z**ip" you can be reminded of City, State and **Z**ip, and these three words begin with the three sounds for the digit zero. You will also notice an envelope near the snake with City, State and **Z**ip written on it. These two aids should make it easy to remember these three sounds. You will find that you will use the letter "S" much more than the other two sounds when applying this system. I hardly ever use the letter "**Z**" or a "Soft C."

A "Soft C" and a "Hard C" make two totally different sounds, so they have two different numbers assigned to them. A "**Hard C**" as in "Cow" equals the number seven as you will recall, and a "**Soft C**" as in "Cent" equals the digit zero.

The following chart with the memory aids for each of the sounds and numbers should be reviewed several times until you are familiar with it. I want you to know it very well before I start to show you its uses. Review it at this time.

Consonant Number System Chart

1 = T or D

A football official holds up one (1) finger on each hand to signal a **T-D** or **T**ouch**D**own.

2 = N

A number two (**2**) on its side looks like a letter "**N**," and a letter "**N**" on its side looks like a number (**2**).

3 = M

A number three (**3**) on its side looks like a letter "**M**," and a letter "**M**" on its side looks like a number (**3**).

4 = R

The number four (4) is the only digit that ends in the letter "**R**" when spelled out (fou**R**).

5 = L

You can form a letter "**L**" with your five (5) fingers by placing your four fingers together and extending your thumb.

6 = J, SH, CH or G - (Soft G)

Engine number six (6) makes the **J**uh-**SH**uh-**CH**uh-**G**uh sound as it chugs down the track.

7 = G, K or C - (Hard G and C)

A number seven (7) is going to **G**o **K**ick a **C**ow.

8 = F or V

A number eight (8) **ate** **F**ruit and **V**egetables.

9 = P or B

A mirror image of a number nine (9) looks like a letter "**P**." Two letter "**P's**" can be used to form a letter "**B**."

0 = Z, S or C - (Soft C)

The digit **Z**ero (0) begins with the letter "**Z**." A **S**nake forms itself into the shape of a Zero and **hisses** at a **C**ent in the center of the Zero shape. Also remember **C**ity, **S**tate and **Z**ip.

Vowels and Vowel Sounds

Remember that **A, E, I, O** and **U** have no number values, because they are vowels. The letters **W, H** and **Y** (**WHY**) also have no number values, because they make vowel sounds.

There are several concepts that must be reviewed before you begin working on some drills that will cause in **The Consonant Number System** to become knowledge to you.

You may remember that I said earlier that vowels and vowel sounds have no value in this number system. That means no number value should come to your mind when you think of a vowel or a vowel sound. The letters **A, E, I, O** and **U** have no number value. The letters **W, H** and **Y** also don't have any number value. **WHY**? Because they make vowel sounds and not consonant sounds. These three letters were all considered actual vowels in old English. Today a **W** and a **Y** are considered vowels in certain uses. In the word "fly" the letter "y" is the only vowel in the word. The "y" sounds exactly like a letter "i" and is a vowel. In the word "baby" the "y" is also a vowel. It sounds exactly like a letter "e" in this word, so it is a vowel. There are many other similar examples of this application that could be shown, but these will suffice. The letter "w" is considered to be a vowel when it follows actual vowels in some words. The word "blow" is an example, and the word "pow" is another example. In the word "blow" the "w" is actually silent and makes no sound. Silent letters will be discussed soon. In the word "pow" the "o" and "w" combine to make the "ow" sound which is a vowel sound and would have no number value. This whole discussion is for the sole purpose of having you understand that vowels and the letters "w," "h" and "y" as in the word "why" are assigned no number value in this system. **WHY**? Because they make vowel sounds and not consonant sounds. Remember we are discussing and you are learning **The Consonant Number System and not The Vowel Number System**. Only consonant sounds have number values in this system. There is no such thing as **The Vowel Number System**. I just made up the words to make the point that vowels do not have any number value in this system.

Shortly I will ask you to participate in practice sessions to improve your knowledge of this system. When you practice, you will begin by changing words into their number values. To make it easier for you to understand this process, I capitalize consonants and put them in **bold type**, but vowels will be lower case without bold type to make the consonants, which have a number value, stand out. This is a standard that I have always used for my own applications. The word "**Ti**R**e**" has four letters with two consonants in it. The "**T**" equals the number one (1), and the letter "**R**" equals the number (4). The other two letters are vowels that have no number values. Therefore, the number value of the word "**Ti**R**e**" is fourteen (14). It could be written as you see it below for more clarification. I have put more space than normal between the letters for a better visual understanding.

T i **R** e
1   4

This exercise is simply a method of practice to know the system better. It is not how the system is applied in learning. Let's examine some other words in this same fashion. The number values in the word "NuMBeR" are 2 for the letter "N," 3 for the letter "M," 9 for the letter "B" and 4 for the letter "R." It can also be shown like this.

N u M B e R
2   3   9   4

The letter "u" and the letter "e" do not have a number value under them, because they are vowels and have no number value.

There are a couple rules and a couple specific letters I want to discuss before giving you some practice drills.

The first rule is the **Silent Letter Rule**. **Silent letters have no number value in this system**, **because they do not make any sounds**. A sound must be made by a letter for it to have a number value, and that sound must be a consonant sound. In the word "kNiFe" for instance, the letter "k" would have no number value assigned to it, because it is silent and makes no sound. The letter "k" in the word "**KiD**" though, would have the number value of seven (7) assigned to it, because it is heard and is not silent. In the word "CoMb" the letter "b" has no number value, because it is silent. There is no "b" sound pronounced when this word is spoken. Pronounce "CoMb" a few times and you will hear no "b" sound. The rule is quite simple, **silent letters have no value**, **because they do not make sounds**.

Since this system is based solely on the sounds made by the letters, certain combinations of letters need to be discussed. The **Double Letter Rule** is very easy to understand. **Double letters only have one number value, since they only make one sound**. In the word "BuTTeR" for instance there are three consonant sounds. The "B" equals the number value of nine as you have learned, and the "R" equals the number four. You have learned those and they cause no concern. The "u" and the "e" are assigned no number value, because they are vowels. The rule we are discussing involves the double letters "**TT**" in this word. When two letters of the same kind appear side by side in a word they are known as **Double Letters**. It might seem obvious at first glance that the "**TT**" letter combination should equal the number 11 or two number one values since there are two letter "T's," but that is not the case. **Double Letters** only make one letter sound. Pronounce the word "BuTTeR" out loud a few times, and you will hear only one "T" sound and not two. There are not two "T" sounds but only one "T" sound, so the number value of the "TT" combination is only one (1) instead of eleven (11). The **Double Letter Rule** is really very easy to understand. **Double Letters only have one number value** and that value is what one of the letters would be on its own. In the word "TuMMy" for instance, the "MM" combination has a value of three (3) and not thirty-three (33). In the word "huRRy" the "RR" combination has a value of four (4) and not forty-four (44). There is an exception to this rule where a set of double letters does make two sounds. In the word "aCCiDeNT" the "CC" combination does make two sounds. Pronounce the word "aCCiDeNT" a few times and you will realize that the first letter "C" makes a "Hard C" sound and equals the number seven (7). The second letter "C" makes a "Soft C" or "S" sound that equals the digit zero (0). This is the only double letter combination that breaks this rule that I know of. As a result, this rule holds firm and true which s that **Double Letters** only make one letter sound and all double letters will have only one number value except the "**CC**" combination in some words.

A couple other letters haven't yet been discussed. The letter "**Q**" always sounds like a letter "**K**." As a result, it always has a number value of seven (7). I don't ever use it in the application of this system, but I mention it, because you will come across it when practicing. The other unusual letter is the letter "**X**." I never ever use it and neither will you. An "**X**" actually makes six different sounds in its various uses. Since you will never use it, just ignore it during practice sessions.

Consonant Number System Practice

There are a few ways to practice this system in what is normally wasted time to know it better and better. First of all review the chart on page 135 so you know the basics well. Practicing to know this system better is simple enough. No doubt you spend a lot of time in an automobile with nothing to do. As you ride, you will notice a myriad of letters, numbers and words. Automobile license plates have letters and numbers on them. When you see letters on license plates, think of their number value; and when you see numbers on license plates, think of their corresponding letter values. License plates are a gold mine for knowledge building practice sessions. When you see words on signs, billboards or street signs, practice changing the consonant sounds in those words to their number values. These practice sessions should be done mentally. You will not have time to write the license plates or words down as you drive. It will have to be a mental process. Participate in as much of this kind of practice as possible. You will not only know this system better, but you will be able to use its applications quicker and more confidently.   As I have already stated, you should always take the time to do the practice drills that I suggest if you want to grow from an **apprentice** to a **Master Mind Mechanic**. You certainly need experience to reach your goal. So please, for you own sake, don't pass up these practice sessions when I assign them. They are vitally important for your growth and improvement. This practice will help you add a more experienced tool to your **mental toolbox**.

I need to discuss some unusual sound combinations so you will understand that it is the sound made by the letters that determines the number value. It is not just the letter itself. Let's examine the word "**TouGH**." The "**T**" equals the number one (1) in this word but what about the "**GH**" letter combination? It equals the number eight (8), because these letters are pronounced like a letter "**F**," which is a number eight. Remember that the number eight (8) ate "**F**ruit" and "**V**egetables." This word phonetically could be written "**TuFF**." I make this point to emphasize that the number value is determined by the sound the letter or letters make and not the appearance of the letter or letters.

In the word "**PHoNe**" a similar situation exists. The "**PH**" letter combination also sounds like a letter "**F**," so this "**PH**" letter combination equals the number eight (8). Of course, the letter "**N**" in this word equals the number two (2). The "**o**" and the "**e**" have no number value, because they are vowels.

In the word "**FRaCTioN**" another unusual situation occurs with the letter "**T**." This word can be displayed with its number values as shown below since phonetically it is pronounced as though it was spelled **FRaCSHioN**.

F R a C T i o N
8 4   7 6   2

At first glance you might think the letter "T" would equal the number one (1), but it does n't, because it does not make a normal letter "T" sound. It actually sounds like the "SH" letter combination which equals the number six (6). Pronounce this out loud a few times, and you will understand why the "T" equals the number six when you hear it for yourself. It sounds like the "SH" letter combination, as if it was spelled **FRaCSHioN**, doesn't it? The number values under the other consonants in this word are standard and easy to understand and, as always, the vowels have no number value. Be aware of unusual pronunciations of this kind when practicing changing letter sounds to numbers and numbers to letter sounds. I want to make one point very clear at this time. Even though you will run into some unusual letter pronunciations when practicing, you will not use unusual letter sounds in actual applications of this system.

It's time to practice for a few days until you are confident that you know **The Consonant Number System** very well. After you practice for a while, return to the book to begin learning applications and uses of this extraordinary tool of learning. As I have already stated, you should always take the time to do the practice drills that I suggest if you want to grow from an **apprentice** to a **Master Mind Mechanic**. You certainly need experience to reach your goal. So please, for you own sake, don't pass up these practice sessions when I assign them. They are vitally important for your growth and improvement. When teaching lengthy seminars, I always allow a week between learning **The Consonant Number System** and teaching its applications and uses.

Using the One Sound Method

Each variation of The **Consonant Number System** is used to make numbers tangible so they can be learned easily. Its main purpose then is to change numbers into pictures so they can be seen and registered in our photographic minds. I call these pictures formed from numbers **Number Memory Words**. I will first teach what is known as **The One Sound Method**.

To begin understanding the application of this learning tool, historical dates will be discussed. Almost everyone knows that Columbus discovered America in 1492, but assume someone didn't know it and needed to learn it. Learning is connecting, and in this case an event must be connected to a date. All learning involves a connection. To begin with, the number 1492 must be changed into a picture so it can be seen. If you and I were studying American history, we wouldn't need to be concerned with the number one (1) at the beginning of this number. Surely we wouldn't think America was discovered in the year 492, and it couldn't possibly have been discovered in 2492. That year hasn't occurred yet. My point is this, we only have to remember the last three numbers in this date and place a number one (1) in front of the three numbers later in actual use. You will recall that I have developed a very basic application rule for all of my systems which is, **use as little as possible to learn as much as possible**. This is a perfect example of that rule. We don't need to learn the beginning number one, so why waste the time?

When using **The One Sound Method** to learn numbers **only one sound is used per number to be remembered**. For instance, with the number 1492, since we are only going to develop an aid to learn the numbers 492, only three sounds are needed for the three numbers.

4   9   2
R   P   N
B

You can see that I have listed the letter sounds of each number under the numbers. Since we have to remember a number 4, I have to use a letter "R" for that purpose. There is no other sound to choose, since the number four only has one letter sound attached to it in this system. However, when it comes to the number nine (9), I must make a choice between two letters. Since the sounds made by a letter "P" or a letter "B" equal the number nine sound, I must use one of these two sounds. But I can only use one or the other sound. If I used them both, the resulting number to be remembered would have two number nines in it instead of just one. Since we have to remember a number 2, I have to use a letter "N" for that purpose. There is no other sound to choose, since the number two only has one letter sound attached to it in this system.

The next step in the process is to use the appropriate letter sounds that correspond to the numbers to be learned and form a **Number Memory Word** using those specific consonant letters and those consonant letters only. We can use any vowels to help us form words, because vowels don't have number values and, as a result, they won't distort our numbers. I thought of the word "**RiBBoN**" for the number 492. The word "**RiBBoN**" can only represent the number 492 based on what you have learned, because "R" equals (4), "B" equals (9) and "N" equals (2) in **The One Sound Method**. There are no other possible numbers that could be represented. The letter "R" will always be a number (4), the letter "B" will always be a number (9) and the letter "N" will always be a number (2). No mistakes can be made in the translations of these sounds to numbers if you have the knowledge of **The One Sound Method**.

We are not yet finished with the learning process for this date and event. We need to connect or associate the event to the date by forming a picture in our mind that ties the two together. How about this. Imagine that Columbus tied a **RiBBoN** to the dock when he left Europe on his voyage so he wouldn't get lost. If he had a problem, he could just follow the **RiBBoN** back to port. It is a silly little picture thought but it will work very nicely. After reviewing this picture thought in your mind a few times, you will always think of Columbus affixing the **RiBBoN** to the dock when he left to discover America. Then, to remember the date, all you have to do is change the letter sounds in your memory aid back into numbers to have the date of the event. **RiBBoN** translates back into the number 492 easily. To remember the date, all you would have to do is drop a number 1 in front of three digits. By doing that we arrive at the date of 1492 which is, of course, the proper date.

This application of **The One Sound Method** involved using one single consonant sound for each digit in the number to be learned. That is why it is called **The One Sound Method**. As you continue to learn how to use it better, you will have choices to make when a digit has more than one potential sound from which to choose. For instance, if you had to remember a digit **eight** in some sort of number, you would have a choice of using a letter "F" or a letter "V." One and only one of them could be used, because only one digit eight would need to be remembered. If you had to remember a digit **seven** in some sort of number, you would have a choice of using one of three letter sounds. You would have to choose a "K," a "Hard C" or a "Hard G." As you will find out, the choice of the letter sound in these kinds of cases will be determined by the rest of the letter sounds represented in the number to be learned. You will want to choose letter sound combinations that enable you to create a picturable and usable word that works well for the memory aid developed to learn the number. The examination of another date will help make this more clear for you.

The Panama Canal was opened in 1915. I want to develop a **Number Memory Word** for this event and date in the same way we did for Columbus discovering America. Once again, we don't have to be concerned with the first number since it is a date.

$$
\begin{array}{ccc}
9 & 1 & 5 \\
P & T & L \\
B & D &
\end{array}
$$

With this number combination I have more choices to make than I did with the last date. I must choose to use a "P" or a "B" for the number nine (9), and I must choose to use a "T" or a "D" for the number one (1). I have no choice with the number five (5). I must use an "L" for it. There are several tangible words I could use for these letter combinations and, of course, the word that is developed should always be a tangible word. I could use a **PooDLe** or a **PuDDLe** or a **PaDDLe** or a **PeDaL** or a **BoTTLe**, for instance. Now I have a choice to make with the next process. I must choose one of these words and connect or associate it to the event to be remembered, which in this case is the opening of the Panama Canal. Here is where our imaginations and creativity come into play. I use my common sense and imagination to use the best possible **Number Memory Word** to make the information as easy as possible to remember. This is a **One-On-One** memory problem, in this case, **one** event and **one** date. Let's examine our choices. I am going to list the **Number Memory Word** choices on one side of the page and the event on the other, so we can examine them more closely.

PooDLe

PuDDLe

PaDDLe   Panama Canal Opened

PeDaL

BoTTLe

I must now decide which one of these **Number Memory Words** on the left will work best for me to help me remember the date of this event. I could imagine that a **PooDLe** was the first to swim through the Panama Canal when it was opened, or I could imagine that the Panama Canal was only a **PuDDLe** when it was opened. I could also imagine that a **PaDDLe** was used to **PaDDLe** the first ship through the Panama Canal, or I could imagine that the first ship to go through the Panama Canal was powered by a **PeDaL**. All of these would work, but I chose to use a **BoTTLe**. I imagined that the first ship to go through the Panama Canal when it was opened was in a **BoTTL**e. I felt this picture would work best for me, because it was more vivid and a bit sillier. Out-of-the-ordinary pictures make better impressions on the mind. I wasn't yet finished. The next step was to record the memory picture that I developed, so I could review it any time I wanted. Every time after that when I thought of the Panama Canal, I imagined that a ship in a **BoTTL**e was the first ship to go through the Panama Canal. All I had to do was change the consonant sounds in the word **BoTTL**e back to numbers and I had the date. The "B" equals 9, the "T" equals 1 and the "L" equals 5. By simply dropping a number one (1) in front of these three numbers, I had the date of 1915. It was that easy to learn and keep because of this simple tool of learning.

I made it a habit of being very organized as I have already stated. I had a special spot where I recorded all of the picture aids I created for dates, for instance. I didn't draw pictures. I simply recorded the picture aid in words for later review. As a student I did this for all of my classes on a daily basis. It didn't take long, and I was keeping up with everything. A quick review of all of my picture aids on the weekend kept me up with everything, and the review solidified the information in my mind more securely. I do the same thing with what I need to remember in my social and business life as well. Being **organized**, **disciplined** and **diligent** is a habit that will reap many dividends. It will also make you an **ODD** person.

Rules for Developing Number Memory Word Pictures

What I have just taken you through lends itself to a simple systematic or rule process when developing **Number Memory Words** to remember numbers. We have only discussed dates to this point, but the process or rules need to be listed just as well. As a beginner you should:

1) **List the sound equivalents** for each digit under the numbers to be remembered as I did for these two dates.

2) **Develop as many tangible Number Memory Words as possible** using those particular letter combinations. Remember that you can only choose one sound for each number. With some numbers, such as the number four (4), you don't have a choice. There will be only one sound to use.

3) **Choose the Number Memory Word you believe will work best** for the number being learned and develop a picture aid. Use your creativity and common sense when developing the picture aid. The more clever the association is, the easier it will be to bring the number back to mind. I will give you examples of this when I begin to discuss phone numbers. As you begin to practice with long digit numbers later, you will have to develop several words to represent the long digit number being learned. You will move on to this application later.

4) **Record the Number Memory Word** of your choice **for later review**. This is a very important step. I will stress this point over and over as I teach.

As you become more experienced, you may not need to list the various words that could be used to represent and picture the number. In time your mind will become more adept at thinking them up as you look at the letters representing the number. For my part, I have enough experience now that I don't even need to list the sounds under the numbers to be remembered. I know the system well enough and have worked with it long enough that it is no longer necessary for me to do those things, but I sure did do it when I first began to use the system. I needed all the help I could get at that time. As a beginner you do too, and I strongly urge you to follow the same procedure listed above as you become more experienced. I will be giving you some other number combinations later to practice this process with.

Let's examine some phone numbers using this same application and procedure. With phone numbers, we need to connect the phone number to the person or business it goes with. There are more numbers in a phone number than a date, but that doesn't matter. **The Consonant Number System** will work for any length numbers. But one step at a time. Let's not get ahead of ourselves. A phone number consists of seven digits that must be transformed into sounds that can be used to develop tangible picture aids. The phone number of one of my friends who is in the construction business is 412-0321. Let's follow the rules for developing number pictures that were previously listed while developing a way to learn this phone number. The **first rule** says that we must **list the sound equivalents** for each digit under the numbers to be remembered. For this phone number, it would look like this:

```
4 1 2 0 3 2 1
R T N Z M N T
  D   S     D
      C
```

You will notice that all of these sounds are listed in the order of the memory aids that helped you learn them. I always list them in this manner. Of course the "C" listed under the zero is a "Soft C." The **second rule** says to **develop Number Memory Words** using the appropriate sound combinations. The first thing that I try to do with phone numbers is develop two words if at all possible. The first of the two words hopefully can be developed from the first three letters of the phone number, and the second word hopefully can be developed from the last four numbers. This process certainly isn't required for the system to work and to work well. That is simply the first possibility for which I look. It works quite nicely for this phone number. First of all we will examine the first three digits and develop possible tangible words for them. Look at this:

```
4 1 2
R T N
  D
```

A possible **Number Memory Word** that could be used is **RouTiNe**, but that is not a good word at all, because it doesn't conjure up a tangible picture in the mind. Remember that the whole purpose of this system is to make numbers tangible. Other possibilities are **RaTTaN** or **RoTTeN**. It is difficult to even think of words using the R - D - N combination without thinking of words that end in "iNG." Technically if a word ends in "iNG" the letter "N" would equal the number two, and the letter "G" would equal the number seven, since the "G" in the "iNG" combination always makes a "Hard G" sound. So then, technically the word "RiDiNG" couldn't be used. It would translate back to the number 4 - 1 - 2 - 7 instead of just 4 - 1 - 2. I will show you how to get around this little technicality a little later, but with your present knowledge, the word "RiDiNG" couldn't be used for the numbers 4 - 1 - 2.

Now we will examine the last four digits in this phone number and develop possible **Number Memory Words** for them. Look at this:

```
0   3   2   1
Z   M   N   T
S           D
C
```

There is only one workable **Number Memory Word** I could think of, and thankfully it worked perfectly for my friend's phone number, as you will soon find out. That word is CeMeNT. By examining the word, we can readily discover that the "Soft C" that begins the word sounds exactly like a letter "S" and equals the digit zero (0). The "M" equals 3, the "N" equals 2 and the "T" equals 1. If I hadn't thought of the word CeMeNT, I probably would have had to develop two words instead of one to picture these four digits.

Rule number three says to **choose the Number Memory Words you believe will work best**. Use your common sense and creativity and be clever when developing the picture aid that connects the number to the use of the number. The more clever you can be, the better the association will work. In the case of this number, my friend was in the construction business. The two words I chose to use to picture his phone number were RoTTeN and CeMeNT. The association picture aid that would work best was very obvious to me. I would imagine that he always used RoTTeN CeMeNT every time he worked on a construction job. **Rule number four** says **to record the Number Memory Words** in a personal phone number file **for later review**. Occasionally I review my phone number picture aids when I have a few moments with nothing to do. When you make up picture aids for phone numbers, you need to remember to always record the aids in your own personal phone number memory file for later review. It was now very easy for me to remember this phone number. In the future every time I thought of him, I remembered that he always uses RoTTeN CeMeNT on his construction sites. By translating the consonant sounds in the words RoTTeN CeMeNT back to numbers, I easily remembered his phone number. It is impossible for me to forget this phone number. All I have to do is think of my friend in the construction business, remember my little picture aids and transform the consonant sounds back into numbers. And, importantly, I can't remember the wrong number if I know **The Consonant Number System**. RoTTeN CeMeNT will always be 412-0321. It can't be anything else. Not only does this system work well, but it also eliminates doubt and confusion. The letter "R" will always be four, so I can't start dialing the number with a wrong number. Obviously, the better you know the system and the more you practice, the faster you will be able to decipher and use this learning tool.

It is a whole lot easier to remember phone numbers, or any numbers for that matter, in this fashion because they have become tangible. And, I think it goes without saying the more numbers you have to learn the more you need to use this system. After a while, masses of numbers just seem to blend together and get lost in the vast land of forgotten numbers.

As I said earlier, a consonant sound must be used for every digit in the number that is to be remembered. I also stated that I try to find two **Number Memory Words** if possible to use for phone numbers. Preferably I would be able to find one word, but it isn't very likely, first of all, that I could find a word with precisely those seven consonants in it. In addition, not only would those seven consonants have to be in the word, but they would have to be in the same order as the order of the numbers. That isn't very likely to happen. It might require the development of three or more words to match those particular numbers in the appropriate order. The important thing is to have the same number of sounds as numbers, and of course, the sounds have to be in the same order as the numbers.

Let's examine another phone number of another one of my friends. This particular friend is an attorney. His phone number is 942-0960. The process or rules to follow from page 71 should become second nature to you after a few more practice applications. First of all we need to list the sound equivalents under the numbers.

```
9  4  2  0  9  6   0
P  R  N  Z  P  J   Z
B        S  B  SH  S
         C     CH  C
               G
```

Once again, you will notice that all of these sounds are listed in the order of the memory aids that helped you learn them. We know that the letter "C's" under the digit zeros are "Soft C's." We also know that the letter "G" under the number six is a "Soft G." As I said before I first try to develop two **Number Memory Words** for phone numbers. You will remember that the first one hopefully, can be developed from the first three numbers. Let's examine the first three digits of this phone number.

```
9  4  2
P  R  N
B
```

Next, we must develop some possible **Number Memory Words** to use for the picture aid. Some possible words for these letter combinations are **PR**aw**N**, **BR**i**N**e and **BR**ai**N** among others. I want to discuss the "iNG" ending that I alluded to earlier with another phone number. I began to discover with practical application of this system that I could have developed some better pictures many times for three digit numbers ending with the digit two (2) if I could have used the "iNG" ending without translating the ending "G" into numbers when remembering the number. One basic rule that I use is, "**Use as little as possible to remember as much as possible.**" Because of the desire to not count the ending "G" in the "iNG" letter combination, I developed another rule that became, "**Break any rule if it makes it easier to remember the information.**" If the "G" on the end of a word ending in "iNG" didn't have to be counted, it would open up many more possibilities for me. Let me show you what I mean by using the beginning three digits in the phone number we are discussing now. The 9-4-2 sequence of numbers could be pictured using the words "**PR**yi**N**g" or "**BoR**i**N**g" if I disregarded the ending "Hard G." I simply decided to never count the ending "G" in a word ending in "iNg." That opened up many more opportunities for me, and this particular phone number is the number that caused me to develop that rule. You will find out why shortly. Let's examine the last four digits of this phone number.

```
0   9   6    0
Z   P   J    Z
S   B   SH   S
C       CH   C
        G
```

We must develop some possible **Number Memory Words** to use for the picture aid using these last four digits. The only truly workable word I could develop using all four digits in one word was the word "**SPeeCHeS**." The word "**SPeeCHeS**" very nicely translates back into the numbers 0-9-6-0. It was time to select the words I wanted to use and create a clever association. I chose to use the word "**BoRiNg**" for the first three letters, and as I said earlier this number caused me to decide not to count the "G" in the word "**BoRiNg**." I have already said that I used the word "**SPeeCHeS**" for the last four digits. Here was the challenge facing me. Connect "**BoRiNg SPeeCHeS**" to my attorney friend. Once again, the association was all too obvious. I imagined that my attorney friend gave very "**BoRiNg SPeeCHeS**." That was awfully close to being a fact anyway. So then, the last and final rule was to record this picture memory aid into my personal phone directory, so I could review the picture aid from time to time when I had some spare time. The truth of the matter is that I have never forgotten either one of the phone numbers I have used as examples for you in this teaching explanation. These are actual numbers of actual friends that I use. They aren't simply made up to make good copy. Now you can see how disappointed I would have been if I would have had to count the letter "G" in the ending "iNg" in the word boring. The number would have translated to 9427-0960 and wouldn't have worked. The **BoRiNg SPeeCHeS** idea was so clever and fit so well that I had to use it and that resulted in the "**break any rule if it makes it easier to remember the information**" rule.

Using the One Word Method

The application of **The One Sound Method** we have been discussing involved using one single consonant sound for each digit in the number to be learned. This application cannot be used effectively in some number combinations. Some number arrangements don't lend themselves to the development of words, because the arrangements put consonants in totally impossible combinations for forming words. I want to describe a phone number that caused me to develop another application method, **The One Word Method**, that opened up a whole new world of possibility for me. The phone number was 489-7061, and it belonged to my **printer**. The first rule of application instructs us to list the sounds under the numbers. Here is what that number looked like after I did that.

```
4   8   9   7   0   6   1
R   F   P   G   Z   J   T
    V   B   K   S   SH  D
            C   C   CH
                    G
```

Once again, you will notice that all of these sounds are listed in the order of the memory aids that helped you learn them. You already know that the "C" under the digit seven (7) is a "Hard C," the "C" under the digit zero (0) is a "Soft C" and the letter "G" under the digit six (6) is a "Soft G." Let's try to examine this phone number like we did the last two. Since I try to use two **Number Memory Words** for phone numbers whenever possible I looked at the first three digits which is always my initial approach to phone numbers. The first three digits look like this.

```
4   8   9
R   F   P
    V   B
```

Can you think of a tangible **Number Memory Word** for those three sound combinations that would have possibilities? I couldn't. Then I examined the last four digits to see if I could find a **Number Memory Word** among those four sound combinations. The four digits look like this.

```
7   0   6   1
G   Z   J   T
K   S   SH  D
C   C   CH
        G
```

You might be able to find one word that might work, but I couldn't. I could easily think of two words but not one. Since I couldn't think of a word for the first three digits or the last four digits, I began to think, "What do I really have to do anyway? I need to develop a sound for each number I have to learn. How could I expand my opportunity of possible words to use without violating this basic principle?" I knew I had to always use a proper sound for each number to be remembered. That was a rule that could never be broken. Then it hit me, "Why not use a **Number Memory Word for each sound** I have to remember **but only count the consonant sound that begins each word**." What an idea! This opened up a whole new world of possibility to me. I thought, "I can use any word that starts with the letter 'R' to represent the first number sound in this phone number. I'm only going to count the first sound anyway. It doesn't matter if that **Number Memory Word** has three, four, five or more sounds in it. I don't have to be concerned with the rest of the sounds, just the first one." Now I began to examine that phone number with a whole different perspective. Let's look at it again.

4	8	9	7	0	6	1
R	**F**	**P**	G	Z	**J**	**T**
		V	B	K	**S**	SH	D
			C	C	CH	
				G		

The sounds I eventually decided to use for this new application are bold. I'm now going to list just those seven sounds.

4	8	9	7	0	6	1
R	**F**	**P**	**C**	**S**	**J**	**T**

You may recall that this was the phone number for my **P**rinter. It only made sense for me to use the word **P**rinter if at all possible with this new application. It seemed as if that application could make the phone number even easier to remember. As I examined the sounds, I saw right away that a letter "**P**" was one of the sounds. I determined immediately that the word, which had to begin with a letter "**P**" with this new application, was going to be the word **P**rinter. It didn't matter that there were four other sounds in the word **P**rinter. I was only going to use and count the first sound when deciphering the number later. I have capitalized and put the beginning letter "**P**" in the word **P**rinter in bold type to make it stand out as the only sound that counted in that word.

I began to examine the sounds further to see what I might come up with. Since **P**rinter was going to be the third word in the memory aid, because the letter "**P**" was the third sound in the number, I began to think about some adjectives that began with the letters "R" and "F" which were the letters in the number that came before the word **P**rinter. I began to think, "What kind of **P**rinter would I like to have? How about a **R**eal **F**ast **P**rinter?" I knew I had what I needed for the first three sounds for sure. I won't go through my entire thinking process for developing the last four words. I'll simply tell you what the words were. They were **C**an **S**ave **J**erry **T**ime. When the seven **Number Memory Words** were put together, I had a **R**eal **F**ast **P**rinter **C**an **S**ave **J**erry **T**ime. By getting my name into the memory aid, it made it even more personal and memorable. Was I excited or what? What a great idea, and it has served me well through the years. If you examine this aid a little bit closer, you will determine that it isn't even a tangible picture, but it is a phrase, actually a sentence, that will work just as well. I recorded the sentence in my phone directory, reviewed it a few times over a short period of time, and I have never forgotten it. I found out that phrases, sentences or even stories that weren't totally tangible could accomplish what I wanted to do in some situations.

I want to talk about this phone number with all of its sounds listed under it once again.

4	8	9	7	0	6	1
R	F	P	G	Z	J	T
		V	B	K	S	SH	D
			C	C	CH	
				G		

I could have used any word that began with the letter "R" for the first digit in this number. I could have used any word that began with the letters "F" or "V" for the second digit. I could have used any word that began with the letters "P" or "B" for the third digit. I could have used any word that began with the letters a "Hard G," "K" or "Hard C" for the fourth digit. I could have used any word that began with the letters "Z," "S" or "Soft C" for the fifth digit. I could have used any word that began with the letters "J," "SH," "CH" or "Soft G" for the sixth digit, and I could have used any word that began with the letters "T" or "D" for the last digit. Here is another idea that would have worked just as well, **R**eally **F**ast **P**rinter **C**ould **S**end **SH**eets **T**oday. There is actually an almost inexhaustible supply of possibilities, almost as many possibilities as there are words in the dictionary that begin with these letters. By the way, the use of a good dictionary has been an invaluable tool for me through the years. The only limit I have in using this idea is the limit of my own vocabulary which, by the way, using my systems will expand dramatically.

I want to review the two methods just discussed and applied. With the first method, **The One Sound Method**, a single consonant sound is used for every digit in the number to be learned, and every sound must be translated back into a digit when the **Number Memory Word** is translated to remember the number. With the second method, **The One Word Method**, an entire word is used for every digit in the number, but only the first sound in the word is translated back into a digit when the memory aid is applied to remember the number. With this method, it doesn't matter how many sounds are in the **Number Memory Words**, since only the first one counts and is translated when applied.

I want to show you a date where I used **The One Word Method**, since we only examined dates using **The One Sound Method** earlier. Perry discovered the North Pole in 1909. As with all dates, we don't need to develop an aid for the beginning number 1. You know by now the process we must follow. Here we go.

$$
\begin{array}{ccc}
9 & 0 & 9 \\
P & Z & P \\
B & S & B \\
  & C &
\end{array}
$$

Of course, the "C" under the zero is a "Soft C." Since I couldn't think of a single **Number Memory Word** for these letter combinations I chose to use **The One Word Method**. Since this date involves the name of **Perry**, I immediately looked for a letter "P" that I might use. I had my choice of a letter "P" in two different places as you can see. Here is the aid I eventually developed, **P**erry **S**aw **P**ole. Those words tell the whole story, because they contain the name of **Perry** and the name of the **Pole** that he discovered. I made sure to record my aid in my date section so I could review it later. I always want to be **organized, disciplined** and **diligent**. How **ODD** can you be?

Using the Combination Method

Later I got another idea, "Why can't I combine both of these methods if it will work better for some numbers." I found out that this idea was also very applicable with certain number combinations. I began to call this **The Combination Method**, because it **combined both of the previous methods** just taught when remembering phone numbers. The phone number that led me to using this idea was 430-7699. You know the procedure by now.

```
4     3     0     7     6     9     9
R     M     Z     G     J     P     P
            S     K     SH    B     B
            C     C     CH
                  G
```

Since I always examine the first three digits of each phone number first, look at these three digits.

```
4 3 0
R M Z
    S
    C
```

I thought of several possible **Number Memory Words** for these sound combinations. I could have used **RaMS**, **RiMS**, **ReaMS**, **RoaMS**, **RooMS** or **RuMS** among others. Let's now examine the last four digits in this number.

```
7   6   9   9
G   J   P   P
K   SH  B   B
C   CH
    G
```

As I began to examine these letter combinations, no word began to come to mind that used all four sounds in the proper order which is always my first choice. See if you can think of one. After not being able to find one word, I began to think about the **One Word Method** instead of the **One Sound Method** for these four digits even though I had already used the **One Sound Method** for the first three digits. This is when I got my idea, "Why not combine these two methods. If I develop and use both methods I will be aware of it, and I am going to record it and review it to lock it in better anyway. Here is the memory aid that I ended up using, **RaMS** Can't Jump Big Pickles. I used the **One Sound Method** for the **first three** digits in the word **RaMS** and the **One Word Method** for the **last four** digits in the four words Can't Jump Big Pickles. When translated back into numbers I had the phone number without a problem.

RaMS Can't Jump Big Pickles
4 30 7   6   9   9

I had a new idea that I began to call The **Combination Method** that opened up even more new horizons and new possibilities for me. As a result of this new idea, I organized my phone numbers into three categories for review purposes. I began to register phone numbers in the following three sections in my personal phone directory:

1)   One Sound Method Numbers

2)   One Word Method Numbers

3)   Combination Method Numbers

With these divisions, I became even more aware of which phone numbers used which of the three methods. It only takes a little review to lock in these memory aids as you will find out when you do it for all of your phone numbers. I also list my numbers in alphabetical order in the three different sections.

There is no special magic in trying to learn the first three and then the last four digits in every phone number. Phone numbers don't have to be learned in that pattern. The first four digits and then the last three digits can be used to form words. Digits in phone numbers can be learned in any combination as long as it works. I try to divide the first three and last four digits, because that is the natural division of phone numbers, but any division of digits will work as long as the consonant sounds match the numbers.

Phone Number Practice

There is no better way for you to practice these three methods for phone numbers than beginning to develop your own personal phone directory for the phone numbers you need to remember and use. Once again, you should always take the time to do the practice drills that I suggest if you want to grow from an **apprentice** to a **Master Mind Mechanic**. You certainly need experience to reach your goal. So please, for you own sake, don't pass up these practice sessions when I assign them. They are vitally important for your growth and improvement. You can decide what you want to use as your personal phone directory. I use a small book that fits comfortably into a pocket or my briefcase. I am going to make an important suggestion. Don't use your phone directory to list the sound combinations under the numbers and the possible **Number Memory Words** that could be used for your memory aids. Use a scratch pad and transfer your final decision to your personal phone directory, so it will remain neat and orderly. This practice will help you add a more experienced tool to your **mental tool box**.

There is no need to get in a hurry when developing these **Number Memory Words**. You want to use your common sense and be clever when developing these aids, so they will be easy to recall. It is important to try to have the **Number Memory Words** contain something that relates to a person's personality or profession if at all possible. You may remember that I used

RoTTeN CeMeNT for a friend in the construction business. These clever aids make it even easier to remember the numbers. That is why I ask you to take your time when developing these aids. By spending a little more time, you might find a really clever aid, and you will get even more experience.

You now have several choices of methods to use to learn numbers. You could use the **One Word Method**, the **One Sound Method** or the **Combination Method**. I use the **One Sound Method** every time I possibly can. It is always my first choice of methods. If the **One Sound Method** doesn't seem to work with the number combinations I have to learn then, and only then, I go on to another method.

As I have already stated, speed is not the most important factor as you start to learn these applications. Speed may never need to be a factor for you. When making up memory aids for phone numbers or any other numbers, take your time and develop several possibilities until you find one that seems to work best for that particular number and its use. One of the times when speed will be helpful is when you call an information operator for a new phone number and don't have anything with which to write it down. You will want to make up a memory aid quickly as you hear the number. That is another reason why practice is important.

I will introduce various other ways to remember long digit numbers including the **Adjective Peg Word Method** later. This method will increase your arsenal of weapons to attack and solve number learning problems. As I said earlier, I want to introduce you to the basics of several systems before fully developing each system. This will allow you to have a better overall grasp of the entire **Lucas Learning System**™ and how to apply it much earlier than if each system were fully taught as soon as it was introduced. Before going on to something else though, I do want to teach another application for numbers.

Area Codes

Area codes are very much a part of phone numbers, but they aren't needed by everyone. Some people don't make many long distance calls, and the very high percentage of their calls occur within their own area code. As a result, they don't have to dial the area code. You may dial long distance calls on a regular basis and remembering the area code would be crucial for you. The overall picture needs to be started with a tangible picture for the area code in these cases. The rest of the phone number would be connected to the area code. I have developed standards for all area codes used in the United States. I will list them for your use. If it is not a U. S. area code it, will say **Not U.S.** after the number. If you think of something you think will work better for a particular area code, use it.

201 - NaSTy	301 - MaST	401 - RuST	501 - LoST
202 - iNSaNe	302 - MoiSteN	402 - ReSiN	502 - LeSSoN
203 - eNZyMe	303 - MuSeuM	403 - Not U.S.	503 - LeaSe Me
204 - Not U.S.	304 - MiSeR	404 - RaCeR	504 - LaSeR
205 - NoZZLe	305 - MuScLe	405 - wReStLe	505 - Low SaiL
206 - NiCe Shoe	306 -	406 - RoSe itCH	506 -
207 - No SocK	307 - MuSiC	407 -	507 - iLL SocK

208 - uNSaFe	308 - MaSSiVe	408 - ReCeiVe	508 -
209 - NewSBoy	309 - MiShaP	409 -	509 - LiSP
210 -	310 -	410 -	510 -
211 -	311 -	411 -	511 -
212 - iNDiaN	312 - MuTiNy	412 - RoTTeN	512 - LighTeN
213 - aNaToMy	313 - MeDiuM	413 - ReDeeM	513 - yuLe TiMe
214 - wiNTeR	314 - MeTeoR	414 - RiDeR	514 -
215 - NooDLe	315 - MoTeL	415 - RaTTLe	515 - LaDLe
216 - NighT watCH	316 - My DitCH	416 -	516 - LaTe Chow
217 - iNDiGo	317 - My DocK	417 - ReTaKe	517 - iLL DoG
218 - NaTiVe	318 - MoTiVe	418 -	518 - LeaD oFF
219 - NighT Pay	319 - MuD Pie	419 - ReTaPe	519 -
601 - CHaSeD	701 - CaSSeTTe	801 - VeST	901 - PoST
602 - CHoSeN	702 - CaSiNo	802 - ViSiNe	902 -
603 - CHooSe Me	703 - CHaSM	803 - FuSSy Ma	903 -
604 - Not U.S.	704 - GeySeR	804 - ViSoR	904 - PaSSeR
605 - CHiSeL	705 -	805 - FiZZLe	905 -
606 - CHewS CHow	706 -	806 - FiSH itCH	906 - PaSSaGe
607 - GooSe eGG	707 - Go aSK	807 -	907 - BaSK
608 - CHaSe oFF	708 -	808 - FaCe oFF	908 -
609 - JuiCe uP	709 -	809 -	909 -
610 -	710 -	810 -	910 -
611 -	711 -	811 -	911 -
612 - SHuTDowN	712 - CoTToN	812 - FaTTeN	912 - BuTToN
613 -	713 - KiD Me	813 - halF TiMe	913 - BoTToM
614 - CHeaTeR	714 - CaTeR	814 - FighTeR	914 - BuTTeR
615 - SHuTTLe	715 - CuDDLe	815 - FiDDLe	915 - BoTTLe
616 - Jet SHoe	716 - CoTTaGe	816 - FooD SHow	916 - PoTaSH
617 - watCH DoG	717 - heCTiC	817 - FaTiGue	917 -
618 - SHuT oFF	718 -	818 -	918 - PaiD oFF
619 -	719 -	819 -	919 - PuT uP

Style or Identification Numbers

Many businesses use various kinds of style or identification numbers to identify products that they inventory. Some companies use a combination of letters and numbers. I will only discuss numbers at this time. I will teach you how to handle a combination of letters and numbers after you learn how to picture and learn letters of the alphabet. You have enough knowledge already so that this explanation only needs to be very brief. This is a simple **One-On-One** learning problem, **one product** and **one style number**. You simply need to connect the inventory item to the style number. You may or may not have to develop a sound-alike word to picture the inventory item. In most cases that won't be necessary, because the inventory items will be tangible and easily pictured. You will definitely have to develop a **Number Memory Word** for the style or identification number using **The Consonant Number System**. I will develop a few as examples first. The example inventory items will be followed by a sample style number and the **Number Memory Word** I developed to picture the style number.

Lamp	685	**SHoVeL**
Table	950	**BeLLS**
Stove	641	**CHaRT**
Toothbrush	170	**TacKS**
Trophy	125	**TuNNeL**
Pencil Sharpener	910	**BaTS**

To learn these style numbers we simply need to connect the inventory item to the **Number Memory Word** and record our memory aid for review purposes. Here are some suggestions.

Lamp - I would see myself using a **SHoVeL** to load these **lamps** onto a storage rack.

Table - I would see this particular **table** covered with **BeLLS**.

Stove - I would see a **CHaRT** burning inside this **stove**.

Toothbrush - I would see **TacKS** on this **toothbrush** instead of bristles.

Trophy - I would imagine that this **trophy** was running in a **TuNNeL**.

Pencil Sharpener - I would see this pencil sharpener being used to sharpen **BaTS**.

These connections would work just fine to allow me to learn the style numbers. If your business has many different lamps or many different tables, I'm sure you can see the difference among all of the lamps or tables in your mind, because they all have a different appearance. If it is your business, you certainly will be able to identify each one by picture. All of the inventory items will have a different style or identification number, so each item would have its own special memory aid picture. Try this idea. It will help you save time.

Prices

Learning prices requires the same application that I just discussed for style numbers. Learning prices is also a simple **One-On-One** learning problem, **one product** and **one price**. You simply need to connect the item to the price. As with style numbers, you may or may not have to develop a sound-alike word to picture the item. In most cases, as was already stated, that won't be necessary, because the items will be tangible and easily pictured. You will have to develop a **Number Memory Word** for the price using **The Consonant Number System**. I will develop a few items and prices as examples. The example items will be followed by a sample price. I would like for you to practice developing the **Number Memory Word** for each item and make the connections yourself. Practice makes perfect. Get some scratch paper to work on. Some of these items have dollars and cents in the prices. You wouldn't have any problem knowing where the decimal point goes, especially if it was your business. Common sense will tell you that a briefcase costs $67.85 and not $6,785. I will show you the **Number Memory Words** I developed for these items later. Remember that you could use the **One Word Method** instead of the **One Sound Method** if you so desire. You could even use the **Combination Method**. I use the **One Sound Method** every time I possibly can though. That is always my first choice of methods as I have stated earlier.

Automobile	$29,404
Tea Set	$49.50
Typewriter	$230.75
Stereo	$99.95
Washing Machine	$485
Briefcase	$67.85
Wastebasket	$5.60
Rug	$21.90

Begin to work on **Number Memory Words** for these items and develop picture memory aids on scratch paper. After you have done that, I want you to fill in your **Number Memory**

Words and **prices** that result from those words in the appropriate blanks below. Since this will be a test, you certainly shouldn't refer to your scratch sheet where your **Number Memory Words** were developed when you take the test. Develop your **Number Memory Words** and connections, review them and then take the test.

Price Test

Please don't look back at the original prices in this book as you take this test.

Item	Number Memory Words	Prices
Automobile	_____	_____
Tea Set	_____	_____
Typewriter	_____	_____
Stereo	_____	_____
Washing Machine	_____	_____
Briefcase	_____	_____
Wastebasket	_____	_____
Rug	_____	_____

These applications will make it easy for you to learn prices. If your business has several different briefcases or rugs or whatever, I'm sure you could easily see a distinct and different picture in your mind for each of them. You would simply develop a **Number Memory Word** and memory aid connection for each item, record it and review it until it becomes knowledge. If two or more items such as briefcases have the same price, use the same **Number Memory Words** for each briefcase with the same price.

CHAPTER 6

The Peg Word System

You may be called upon to learn information at a numbered position, such as the number of an element in the periodic table. **The Peg Word System** has many uses but the first and foremost use is for remembering information by number or at numbered positions. For instance, you may need to learn which element is at number 30 or is the 30th element in the periodic table. The 30th element is zinc, the 94th element is plutonium, and the 10th element is neon and so forth. This is a simple One-On-One learning problem. You would simply need to connect a number to an element, but you would have a problem being able to picture numbers. After studying, you would want to know the 30th element immediately, or the 50th element immediately. To do this, you need a system that will enable you to picture any number immediately for instant retrieval. **The Peg Word System** will give you that ability.

This system is based on the knowledge you learned in **The Consonant Number System**, so you don't have any basic new fundamentals to learn for this system. You simply have to learn how to apply and adapt some of your present knowledge to this new technique. **A Peg Word can be defined as a standard picture for a number**. The basic idea is to have a standard way to picture the numbers 1 through 100, so you can conjure up a tangible identity for any of these numbers immediately like you can for a cow, a horse or a giraffe.

You can't use it before you learn it, so let's get started. In developing standard pictures for the numbers 1 through 100, I use the **One Sound Method** that you learned with **The Consonant Number System**. As I previously stated, this system is based on the knowledge you already learned from **The Consonant Number System**. Only one sound will be used for each digit in the numbers 1 through 100. Since the number one (1) is a single digit number, the standard word created to picture it can only contain one consonant sound. The **One Sound Method** demands that we use only one consonant sound for each digit in the number. There are many potential words I could have chosen for the standard picture for the number one (1). I could have used a Tie, a Toe, a Doe, Dew or several other words that contain only one sound for the number one (1). In choosing and developing these standard pictures, I had to keep in mind that none of them could cause confusion with any other peg word. I certainly didn't want to think of a number and have any confusion about how I pictured it, nor did I want any two peg words to be so similar in nature that they caused confusion. Why this concept is so important will become apparent to you as the complete **Peg Word System** is developed.

The standard word I chose to picture the number one (1) is Tie. We can easily see a Tie in our minds, and a **Tie** can only represent the number one based on our knowledge of **The Consonant Number System**. The letter "T" equals the number one (1), and the "i" and "e" are vowels and have no number value in **The Consonant Number System**. This peg word has become such a standard for me that I automatically see a **Tie** in my mind every time I think of the number one (1) in the same way that I automatically see a cow in my mind when I think of it. You see a picture for this peg word below. All 100 peg words have become that tangible in my mind. That is the whole purpose of **The Peg Word System**, to be able to automatically see a standard picture for the numbers 1 through 100.

The peg word for the number two (2) is **Noah**. Noah can only equal the number two, because it has only one consonant sound, and that sound is the sound made by the letter "N." The two vowels and the letter "h" in the word do not make consonant sounds, so they have no number value. I use the word **Noah** for the peg word for number two for several reasons, the least of which is that the animals went onto the ark **two by two**. This seems to make it a little easier to remember. Whatever word was used for the number two (2) had to have only one consonant sound in it, because the number two (2) is a single digit number. That sound had to be the sound made by the letter "N" based on what was learned in **The Consonant Number System**. To picture this peg word, I see **Noah**'s ark or imagine what I need to remember entering the ark in some unusual way. With the number one (1), I had a choice of using a "T" or a "D" in the peg word, but with the number two (2) I had no choice since there is only one sound used for the number two. You see a picture for this peg word below.

Since the number three (3) is also a single digit number, the peg word for this number must also have only one consonant sound in it, and that sound must be the sound made by the letter "M" since that is the only sound used for the number three (3). The peg word for the number three is **M**a. The word **M**a can only represent the number three, because the letter "M" can only equal the number three based on what you have learned, and the letter "a" has no number value. To picture this peg word, I simply see a **M**a or a mother in my mind. To make it more vivid, I picture my own **M**a or mother for this peg word. You see a picture for this peg word below.

Since the number four (4) is also a single digit number, the peg word for this number must also have only one consonant sound in it, and that sound must be the sound made by the letter "R" since that is the only sound used for the number four (4). The peg word for the number four is **R**ye. The word **R**ye can only represent the number four, because the letter "R" can only equal the number four based on what you have learned, and the "y" and "e" have no number value. To picture this peg word, I simply see a loaf of **R**ye bread or a **R**ye bread sandwich. You see a picture for this peg word below.

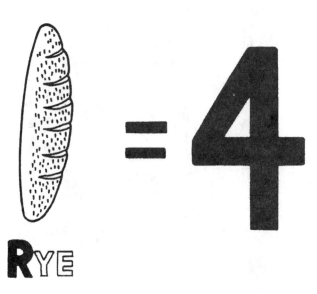

Since the number five (5) is also a single digit number, the peg word for this number must also have only one consonant sound in it, and that sound must be the sound made by the letter "L" since that is the only sound used for the number five (5). The peg word for the number four is **Law**. The word **Law** can only represent the number five, because the letter "L" can only equal the number four based on what you have learned, and the "a" and "w" have no number value. To picture this peg word, I simply see a **Lawman** or a policeman. You see a picture for this peg word below.

Peg Word Review

Before establishing any more peg words, I want you to review the first five peg words by asking you some questions. When reviewing peg words there is a standard procedure to follow. Ideally you would never have to go beyond suggestion number one (1) in the list below before remembering the peg word, but if suggestion number one doesn't work there are some backup suggestions in this procedure.

1) **Think of the peg word number**. In this case it will only be the numbers 1 through 5. After you learn all of the peg words, study them and know them better. You may not have to go past this suggestion before the peg word pops into your mind.

2) **Remember the consonant sounds** for the digit or digits. Hopefully the peg word will pop into your mind at this point if it hasn't already.

3) **Refer to the Peg Word Picture** for help. **Peg Word Pictures** are not individual pictures of the peg words like I have shown you for the first five peg words. **Peg Word Pictures** contain the pictures of ten peg words that have been linked together to help you remember them better, but they are only introduced after ten peg words are established, so you won't have them for this review. There is a **Peg Word Picture** for the peg words 1 through 10, another one for the peg words 11 through 20, another one for the peg words 21 through 30 and so forth. It is necessary to list this step in the review process even

though you can't use the actual **Peg Word Picture** for this review. I showed you the individual pictures of these first five peg words, so you would at least have an individual picture of each for your review.

4)   **Mentally place vowels after or between the appropriate consonant sounds to help recall the peg word.** If all of the previous suggestions have failed, begin to **place vowels** in the A, E, I, O, U order **after** a single digit consonant sound for single digit peg words **or between the appropriate** double digit **consonant sounds** for double digit peg words **to help recall the peg word**. Even though some peg words, especially single digit numbers, have more that one vowel in them, this step can still be helpful. Most double-digit peg words have only one vowel between the consonant sounds. If all of these suggestions fail, you have not spent enough time learning the peg words and will need to review and study the peg words and peg word pictures some more.

Look at these four review rules as you try to remember the first five peg words. Do that now. If you couldn't remember one of them, go back and review my teaching until you know all of them well.

The number six (6) is a single digit number, so the peg word for this number must have only one consonant sound in it. The peg word for the number six (6) is **SH**oe. **SH**oe can only equal the number six, because it has only one consonant sound, and that sound is the six sound made by the letters "SH." The two vowels in this word do not make consonant sounds, so they have no number value. With this number I had a choice of using a "J," "SH," "CH" or "Soft G" sound in the peg word, since all of these sounds equal the number six (6). I chose a **SH**oe, because it is easy to picture and is very versatile in application. Simply see a **SH**oe in you mind to picture this peg word. Some of my students see a fancy **SH**oe to make it more vivid, perhaps an old fashioned high-top **SH**oe. You see a picture for this peg word below.

SHOE

The number seven (7) is a single digit number, so the peg word for this number must have only one consonant sound in it. The peg word for the number seven (7) is Cow. Cow can only equal the number seven, because it has only one consonant sound, and that sound is the sound made by the **hard** letter "C." The two vowels in the word do not make consonant sounds, so they have no number value. With this number I also had a choice of using a "Hard G," "K" or a "Hard C" sound in the peg word, since all of these sounds equal the number seven (7). The choice of this peg word was easy, because Cow is a word in the little memory aid that helped you recall the sounds for the digit seven when learning **The Consonant Number System**. You see a picture for this peg word below

Since the number eight (8) is also a single digit number, the peg word for this number must also have only one consonant sound in it, and that sound must be the sound made by the letters "F" or "V," since those are the only sounds used for the number eight (8). The peg word for the number eight is iVy. The word iVy can only represent the number eight, because the letter "V" can only equal the number eight based on what you have learned, and the other two letters are vowels and have no number value. This peg word is different from all other peg words, because it doesn't begin with a consonant sound. Even though it doesn't, it makes no difference. It still has only one consonant sound in it, and that is "V" which equals eight. With this number, I also had a choice of using an "F" or a "V" sound in the peg word, since both of these sounds equal the number eight (8). To picture this peg word, I simply see growing iVy. To make it more vivid, I picture poison iVy. You see a picture for this peg word below.

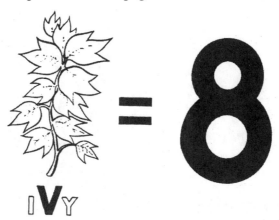

Since the number nine (9) is also a single digit number, the peg word for this number must also have only one consonant sound in it, and that sound must be the sound made by the letters "P" or "B," since those are the only sounds used for the number nine (9). The peg word for the number nine is **B**ee. The word **B**ee can only represent the number nine, because the letter "B" can only equal the number nine based on what you have learned, and the two vowels have no number value. With this number, I also had a choice of using a "P" or a "B" sound in the peg word, since both of these sounds equal the number nine (9). To picture this peg word, I see an oversized honey **B**ee. This peg word is also easy to remember, because the word **B**ee sounds exactly like one of the two sounds that represent the number nine in **The Consonant Number System**. "P" and "B" are the sounds for the number nine, and "B" sounds exactly like **B**ee. You see a picture for this peg word below.

Since the number ten (10) contains two digits, the peg word for this number must also have two consonant sounds in it, and those sounds must correspond to the sounds made by the digits one (1) and zero (0). We must always have an equal number of sounds for the number of digits in any number. The peg word for the number ten (10) is **T**oe**S**. The word **T**oe**S** can only represent the number ten, because the sound made by the letter "T" can only equal the number one (1), and the letter "S" can only equal zero (0) based on what you have learned. The two vowels in the word have no number value. To picture this peg word, I simply see my ten **T**oe**S**. Notice I said my **ten T**oe**S**. Since this is the peg word for the number **ten** (10), having **ten T**oe**S** makes the peg word easier to remember. You see a picture for this peg word below.

Learning Ladders

Before showing you the **Peg Word Picture** for the peg words 1 through 10, I want to introduce another concept that I call **Learning Ladders**. **Learning Ladders** are ladders that contain ten (10) peg words spelled out. They do not show the drawn picture of the peg words as the **Peg Word Pictures** do. These special ladders simply list the peg words in ascending order to help you see and review them in another way. Here is the first of the ten **Learning Ladders**.

As you can see, there are ten rungs, or **Pegs,** representing the **Peg Words**, on the ladder pictured below. To the left of each **Peg** space are the sound or sounds that correspond to the sounds learned in **The Consonant Number System**. The sounds used for each peg word are **bold**. This listing is a helpful reference. These sounds start at the bottom of the ladder and work up the same way the peg words do. Several clichés come to mind as I look at this ladder, "Start at the bottom and work your way up," or "Step up to success," or "Climb the ladder of success." These clichés are apropos for this ladder, because it will help you with all of those thoughts. The first peg word, **T**ie, is on the **first peg**, the second peg word, **N**oah, is on the **second peg**, the third peg word, **M**a, is on the **third peg** and so on. Spend some time examining and studying this **Learning Ladder**. It will help solidify the first ten peg words in your mind.

T or D & **Z, S** or Soft C	10 - Toe**S**
P or **B**	9 - **B**ee
F or **V**	8 - i**V**y
Hard G, K or Hard **C**	7 - **C**ow
J, **SH**, CH o r Soft G	6 - **SH**oe
L	5 - **L**aw A **L**awman or policeman
R	4 - **R**ye
M	3 - **M**a
N	2 - **N**oah
T or D	1 - **T**ie

Peg Word Pictures

As I have already stated, **Peg Word Pictures** contain the pictures of ten peg words that have been linked together to help you remember them better. The **Peg Word Picture** for the peg words 1 through 10 is pictured below.

Tie - Noah - Ma- Rye - Law - SHoe - Cow - iVy - Bee - ToeS

As you can see, the picture starts with a **T**ie that is worn by **N**oah. **N**oah is holding hands with a **M**a. With her other hand the **M**a is holding a loaf of **R**ye bread like a baby. The **R**ye bread is handcuffed to the **L**aw. The **L**aw, a policeman, is placing a **SH**oe on a **C**ow while the **C**ow is munching on some i**V**y. A **B**ee on the i**V**y is stinging some **T**oe**S**. This picture not only depicts the first ten (10) peg words, but it also connects or links them together in order. Study this picture for a while and then go through a review of the first ten (10) peg words listed below the picture.

I have repeatedly told you to be organized, disciplined and diligent, or you won't become a **Master Mind Mechanic**. I have been disciplined and diligent enough to develop and organize the **Learning Ladder** and **Peg Word Picture** for you, so you should certainly be disciplined and diligent enough to organize yourself to study and learn them until they become knowledge, knowledge you can call upon and use at any time.

Using the Peg Word System

The main use of the **Peg Word System** is to remember items in and out of order by number. Since you have learned the first ten peg words, I am going to show you how to use them to learn the first ten elements in the periodic table taught in chemistry. If you tried to learn this information by repetition, it would take a long time and be very boring. This application will require using two tools at the same time even though the learning problem is a simple **One-On-One** learning problem. It is a **One-On-One** problem, because we only have to connect the name of an element to a number, one element to one number. Two tools have to be used to accomplish this. We have to use the **Sound-Alike System** to change the intangible name of the element to a tangible picture, and the **Peg Word System** is used to picture the numbers 1 through 10.

I want you to think of sound-alike words for the elements for further practice. The more practice you can get, the more qualified you will become. This practice will help you add a more experienced tool to your **mental toolbox**. I will list the elements with a phonetic pronunciation after each element. Write in the sound-alike word you think of on the blank following each element. You will read what my sound-alike words for these ten elements are later. Remember to say each syllable slowly as you develop sound-alike words. Sometimes you don't have to develop actual, technical sound-alike words. The first element, for instance, is **hydrogen**. I simply picture a **hydrogen bomb** for that element. A technically correct sound-alike word picture for hydrogen would have to contain the three syllables in the word which are **high-dro-gin**. My sound-alike words won't necessarily work any better than yours. As long as a sound-alike word sounds like the original word and can be pictured, it will work. A clever connection will make it work. I do want to point out that many of the elements end with the letters "ium," and I don't even worry about developing a sound-alike for these three ending letters. When they are studied, our original awareness will make us aware of that ending, because we will have seen the actual words many times. The first ten elements are:

1)   Hydrogen - (High-dro-gin) - <u>You already know that I use a hydrogen bomb.</u>

2)   Helium - (He-lee-um) _____

3)   Lithium - (Lith-e-um) _____
         (I only do the "lith" sound for this element.)

4)   Beryllium - (Burr-ill-e-um) _____
         (I only do the "burr" and "ill" sounds for this element.)

5)   Boron - (Bore-on) _____

6)   Carbon - (Car-bun) _____

7)   Nitrogen - (Nigh-tro-gin) _____

8) Oxygen - (Ox-ih-gin)

9) Fluorine - (Floor-een)

10) Neon - (Knee-on)

Here are the sound-alike words I developed for these ten elements.

1) Hydrogen - (High-dro-gin) - You already know that I use a **hydrogen bomb**.

2) Helium - (He-lee-um) - I simply use a **helium balloon**. No other sound-alike we could develop will work better. I always take advantage of the obvious as in this case.

3) Lithium - (Lith-e-um) - I use a lisp or a "**lith**p" if you will. The "e" and "um" sounds are not needed. They will be remembered naturally, because of the student's general knowledge of the subject.

4) Beryllium - (Burr-ill-e-um) - I use "**brr**" as though someone was cold and "**ill**." I picture a thermometer to see the word "ill." The "e" and "um" sounds are needed. They will be remembered naturally.

5) Boron - (Bore-on) - I use a wild "**boar**" that is "**on**" something.

6) Carbon - (Car-bun) - I use a "**car**" and a "**bun**."

7) Nitrogen - (Nigh-tro-gin) - I use a crescent shaped moon. It comes out at "**night**," the word "**row**" and "**gin**ger ale." As you can see I combined part of the first two syllables when developing the first part of this sound-alike. That doesn't matter at all. I can break any pronunciation rule if it works for me, and this works for me.

8) Oxygen - (Ox-i -gin) - I use an "**ox**" and "**gin**ger ale." As you can see I have eliminated the middle syllable in my sound-alike. Once again, so what? It works and it works well. You should never get hung up on thinking that you have to absolutely use every syllable in the original word in the sound-alike. Use whatever works. As you already know one of my famous rules is **use as little as possible to remember as much as possible**.

9) Fluorine - (Floor-een) - I use a "**floor**" with a high "**sheen**" or shine on it. Here is an example where I used only the last three letters in a five letter word. Again I say, "So what! It works."

10) Neon - (Knee-on) - I simply use a "**neon**" sign. No other sound-alike we could develop will work better. This is an obvious case as was helium.

I am going to use these sound-alikes in my teaching. It doesn't mean that they are any better than yours, but you may have learned something from how I developed them. I have developed many standards for certain sounds that I will provide for you later. They are very helpful when developing sound-alike words. To learn these first ten elements by number, we simply need to connect the sound-alike word for the element with the peg word for its number position. When I teach this application in my seminars, I don't show tangible pictures of the connections or associations. I ask my students to see mental pictures, but since this is your first list to be learned with the Peg Word System, I will show you actual pictures. Here we go!

1)   For element **number one (1)**, we must connect **Tie**, the peg word for number one (1), to a **hydrogen bomb**, the sound-alike for the element **hydrogen**. In the picture below, you see a man wearing a **hydrogen bomb** around his neck instead of a **Tie**. The Substitution Rule from the **ADEOS** rules was used here. See the picture clearly before continuing.

2)   For the second element, **helium**, we simply need to connect **Noah**, the peg word for the number two (2), to a helium balloon, our sound-alike picture for this element. In the picture you see that Noah's ark is being held up by helium balloons. I simply imagined that God attached helium balloons to the ark to help it float better. See the picture clearly.

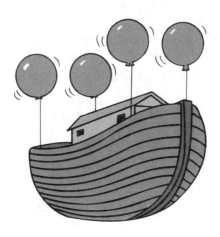

3)   Element number three (3) is **lithium**. The peg word for number three (3) is **Ma**. Below, you see a picture of a **Ma** with her baby. The **Ma** says, "I have a **lith**p!" As I mentioned before, the ending sounds of "e" and "um" don't need to be part of the picture. They will be remembered by a student familiar with chemistry. Pay particular attention to this picture, because there isn't really any action to make it more memorable.

4)   Element number four (4) is **beryllium**. The peg word for number four (4) is **Rye**. In the picture you see a loaf of **R**ye bread that is very cold. It is so cold that it says, "**Brr**." The cold has caused it to get **ill** as you can see by the thermometer. Once again, the sounds of "e" and "um" don't need to be part of the picture.

5)   Element number five (5) is **boron**. The peg word for number five (5) is **Law**. In the picture you see a **Law** man, a policeman, directing traffic with a wild **boar on** his head. What a funny thing to do! The silliness of the picture causes better registration.

6)   Element number six (6) is **carbon**. The peg word for number six (6) is **SH**oe. In the picture you see some very unusual **SH**oes. They are a **car** with a flip **bun** top.

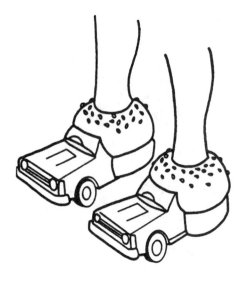

7)   Element number seven (7) is **nitrogen**. The peg word for number seven (7) is Cow. In the picture you see a stubborn Cow being pulled toward some water. The Cow is being pulled by a moon, which is my standard for the word **night**. The moon is **row**ing the boat with a bottle of **gin**ger ale.

8)   Element number eight (8) is **oxygen**. The peg word for number eight (8) is iVy. In the picture, you see an **ox** sitting in iVy while drinking a bottle of **gin**ger ale. As I said earlier, I don't think the middle syllable is necessary to remember this element.

9)   Element number nine (9) is **fluorine**. The peg word for number nine (9) is **B**ee. In the picture below, you see a **B**ee mopping and shining a **floor** to a very high sh**een**. The last three letters in the word sh**een** are the only letters used in the sound-alike word picture.

10)   **Neon** is element number ten, and I use neon lights to picture neon. Since **ToeS** is the peg word for the number ten (10), we must connect **ToeS** with neon. In the picture, you see some **ToeS** flashing on and off like **neon** lights. Imagine that they are made of neon lights. Imagine that your own **ToeS** are made of neon.

Element Test by Number

Go back over these pictures a couple of times more before taking this test. I normally conduct a review after the first five elements. That is why I want you to review them again to make sure the pictures are locked into your mind. As you review the pictures again, say the peg words and elements a few times as you look at each picture, and you will know them.

1)   Think of a **Tie** (1). What did the man have around his neck instead of a **Tie**? So then what is element number one (1) in the periodic table?

2)   Think of **Noah** (2). What was helping hold up **Noah's** ark? So then, what is element number two (2) in the periodic table?

3)   Think of a **Ma**. What did the **Ma** say was wrong with her? What is element number three (3)?

4)   Think of **Rye** bread. What was the **Rye** bread saying, and why was it saying it? What was its condition? What is element number four (4)?

5)   Think of the **Law**, a policeman. While he was directing traffic, what was on his head? What is element number five (5)?

6)   Think of a **SH**oe. You saw some very unusual **SH**oes. What were they made to look like? What is element number six (6)?

7)   Think of a **Cow**. What was happening to the **Cow**, and what was doing it to the **Cow**? What is element number seven (7)?

8)   Think of some i**V**y. What was sitting in the i**V**y, and what was it drinking? What is element number eight (8)?

9)   Think of a **Bee**. The **Bee** was busy doing what to what? What is element number nine (9)?

10)   Think of **ToeS**. What were the **ToeS** in the picture made of? What is element number ten (10)?

That worked for you, didn't it? But it wasn't done in and out of order. The beauty of the Peg Word System is that you can easily know any item in any list, in and out of order by number. Now I will simply list the ten peg words in a haphazard order. When you see the peg word, think of the picture and fill in the name of the element on the blank line after the peg word.

Law (5) _____

iVy (8) _____

Noah (2) _____

Bee (9) _____

Rye (4) _____

Cow (7) _____

Tie (1) _____

ToeS (10) _____

SHoe (6) _____

Ma (3) _____

That's exciting, isn't it? You knew them out of order as well starting with the peg word first. Now I want to test you by naming the element and have you write the peg word and its number in the blank following each element.

Boron   Peg Word _____   Number _____

Neon   Peg Word _____   Number _____

Helium   Peg Word _____   Number _____

Fluorine   Peg Word _____   Number _____

Carbon   Peg Word _____   Number _____

Lithium   Peg Word _____   Number _____

Hydrogen   Peg Word _____   Number _____

Oxygen   Peg Word _____   Number _____

Beryllium   Peg Word _____   Number _____

Nitrogen   Peg Word _____   Number _____

You had no trouble with that either, did you? Now I want to test you with a combination of questions. Some will start with the number, and some will start with the name of the element. If it starts with the number, think of the peg word, see the picture and fill in the name of the element. If it starts with the element, think of the sound-alike word, see the picture and fill in the peg word number.

Boron   _____

Seven (7)   _____

Three (3)   _____

Neon   _____

Six (6)   _____

Helium   _____

Four (4)   _____

Eight (8)   _____

Hydrogen   _____

Nine (9)   _____

In just a moment I want you to put this book aside and mentally go through the numbers and peg words for the numbers one (1) through ten (10). As you do, the element pictures will pop into your mind and you will see that you easily know them by number. After doing that, think of the numbers one (1) through ten (10) randomly, and you will recall each element at that number as you do. This will be proof enough that this system works. Do that now!

That is proof enough that you learned the first ten elements in any order or in any way you could possibly be questioned, isn't it? As always, if you didn't have these pictures but had developed mental pictures, the memory aids should be organized and recorded, so they could be reviewed at any time. I have pictures of all of the elements in the periodic table. Doesn't it make sense that chemistry students, and all students and business people, learn the entire Peg Word System and how to use it effectively? I don't think there is any doubt that you agree after this little demonstration.

The first time I ever demonstrated my ability to remember a list of items in and out of order by number was as a freshman at Ohio State University. My roommate was John Havlicek, all-time great Hall of Fame player for the Boston Celtics. We had been in school for about three weeks when one evening John said, "Jerry, if you don't start studying, you are going to flunk out of school." You see, John was being very diligent to study several hours a night, and I only was spending thirty to forty-five minutes per night. What he didn't know was that I was diligently developing and recording the pictures I needed to learn my lessons. He also wasn't aware that I was spending a couple of hours on the weekend reviewing my picture memory aids.

I answered John by saying, "John, I don't have to study as long as you do, because I use learning systems to make it easier to learn." He replied, "I've never heard of learning systems. What in the world are you talking about?" I excitedly said, "John, let me give you a little demonstration." I had never done that for anyone before. My parents or my brother didn't even know that I was doing these things. I had never told anyone. They didn't even know I could spell alphabetically. I had just done it and improved without telling anyone. I continued, "John, call out a word, and I will rearrange the letters in the word and spell it back to you alphabetically." John quipped, "There is no way you can do that." I said, "Give it a try." He called out a word, and I spelled it back alphabetically faster than he could understand the letters. He said, "Wait a minute! How do I know if you are right or not?" I answered, "Let me call out the letters slower." I called out the letters much slower and explained that they were in perfect alphabetical order. He gaped and said, "I can't believe that." I said, "Try another word." He not only tried another word, but many more words, each seemingly more complicated than the last. I spelled every one of them in perfect alphabetical order. He immediately said, "What in the world are you, some sort of genius or something?" I wasn't a genius. I had been practicing spelling words alphabetically since I had been in about the third grade. The only genius to what I was able to do was several years of practice.

After that demonstration, I asked John to get a pencil and paper and said, "John, get on the other side of the room where I can't see the paper and do the following. Write the numbers one (1) through twenty-five (25) vertically, one under the other, on the left hand side of the page." When he finished doing that I gave these instructions, "Now call out any number and any object and write that object next to that number. After doing that, call out all of the other numbers randomly and call out another object after each number and write that object next to that number. When you have finished with the entire list, I will do another little demonstration for you." When John finished the list I said, "Pick up the list and look at it. First I will tell it to you backwards." I did and his mouth fell open. I continued, "John, call out any number, and I will tell you the object you wrote next to it, or call out any object, and I will tell you at which number you wrote it." John was amazed after that demonstration. Then I said, "Now you get a little idea of why I don't have to spend a lot of time studying. I have developed some learning methods that make it easier for me to learn." My systems certainly weren't as expansive or sophisticated as they are today, but I used them well enough to be a straight "A" student my whole freshman year. All I did to learn the list was simply use the first twenty-five peg words to picture each number. As John called out a number and an object, I simply formed an action picture in my mind between the picture for the peg word and the tangible object he called out at each number. It was easy later to recall the peg word for the number and see the object I had connected to it with my mental picture. I could just as easily think of the object, recall the picture and see the peg word.

I want to tell you a little secret about John Havlicek. When he learned that I had that skill, he won a lot of money on campus in the next few weeks. Some interesting bets on my ability were placed in the next few days. It seemed to me that some of my freshmen teammates might have taken part in this money scheme as well. One of my classmates was Bobby Knight, the great

Hall of Fame coach for the Indiana Hoosiers.

As word about my ability spread around campus, John's little scheme lost its viability. There seemed to be no more suckers available. But one Wayne Woodrow "Woody" Hayes, the Ohio State football coach, heard about it and called me into his office. I was kind of nervous about the meeting, because I thought he was going to lecture me on the vice of sucker baiting. I needn't have been nervous. Woody always wanted the best for his football players, his "boys" as he called them. He thought of his players like a father would his sons. My coach, Fred Taylor, was very much like that in his approach to us as well. Woody asked if I could help some of his players who were having a tough time with the books. He wondered if my methods might help them. I began to teach some of his players with great success, so Woody Hayes was the first person who ever officially asked me to teach my systems.

A little later when you learn some more peg words and know them well, you should demonstrate your abilities to some of your friends as well. The experience and pressure of having to perform will be good for you. It's time to get back to some more peg words.

Peg Words 11 through 20

The **Learning Ladder** for the peg words 11 through 20 is pictured on the next page. To the left of each ladder rung or **Peg** you will see the choices of sounds that were available to develop the peg word based on the sounds from **The Consonant Number System**. The sounds that are used in each peg word are **bold**. Examine each peg word carefully.

N & **Z**, **S** or Soft C	20 - NoSe	
T or D & P or **B**	19 - TuB	
T or **D** & F or **V**	18 - DiVe	
T or **D** & Hard G, **K** or Hard C	17 - TacK	"cK" only makes one sound
T or **D** & J, **SH**, CH or Soft G	16 - DiSH	
T or D & **L**	15 - ToweL	
T or D & **R**	14 - TiRe	
T or D & **M**	13 - ToMb	Silent "b" = No number value
T or D & **N**	12 - TiN	
T or D & **T** or D	11 - ToT	A baby in diapers

I see a baby in diapers to picture a **ToT**, the peg word for number eleven (11). See a **TiN** can to picture the peg word for number twelve (12). Some people have chosen to see Rin **TiN TiN**, the movie dog, for this peg word. I see a **ToMb**stone for number thirteen (13). To the right of the word **ToMb**, I have pointed out that the letter "B" in the word **ToMb** is silent, so it has no number value. As a result, **ToMb** can't equal 139 but just 13. Simply see an automobile **TiRe** to picture number fourteen (14). Seeing any **ToweL** will work for number fifteen (15). Picturing any **DiSH** will work for number sixteen (16). Any small **TacK** will work for number seventeen (17). I also want to point out that the letters "cK" only make one seven sound and not two. I picture a person preparing to **DiVe** into a pool for number eighteen (18). I simply picture a **TuB**, a bath**TuB**, for number nineteen (19). Peg words 11 through 19 had to start with a "T" or a "D," because all of those numbers start with the digit one (1), but the number twenty (20) is another story. The peg word must start with a letter "N," because this number starts with a the digit two (2). The peg word for twenty (20) is a **NoSe**, and I picture a very large **NoSe**, perhaps a Jimmy Durante type **NoSe**. **Memory Tip** - To help in your review of these peg words, I want to point out that the peg words 16 through 18 begin with a letter "D" instead of the letter "T."

The **Peg Word Picture** for the peg words 11 through 20 is pictured below. The picture begins with a **ToT** rolling on a **TiN** can. He rolled the **TiN** can into a **ToMb**. A **TiRe** jumped off of the **ToMb** and is being handed a **ToweL** by a **DiSH**. A **TacK** loves to **DiVe** into the **TuB**. A goofy looking **NoSe** is the lifeguard at the unusual pool.

By using the **Learning Ladder** and **Peg Word Picture** for the peg words 11 through 20, you shouldn't have any trouble learning these ten peg words. Learning the peg words will demand more of your time than learning any other system. Don't get in a hurry with them. Make sure you know all of the peg words you have reviewed before going on to the next ten peg words. Don't go on until the previous peg words have become knowledge.

Don't get in a hurry when learning these peg words. They are a vital part of these over-all tools but shouldn't be rushed. Learning the peg words should be a gradual process. Set a goal of about twenty (20) peg words a week and stick with it.

I am going to provide a list in random order as though I was calling out twenty (20) items for you to learn in and out of order. This is the same thing that I described that John Havlicek did to me when we were freshmen in college. I will list a number and an object. When you see the number, think of the peg word and then connect it to the listed object by seeing a silly and vivid picture between them. Take a little time between each object to make sure you see the picture clearly. You will get faster and faster with this application with experience and practice. This is very good practice. You must know the first twenty (20) peg words well before doing this, so make sure you know them before proceeding with this test.

11 - Eyeglasses

4 - Flag

17 - Soap

1 - Ski Pole

9 - Hammer

19 - Umbrella

6 - Apron

18 - Gas Pump

12 - Bandage

15 - Chopsticks

14 - Pig

3 - Door

7 - Bullet

10 - Turkey

16 - Skull

20 - Lamp

5 - Frypan

13 - Torch

2 - Pillow

Now that you have studied and learned the list, I will provide two different tests. In the first test you must list the learned objects in order backwards. Simply write the objects at the appropriate numbers. In the second test I will list the objects, and you must list the number at which each object was learned.

20 - _____	Skull	_____
19 - _____	Pig	_____
18 - _____	Bandage	_____
17 - _____	Hammer	_____
16 - _____	Razor	_____
15 - _____	Flag	_____
14 - _____	Lamp	_____
13 - _____	Turkey	_____
12 - _____	Pillow	_____
11 - _____	Apron	_____
10 - _____	Eyeglasses	_____
9 - _____	Soap	_____
8 - _____	Torch	_____
7 - _____	Door	_____
6 - _____	Ski Pole	_____
5 - _____	Bullet	_____
4 - _____	Frypan	_____
3 - _____	Chopsticks	_____
2 - _____	Umbrella	_____
1- _____	Gas Pump	_____

Peg Words 21 through 30

The **Learning Ladder** for the peg words 21 through 30 is pictured on the next page. To the left of each ladder rung or **Peg**, you will see the choices of sounds that were available to develop the peg word based on the sounds from **The Consonant Number System**. The sounds that are used in each peg word are **bold**. Examine each peg word carefully.

M & Z, **S** or Soft C	30 - **M**oo**S**e
N & **P** or B	29 - **N**no**B**
N & F or **V**	28 - k**N**i**F**e
N & Hard G, **K** or Hard C	27 - **N**ec**K** "c**K**" only makes one sound
N & J, SH, **CH** or Soft G	26 - **N**ot**CH** Silent "t" = No number value
N & **L**	25 - **N**ai**L**
N & **R**	24 - **N**e**R**o
N & **M**	23 - **N**a**M**e A **N**a**M**e tag
N & **N**	22 - **N**u**N**
N & **T** or D	21 - **N**e**T**

I see a fishing dip **NeT** or a casting **NeT** to picture a **NeT**, the peg word for number twenty-one (21). See a **NuN** to picture the peg word for number twenty-two (22). I see either a **NaMe** tag or someone signing his or her signature or **NaMe** for number twenty-three (23). I see a Roman in a toga playing a fiddle, as in **NeRo** fiddled as Rome burned, to picture the peg word for number twenty-four (24). I sometimes just see a fiddle for this peg word. Seeing any **NaiL** will work for number twenty-five (25). Seeing a **NotCH** in something is how I picture the peg word for number twenty-six (26). I like to see it all **NotCH**ed up in an unusual way. Of course, the letter "T" in this word is silent and isn't assigned a number value. I don't see just any **NecK** for the number twenty-seven (27). I like to see an unusual **NecK**, so I see either a giraffe's **NecK** or a long dinosaur **NecK**. Once again, I want to point out that the letters "cK" only make one seven sound and not two. I picture a very large **kNiFe** to see the peg word for number twenty-eight (28). I see a door**kNoB** to picture the peg word for number twenty-nine (29). Peg words 21 through 29 have to start with an "N" sound, because all of those numbers start with the digit two (2), but the number thirty (30) is another story. The peg word must start with a letter "M," because this number starts with the digit three (3). The peg word for thirty (30) is **MooSe**, and I picture a very large **MooSe** with very large antlers. **Memory Tip** - All of the peg words 21 through 29 must begin with a letter "N" sound.

The **Peg Word Picture** for the peg words 21 through 30 is pictured below. The picture begins with a **NeT** being tossed by a **NuN**. The **NuN** tossed the **NeT** over a **NaMe** being written on the Declaration of Independence. **NeRo** is signing the **NaMe** with a **NaiL**. **NeRo** swung the **NaiL** and put a **NotCH** in the **NecK** of a giraffe before he signed his **NaMe**. The giraffe just walked past a large **kNiFe**. The **kNiFe** is being used to pry a door**kNoB**. A **MooSe** is trying to remove the door**kNoB**.

By using the **Learning Ladder** and **Peg Word Picture** for the peg words 21 through 30, you shouldn't have any trouble learning these ten peg words. Don't get in a hurry when learning these peg words. Make sure you know all 30 peg words before going on to the next ten peg words. Don't go on until the previous peg words have become knowledge.

Now that you know a few more peg words, I want to show you how a few of them could be used to learn the numerical position of more elements in the periodic table. I have developed pictures for the entire periodic table, but I'm not going to show you all of them. A few of them after every 20 or 30 peg words will continue to show you how well the peg words work for learning information at numerical positions and knowing it instantly if you know the peg words. That is why it is so important to know this tool and all tools well. The better you know them the more adept and quick you will be with your applications.

Element number thirteen (13) is **aluminum**. We simply need to associate a picture for **aluminum** to a **ToMb**, the peg word for number thirteen. This picture will work very well. You see **aluminum** foil wrapped around a **ToMb**.

Element number twenty-six (26) is **iron**. The peg word for number twenty-six (26) is **NotCH**. The following picture works very well to lock those two pieces of information together. You see an **iron** with a large **NotCH** in it.

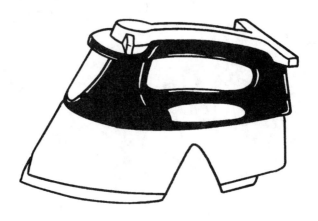

Element number thirty (30) is **zinc**. The peg word for number thirty (30) is **MooSe**. This picture of a **MooSe** taking a drink out of a kitchen **zink** will work nicely. I took a little liberty with the word "sink," but so what. It works!

A brief review of these three pictures will lock the information into your mind if you know the peg words well. It works just as well with all of the elements if you know the peg words well. I keep saying this to impress upon you the importance of fundamentals. Learning the peg words will be the most "study" you will be called upon to apply for all of my systems, but even that is made much easier with the learning ladders and the peg word pictures.

Some people feel there might be potential confusion with peg lists if peg words were used to remember more than one list at a time. They think they might confuse items of the same number in different lists. I have never had a problem with this. When you think about it logically, it would be difficult to confuse a list from economics with a list from chemistry. The difference should be obvious in the material itself. If you feel there would be a potential for confusion, a standard for each list could be incorporated into the pictures to eliminate any possible confusion. There are other solutions as well as you will learn later. One of the best qualities of these systems and tools is that they eliminate confusion. You certainly can't confuse the peg words **Cow** and **TiRe**, for instance, just as you can't possibly confuse a lion with a zebra in your mind. Your photographic mind automatically makes the distinction for you. The photographic capability of the mind is incredible and should be used to our advantage.

Peg Words 31 through 40

The **Learning Ladder** for the peg words 31 through 40 is pictured below. To the left of each ladder rung or **Peg**, you will see the choices of sounds that were available to develop the peg word based on the sounds from **The Consonant Number System**. The sounds that are used in each peg word are **bold**. Examine each peg word carefully.

R & Z, S or Soft C	40 - RoSe	
M & P or B	39 - MoP	
M & F or V	38 - MoVie	
M & Hard G, K or Hard C	37 - MuG	
M & J, SH, CH or Soft G	36 - MatCH	Silent "t" = No number value
M & L	35 - MaiL	
M & R	34 - MoweR	A lawnMoweR
M & M	33 - MuMMy	"MM" only make one sound
M & N	32 - MooN	
M & T or D	31 - MaT	A welcome MaT

I see a welcome **MaT** for the peg word for number thirty-one (31). See the **MooN** to picture the peg word for number thirty-two (32). I picture a partial, crescent **MooN** instead of a full **MooN**. A **MuMMy** is a vivid picture for number thirty-three (33). I see a lawn **MoweR** to picture the peg word for number thirty-four (34). Seeing any **MaiL** box will work for number thirty-five (35). I see a large old-fashioned **MatCH** to picture the peg word for number thirty-six (36). Of course, the letter "T" in this word is silent and isn't assigned a number value. I picture a **MuG** with foam spilling out of it for the peg word for number thirty-seven (37). I picture a **MoVie** screen or a **MoVie** camera for the peg word for number thirty-eight (38). I see an old fashioned **MoP** to picture the peg word for number thirty-nine (39). Peg words 31 through 39 have to start with an "M," because all of those numbers start with the digit three (3), but the number thirty (40) is another story. The peg word for number forty (40) must start with a letter "R," because this number starts with the digit four (4). The peg word for forty (40) is **RoSe**, and I picture a **RoSe** with thorns. **Memory Tip** - All of the peg words 31 through 39 must begin with a letter "M."

The **Peg Word Picture** for the peg words 31 through 40 is pictured below. The picture begins with a welcome **MaT** with a **MooN** standing on it. The **MooN** is watching a **MuMMy** that is using a **MoweR** to cut the grass around a **MaiL** box. The **MaiL** box is next to a **MatCH** drinking from a **MuG**. The **MatCH** and **MuG** are in a **MoVie** house. A **MoP** is being used by a **RoSe** to clean the aisle.

By using the **Learning Ladder** and **Peg Word Picture** for the peg words 31 through 40, you shouldn't have any trouble learning these ten peg words. Don't get in a hurry when learning these peg words. Make sure you know all 40 peg words before going on to the next ten peg words. Don't go on until the previous peg words have become knowledge.

Peg Words 41 through 50

The **Learning Ladder** for the peg words 41 through 50 is pictured below. To the left of each ladder rung or **Peg**, you will see the choices of sounds that were available to develop the peg word based on the sounds from **The Consonant Number System**. The sounds that are used in each peg word are **bold**. Examine each peg word carefully.

L & Z, S or Soft C	50 - LaCe	
R & P or B	49 - RoPe	
R & F or V	48 - RooF	
R & Hard G, K or Hard C	47 - RuG	
R & J, SH, CH or Soft G	46 - RoaCH	
R & L	45 - RaiL	A RaiL on a RaiLroad
R & R	44 - RoweR	A person rowing a boat
R & M	43 - RaM	
R & N	42 - RaiN	
R & T or D	41 - RaT	

I see a big, ugly **RaT** for the peg word for number forty-one (41). See the **RaiN** in a downpour to picture the peg word for number forty-two (42). A **RaM** with long curled horns is what I use as the peg word picture for number forty-three (43). I see a **RoweR** to picture the peg word for number forty-four (44). Simply see a picture of a person rowing a boat. Seeing a **RaiL** in a **RaiL**road or any **RaiL**road works well for number forty-five (45). I see a big ugly **RoaCH** to picture the peg word for number forty-six (46). I picture a **RuG** for the peg word for number forty-seven (47). I picture a **RooF** for the peg word for number forty-eight (48). If you have a particular style of **RooF** that you prefer, use it. I see **RoPe** to picture the peg word for number forty-nine (49). Peg words 41 through 49 have to start with an "R," because all of those numbers start with the digit four (4), but the number fifty (50) is another story. The peg word for number fifty (50) must start with a letter "L," because this number starts with a the digit five (5). The peg word for fifty (50) is **LaCe**, and I picture a **LaCe** doily. **Memory Tip** - All of the peg words 41 through 49 must begin with a letter "R."

The **Peg Word Picture** for the peg words 41 through 50 is pictured below. The picture begins with a big ugly **RaT** with **RaiN** pouring down on it. The **RaiN** splashes off of the **RaT** toward a **RaM** that is a **RoweR**. It has rowed toward a **RaiL** of a **RaiL**road. A **RoaCH** standing next to the **RaiL** is lifting a **RuG** with a **RoPe**. A **LaCe** doily is pulling on the other end of the **RoPe** to help lift the **RuG**.

By using the **Learning Ladder** and **Peg Word Picture** for the peg words 41 through 50, you shouldn't have any trouble learning these ten peg words. I always instruct you not to get in a hurry when learning peg words. Make sure you know all 50 peg words before going on to the next ten peg words. Don't go on until the previous peg words have become knowledge. You may feel that learning all of these peg words is a little tedious, but you must learn them and know all of their uses before you can reach your goal of becoming a **Master Mind Mechanic**. They were harder for me to learn without the **Learning Ladders** and **Peg Word Pictures** that I have developed for you.

Peg Words 51 through 60

The **Learning Ladder** for the peg words 51 through 60 is pictured below. To the left of each ladder rung or **Peg**, you will see the choices of sounds that were available to develop the peg word based on the sounds from **The Consonant Number System**. The sounds that are used in each peg word are **bold**. Examine each peg word carefully.

J, SH, **CH** or Soft G & Z, **S** or Soft C	60 - **CH**ee**S**e
L & **P** or B	59 - **L**i**P**
L & F or **V**	58 - **L**a**V**a
L & Hard G, **K** or Hard C	57 - **L**oc**K**
L & J, SH, **CH** or Soft G	56 - **L**ee**CH**
L & **L**	55 - **L**i**L**y
L & **R**	54 - **L**u**R**e
L & **M**	53 - **L**a**M**b
L & **N**	52 - **L**io**N**
L & **T** or D	51 - **L**o**T**

57 - **L**oc**K**   "c**K**" only make one sound

54 - **L**u**R**e   A fishing **L**u**R**e

53 - **L**a**M**b   Silent "b" = No number value

I see a **LoT** For Sale sign or an open **LoT** for the peg word for number fifty-one (51). See the king of the beasts, a **LioN**, to picture the peg word for number fifty-two (52). Then see a timid **LaMb** for the peg word picture for number fifty-three (53). The letter "b" in **LaMb** is silent and has no number value. A fishing **LuRe** is pictured for the peg word for number fifty-four (54). See an Easter **LiLy** for number fifty-five (55). A big ugly blood sucking **LeeCH** is what I use to picture the peg word for number fifty-six (56). I picture a **LocK** for the peg word for number fifty-seven (57). I suppose any kind of **LocK** would suffice, but I picture a regular pad**LocK**. I picture **LaVa** flowing out of a volcano for the peg word for number fifty-eight (58). I see a big set of **LiPs** to picture the peg word for number fifty-nine (59). **LiPs** is a plural word and in actuality would equal 590, but I know it is the peg word, and the singular **LiP** is all that I translate back into numbers. Peg words 51 through 59 have to start with an "L," because all of those numbers start with the digit five (5), but the number sixty (60) does not. The peg word for number sixty (60) can start with a letter "J" or "SH" or "CH" or a "Soft G," because these are the sounds for the digit six (6). The peg word for sixty (60) is **CHeeSe**, and I picture a piece of Swiss **CHeeSe**. **Memory Tip** - All of the peg words 51 through 59 must begin with a letter "L."

The **Peg Word Picture** for the peg words 51 through 60 is pictured below. The picture begins in a **LoT**. A **LioN** and a **LaMb** are standing in the **LoT**. They are casting a fishing **LuRe** that looks like an Easter **LiLy**. A **LeeCH** is using a **LocK** to try to stop molten **LaVa** flowing from a volcano. Hanging from its **LiPs** is a big piece of **CHeeSe**.

Using the **Learning Ladder** and **Peg Word Picture** for the peg words 51 through 60 will make these ten peg words easier to learn. As always, don't get in a hurry when learning peg words. Make sure you know all 60 peg words before going on to the next ten peg words. Don't go on until the previous peg words have become knowledge.

Peg Words 61 through 70

The **Learning Ladder** for the peg words 61 through 70 is pictured below. To the left of each ladder rung or **Peg** you will see the choices of sounds that were available to develop the peg word based on the sounds from **The Consonant Number System**. The sounds that are used in each peg word are **bold**. Examine each peg word carefully.

Hard G, K or Hard **C**
&
Z, **S** or Soft C

70 - Ca**S**e

A wooden Ca**S**e or box

J, SH, CH or Soft G & **P** or B

69 - **SH**i**P**

J, SH, CH or Soft G & F or **V**

68 - **SH**a**V**e

J, SH, CH or Soft G
&
Hard G, **K** or Hard C

67 - Jac**K**

"c**K**" only make one sound

J, SH, CH or Soft G
&
J, SH, **CH** or Soft **G**

66 - Jud**G**e

Silent "d = No number value

J, SH, CH or Soft G & **L**

65 - Jai**L**

J, SH, CH or Soft G & **R**

64 - Ja**R**

J, SH, CH or Soft G & **M**

63 - Ja**M**

J, SH, **CH** or Soft G & **N**

62 - **CH**ai**N**

J, SH, CH or Soft G & **T** or D

61 - Je**T**

I see a **JeT** airplane for the peg word for number sixty-one (61). I see a big **CHaiN** to picture the peg word for number sixty-two (62). Delicious **JaM** is pictured for the peg word picture for number sixty-three (63). A **JaR** is pictured for the peg word for number sixty-four (64). See a **JaiL** for number sixty-five (65). A **JudGe** in a flowing robe is what I see to picture the peg word for number sixty-six (66). The letter "d" in **JudGe** is silent and has no number value. I picture a toy **JacK** or a car **JacK** for the peg word for number sixty-seven (67). I see someone **SHaVing**, **SHaVe**, to see the peg word for number sixty-eight (68). I see a large **SHiP** to picture the peg word for number sixty-nine (69). Peg words 51 through 59 have to start with a "six sound," because all of those numbers start with the digit six (6), but the number seventy (70) does not. The peg word for number seventy (70) could start with a "Hard G," "K" or a "Hard C," because these are the sounds for the digit seven (7). The peg word for seventy (70) is **CaSe**, and I picture a wooden **CaSe** or box. **Memory Tip** - All of the peg words 61 through 69 begin with the letter "J" except number 62.

The **Peg Word Picture** for the peg words 61 through 70 is pictured below. The picture begins with a **JeT** airplane flying overhead. A long **CHaiN** with **JaM** attached to it is connected to the plane. The **JaM** is in a **JaR**. The **JaR** hit a **JaiL**. The **JudGe** in the **JaiL** is standing on a large toy **JacK**. The **JudGe** is taking his morning **ShaVe**. A **SHiP** is anchored outside. A **CaSe** on the **SHiP** is for the **JudGe**.

Using the **Learning Ladder** and **Peg Word Picture** for the peg words 61 through 70 will make these ten peg words easier to learn. As always, don't get in a hurry when learning peg words. Make sure you know all 70 peg words well before going on to the next ten peg words. Don't go on until the previous peg words have become knowledge.

Peg Words 71 through 80

The **Learning Ladder** for the peg words 71 through 80 is pictured below. To the left of each ladder rung or **Peg**, you will see the choices of sounds that were available to develop the peg word based on the appropriate sounds from **The Consonant Number System**. The sounds that are used in each peg word are **bold**. Examine each peg word carefully.

F or **V** & Z, **S** or Soft C	80 - **FaCe**
Hard G, K or Hard **C** & **P** or B	79 - **CaPe**
Hard G, K or Hard **C** & **F** or **V**	78 - **CaVe**
Hard G, K or Hard **C** & Hard G, **K** or Hard C	77 - **CaKe**
Hard G, K or Hard **C** & J, SH, CH or Soft **G**	76 - **CaGe**
Hard G, K or Hard **C** & **L**	75 - **CoaL**
Hard G, K or Hard **C** & **R**	74 - **CaR**
Hard G, K or Hard **C** & **M**	73 - **CoMb**	Silent "b" = No number value
Hard G, K or Hard **C** & **N**	72 - **CaN**
Hard G, K or Hard **C** & **T** or D	71 - **CaT**

I see a **CaT**, an alley **CaT**, for the peg word for number seventy-one (71). I see a big garbage **CaN** to picture the peg word for number seventy-two (72). There is a potential confusion of peg words here if you don't see a big garbage **CaN** for this peg word, because a **TiN** can is used for number 12. A small **TiN** can and a very large garbage **CaN** certainly won't be confused. No peg word should ever be confused with any other peg word. A **CoMb** is pictured for the peg word picture for number seventy-three (73). A **CaR** is pictured for the peg word for number seventy-four (74). There is also a potential point of confusion with **CaR** and **JeeP**. The **CaR** I see, as a result, is a long limousine type **CaR**. I certainly can't confuse that with a small Army **JeeP**. I see a pile of **CoaL** for number seventy-five (75). A **CaGe** for a bird is what I see to picture the peg word for number seventy-six (76). I picture a birthday **CaKe** for the peg word for number seventy-seven (77). I picture a **CaVe** to see the peg word for number seventy-eight (78). I see a long **CaPe** like Sherlock Holmes might wear to picture the peg word for number seventy-nine (79). Peg words 71 through 99 have to start with a "seven sound," because all of those numbers start with the digit seven (7), but the number eighty (80) does not. The peg word for number eighty (80) could start with a "F" or a "V," because these are the sounds for the digit eight (8). The peg word for eighty (80) is **FaCe**, and I picture a **FaCe** with a lot of makeup or a false **FaCe**. **Memory Tip** - All of the peg words 71 through 79 begin with the letter "C," even though two other letters could have been used. As a result, when you review the peg words 71 through 79, you won't have to bother yourself with even thinking of the other two letters to start the peg words.

The **Peg Word Picture** for the peg words 71 through 80 is pictured below. The picture begins with an alley **CaT** climbing out of a large garbage **CaN** while using a **CoMb** to **CoMb** its fur. A **CaR** crashes into a pile of **CoaL**. A bird in a **CaGe** crashed the **CaR**, because it took its eyes off of the road to watch the **CaT**. Icing from a birthday **CaKe** in a **CaVe** was blown toward the **CaGe**. A long **CaPe** has a **FaCe** on it. The **FaCe** blew on the candles.

Using the **Learning Ladder** and **Peg Word Picture** for the peg words 71 through 80 will make these ten peg words easier to learn. As always, don't get in a hurry when learning peg words. Make sure you know all 80 peg words well before going on to the next ten peg words. Don't go on until the previous peg words have become knowledge.

Peg Words 81 through 90

The **Learning Ladder** for the peg words 81 through 90 is pictured below. To the left of each ladder rung or **Peg**, you will see the choices of sounds that were available to develop the peg word based on the sounds from **The Consonant Number System**. The sounds that are used in each peg word are **bold**. Examine each peg word carefully.

P or **B** & Z, **S** or Soft C	90 - **BuS**	
F or V & P or **B**	89 - **FoB**	A pocket watch chain
F or V & **F** or V	88 - **FiFe**	A small flute
F or V & Hard **G**, K or Hard C	87 - **FoG**	
F or V & J, **SH**, CH or Soft G	86 - **FiSH**	
F or V & **L**	85 - **FiLe**	
F or V & **R**	84 - **FuR**	
F or V & **M**	83 - **FoaM**	
F or V & **N**	82 - **FaN**	
F or **V** & **T** or D	81 - **FaT**	

I see a very **FaT** person for the peg word for number eighty-one (81). A **FaN** is the picture for the peg word for number eighty-two (82). **FoaM** is pictured for the peg word picture for number eighty-three (83). A luxurious **FuR** is pictured for the peg word for number eighty-four (84). See a fingernail **FiLe** or a carpenter's **FiLe** for the peg word for number eighty-five (85). A **FiSH** is the peg word for number sixty-six (66). I prefer seeing a sail **FiSH**, because I believe it is more vivid. A blanketing **FoG** is pictured for the peg word for number eighty-seven (87). I see a **FiFe**, which is a small flute, to see the peg word for number eighty-eight (88). I see a **FoB** to picture the peg word for number eighty-nine (89). There could be some possible confusion between a **CHaiN** and a **FoB**. That is why I see a large, long **CHaiN** for 62 and a small watch chain with a pocket watch on it for a **FoB** or 89. Peg words 51 through 59 have to start with an "eight sound," because all of those numbers start with the digit eight (8), but the number ninety (90) does not. The peg word for number ninety (90) could start with a "P" or a "B," because these are the sounds for the digit nine (9). The peg word for ninety (90) is **BuS**, and I picture a school **BuS** for this peg word. **Memory Tip** - All of the peg words 81 through 89 begin with the letter "F" except number 81.

The **Peg Word Picture** for the peg words 81 through 90 is pictured below. The picture begins with a **FaT** lady looking at an electric **FaN** that is blowing **FoaM** in the water. A **FuR** is worn by the lady. She is using a large **FiLe** on her fingernails. A **FiSH** watches her **FiLe** her nails. The **FiSH** opened its mouth and a heavy **FoG** came out of its mouth. A **FiFe** with a **FoB** hanging on it is above the **FiSH**. The boy playing the **FiFe** is in a **BuS**.

Using the **Learning Ladder** and **Peg Word Picture** for the peg words 81 through 90 will make these ten peg words easier to learn. As always, don't get in a hurry when learning peg words. Make sure you know all 90 peg words well before going on to the next and final ten peg words. Don't go on until the previous peg words have become knowledge.

Peg Words 91 through 100

The **Learning Ladder** for the peg words 91 through 100 is pictured below. To the left of each ladder rung or **Peg**, you will see the choices of sounds that were available to develop the peg word based on the sounds from **The Consonant Number System**. The sounds that are used in each peg word are **bold**. Examine each peg word carefully.

Pictures for the numbers 00 to 1,000 are listed on page 293. I call this The Consonant Number Dictionary.

T or **D** & **Z**, **S** or Soft C & **Z**, **S** or Soft C	100 - **DiSeaSe**	Three (3) sounds are required
P or B & **P** or B	99 - **PiPe**	
P or B & F or **V**	98 - **PuFF**	
P or **B** & Hard G, **K** or Hard C	97 - **BiKe**	
P or **B** & J, **SH**, CH or Soft G	96 - **BuSH**	
P or **B** & **L**	95 - **BaLL**	"LL" only make one sound
P or **B** & **R**	94 - **BeaR**	
P or **B** & **M**	93 - **BuM**	
P or **B** & **N**	92 - **BuN**	
P or **B** & **T** or D	91 - **BaT**	

I see a baseball **BaT** for the peg word for number ninety-one (91). See a tasty **BuN** to picture the peg word for number ninety-two ((2). A **BuM** is pictured for the peg word picture for number ninety-three (93). A grizzly **BeaR** is pictured for the peg word for number ninety-four (94). See a **BaLL** for number ninety-five (95). Even though **BaLL** has two letter "L's" in it, the **Double Letter Rule** tells us that the letter "L's" only make one sound. A **BuSH** is used to picture the peg word for number ninety-six (96). I picture a **BiKe** for the peg word for number ninety-seven (97). Sometimes I use a **BiKe** built for two if I have extra information to remember at the number ninety-seven (97). I picture a large **PuFF** of smoke to see the peg word for number ninety-eight (98). I see a **PiPe** to picture the peg word for number ninety-nine (99). Peg words 91 through 99 have to start with a "nine sound," because all of those numbers start with the digit nine (9), but the number one-hundred (100) is another story. The peg word for number one-hundred (100) must have three sounds in it, because there are three digits in the number. The peg word for one-hundred (100) is **DiSeaSe**, and I picture a person with measles, because the spots are so easy to recognize. **Memory Tip** - All of the peg words 91 through 99 begin with the letter "B" except number 98 and 99 which begin with a letter "P."

The **Peg Word Picture** for the peg words 91 through 100 is pictured below. The picture begins with a baseball **BaT** eating a tasty **BuN**. It is watching a **BuM** help a circus **BeaR** learn to roll on a **BaLL**. A man crashes into a **BuSH** while riding a **BiKe** as he watched. A **PuFF** of smoke comes from his **PiPe**. You will notice that the smoke can cause a **DiSeaSe**.

Using the **Learning Ladder** and **Peg Word Picture** for the peg words 91 through 100 will make these ten peg words easier to learn. As always don't get in a hurry when learning these ten peg words. Make sure you know all 100 peg words well before going on to my next instruction.

Peg Word Chart

The following **Peg Word Chart** contains all 100 peg words for quick and easy reference. This chart will be very helpful in the review and learning process.

10 ToeS	20 NoSe	30 MooSe	40 RoSe	50 LaCe	60 CHeeSe	70 CaSe	80 FaCe	90 BuS	100 DiSeaSe
9 Bee	19 TuB	29 kNoB	39 MoP	49 RoPe	59 LiP	69 SHiP	79 CaPe	89 FoB	99 PiPe
8 iVy	18 DiVe	28 kNiFe	38 MoVie	48 RooF	58 LaVa	68 SHaVe	78 CaVe	88 FiFe	98 PuFF
7 Cow	17 TacK	27 NecK	37 MuG	47 RuG	57 LocK	67 JacK	77 CaKe	87 FoG	97 BiKe
6 SHoe	16 DiSH	26 NotCH	36 MatCH	46 RoaCH	56 LeeCH	66 JudGe	76 CaGe	86 FiSH	96 BuSH
5 Law	15 ToweL	25 NaiL	35 MaiL	45 RaiL	55 LiLy	65 JaiL	75 CoaL	85 FiLe	95 BaLL
4 Rye	14 TiRe	24 NeRo	34 MoweR	44 RoweR	54 LuRe	64 JaR	74 CaR	84 FuR	94 BeaR
3 Ma	13 ToMb	23 NaMe	33 MuMMy	43 RaM	53 LaMb	63 JaM	73 CoMb	83 FoaM	93 BuM
2 Noah	12 TiN	22 NuN	32 MooN	42 RaiN	52 LioN	62 CHaiN	72 CaN	82 FaN	92 BuN
1 Tie	11 ToT	21 NeT	31 MaT	41 RaT	51 LoT	61 JeT	71 CaT	81 FaT	91 BaT

One of the best ways to review the peg words for learning purposes is to review them by tens as in the horizontal rows above. By that I mean thinking of the peg word for number one (1), then the peg word for number eleven (11), then the peg word for number twenty-one (21), then the peg word for number thirty-one (31). This would be done up to the peg word for number ninety-one (91). Of course, you do this without looking at the peg word chart. By doing this, you group like numbers together for more productive review. Later it is good to have a friend or relative hold the peg word chart and call out numbers at random to test you. You need to get to the point where you know all 100 peg words almost immediately. This will take more study time than anything will with these systems and tools, but it is vital.

CHAPTER 7

The Associate Link

As was stated when the learning tools were listed briefly earlier, **The Associate Link System** connects or **associates the items in a list to something else that you are familiar with.** This adaptation to the **Pure Link System** can be used to learn almost anything that needs to be learned in order. I have used this system for rather simple to very complex information. As a matter of fact, I used this tool to learn the entire New Testament, all 260 chapters, so it is very versatile. There are many, many possibilities for using this tool. All you need is a knowledge of something that is already in order that you can easily see and recreate in your mind. You may recall some of the questions I asked you earlier when proving the point that tangible items are easier to remember than intangible ones. I asked you if you could name the furniture in your living room from left to right, name the parts of an automobile from front to back, not including the internal working parts, or describe the houses on the street where you live. I was confident that you could. This knowledge, other knowledge that you already possess and other knowledge you could obtain can all be used as **associate lists** to remember information. An associate list is simply the knowledge of something that you know in order to which information can be connected. Since you know the associate list in order you will remember the information in order.

The basic idea is quite simple. Information that needs to be learned is made tangible and then connected to the items in the **associate list** in the order that they need to be learned. This idea actually originated thousands of years ago when Greek and Roman orators had to remember lengthy speeches. Their idea was to connect the thoughts in their speech to the furniture in their homes. They would picture a thought and then connect the picture for that thought to the first piece of furniture on the left as they walked into their living room. The next thought they wanted to discuss was pictured and connected to the next or second piece of furniture. The next thought was pictured and connected to the next or third piece of furniture. This process continued until all of the furniture in the room was used. They made sure they could see each picture on each piece of furniture, and the thought connected or pictured on it, clearly in their mind. When they could leave the room, recreate a mental picture of the room along with the pictured thoughts on each piece of furniture, they went to another room and did the same thing in that room if they had more thoughts to discuss while delivering their speech. The rooms had a predetermined order in their mind. To deliver the speech, they simply stood up, created a mental picture of the rooms in their home, took a mental trip through the rooms and spoke about the thoughts pictured on each piece of furniture. Since they knew the furniture in order, the speech was delivered in order. This application was called the **loci** principle or method of learning. Loci means "**place**" in English. So, the orators had pieces or thoughts of information in these various **loci or places**. Certain information was in the first place or loci, other information was in the second place or loci and other information was in the other places or loci. This is how the phrases, "In the first place, in the second place," and so on crept into our language.

This basic idea of connecting information that needs to be learned in order to something already familiar, like furniture in a room, is what **The Associate Link System** is based on. Since you know the **associate list** in order, you will recall the learned information in order when you recall the **associate list** and mentally see the pictures connected to each item in the **associate list**. I have used a variety of things for **associate lists**. Of course, as has already been stated, I have used furniture in rooms as the Greeks and Romans did. I have also used parts of an automobile or truck, animals in alphabetical order, athletic teams in alphabetical order, parts of my body from head to toe and other **associate lists** that I had knowledge of. I even made up **associate lists** that worked extremely well for me. I will teach you how to do that as well. **The Associate Link System** is one of the most useful and versatile learning tools available to you.

Room System

Let me show you how it works by teaching you some basic information in a chapter of the Bible in order. By doing this, I'm not trying to recruit you for any church, synagogue, temple or denomination. I'm just showing you how a system works. I believe this to be a very useful demonstration of the system's potential, because as I said earlier, I used this idea to learn the entire New Testament basically word for word, even though I'm only going to teach you some basics in a chapter as a teaching session. When I began to learn the New Testament, I used a room for each chapter. I learned the furniture in the room in order. Actually I started using homes I was already familiar with. I then connected the basic information in the chapter in order to the furniture in order. Of course, this meant I had to use the **Sound-Alike System** to change intangible words in each chapter to a tangible picture. The pictures were then connected to the furniture in the room in order, so the basic information could be learned in order. Initially I learned the information by seeing only mental pictures, and they worked very well for me. At first I learned only the basics of each chapter or a skeleton outline. Eventually I began to add more detailed information to each chapter and began to put more meat on the skeleton, if you will. I even had professional artists draw not only pictures of the rooms, but also individual detailed pictures of each piece of furniture with the information to be learned pictured on them to make it easier for other people to learn the information. I have always done as much as possible to make the learning process easier and easier for everyone. I used a sound-alike word for the name of the books of the Bible and a peg word for the chapter number and connected those to the beginning of the room. That way I could easily open up the correct room in my mind when I thought of a certain chapter.

I want to get back to the learning process and show you the room I used to learn Mark chapter one (1) of the New Testament. The room is pictured below. It isn't a room at all but a garage, but it functions the same as a room does.

Furniture or Items

1) Door	2) Stack of Boxes	3) Ice Chest	4) Bobsled	5) Extension Cord
6) Toolbox	7) Wagon	8) Motorcycle	9) Bicycle	10) Tyke's Bike
11) Window	12) Tanks	13) Grill	14) Basket on Bike	15) Garage Door
16) Freezer	17) Refrigerator	18) Ironing Board	19) Soda Bottles	

I even had professional artists draw special link pictures of the furniture linked together to make it easier for my Bible memory students to learn the furniture. I will teach a few basics from this chapter to show you how this system works. The items, or pieces of furniture, were learned in order from left to right, so the information would be learned in order. I will list a few items, the information and the mental picture for you to see on the item. You should not only see the mental picture clearly but also imagine that you see the action actually taking place. The more real the picture is in your mind, the better it will work.

Door - The beginning of the gospel of Jesus Christ. - Imagine that a baseball scoreboard is on the door. A team had a **big inning**, **beginning**, on the scoreboard. Then imagine that a **cross** for **Jesus Christ** is pulling gauze through the keyhole of the door. **Gauze pull** equals **gospel**. Go over this a few times and you will easily know this basic information.

Stack of Boxes - John the Baptist began preaching in the wilderness. - Imagine that **John the Baptist** is standing on the boxes behind a **pulpit preaching** to a bunch of **trees**, a **wilderness**. Review this picture.

Ice Chest - John the Baptist baptized Jesus in the Jordan. - Imagine that **John the Baptist** placed a cross, **Jesus**, under some water in the bottom of the ice chest and **baptized** it. Also imagine that a jar is down **in the** bottom of the chest. **Jar down** equals **Jordan**. Review this picture.

Bobsled - Jesus is tempted by Satan in the wilderness. - Imagine that **Satan** pushed a cross, **Jesus**, that was in a tent, **tempted**, in the bobsled. Also imagine that the bobsled was pushed through a bunch of trees, a **wilderness**. Review this picture.

Extension Cords - John the Baptist is taken into custody. - Imagine that **John the Baptist** is wrapped up with the extension cord and **taken into custody**. Review this picture.

Tool Box - Jesus began to preach in Galilee. - Imagine that a cross, **Jesus**, opens the tool box, stands behind a pulpit and begins to **preach** to an art gallery, **Galilee**, in the tool box. Review this picture.

Wagon - Jesus called his first four apostles. - A cross, **Jesus**, sat on **four** puzzles, **apostles**, in the wagon and **called** on a phone. Review this picture.

Motorcycle - Jesus began to teach in Capernaum on the Sabbath. - A cross, **Jesus**, rode the motorcycle into a classroom and **began to teach**. The cross was wearing a **cap** that was **burning**, **Capernaum**. The cross ran into a bathroom and stuck the burning cap into a **sad bath** tub, **Sabbath**. Review this picture.

Bicycle - News about him went out everywhere. - Imagine that a newspaper delivery boy is using the bicycle to deliver the **news**. The news has a picture of a boxer and **a bout** he fought. The delivery boy is singing a **hymn** as he delivers the news **everywhere**. Review this picture.

I could go on with more items and more information, but I think you have gotten the idea. Go back and review the items, pieces of furniture normally, in order until you know them. Then review the mental pictures until you can see them clearly in your mind. After doing that, simply think of each item in order, and the picture providing the information should pop into your mind.

This works beautifully for massive amounts of information that needs to be learned. Try it on information that you need to learn after reading the rest of this section on the room system, and you will be very pleased.

Becoming an Interior Decorator

While learning the New Testament using already existing rooms, I got what I felt was a great idea. Why not add furniture to rooms that would better fit the information in each chapter. For instance, if a baptism was taking place in a chapter, you need water for a baptism. I could put an aquarium or a vase full of water in the appropriate place where that information appeared, remembering, of course, that the information needed to be learned in order. I didn't benefit enough from that idea when learning the New Testament, because I didn't think of it soon enough. But I began to use the idea in some chapters and for other information later, and so can you. So you see, I'm not so smart after all, or I would have come up with this idea before I used already existing rooms for the 260 chapters in the New Testament. I was so **ODD** I just plowed ahead with my efforts to learn all 260 chapters without doing enough of this.

I will provide actual rooms professional artists have drawn for your use as learning aids. I used some of them for Bible memory, so you will notice some unusual items in a few places. It doesn't matter. When you learn these rooms you can use them to learn any information. I don't know the New Testament the way I used to, because I haven't had the opportunity to review for over fifteen years. I felt it was more important for me to create learning tools for others and to teach others than to spend all of my time on my own pursuits.

I say all of this to let you know that you can become an interior decorator yourself. You can create rooms to use to remember almost anything. Simply make them up to match what you need to learn. A picture of an airplane on a wall would work well for some information you had to learn about aviation, for instance. Simply use your own imagination to do this for what you need to learn.

Later I will show you the whole process by teaching you how one of my students who was a commercial airline pilot used the Room System to learn very long and complicated information related to his work.

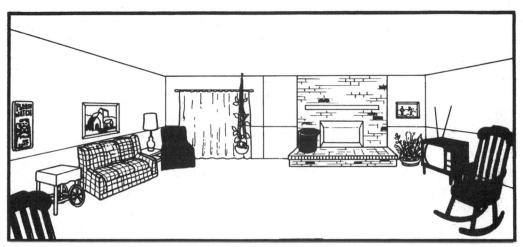

Furniture or Items

1) Rocking Chair	2) Please Watch Sign	3) Serving Cart	4) Picture	5) Couch
6) lamp	7) Table	8) Chair	9) Drapes	10) Plant
11) Ash Bucket	12) Fireplace	13) Mantle	14) Picturee	15) Flowers
16) Television	17) Other Rocking Chair			

Furniture or Items

1) Bean Bag Seat	2) Square Hole	3) Shoes	4) Clothes	5) Black Box
6) Gumball Machine	7) Linus Pennant	8) Player	9) Record Rack	10) Shade
11) Curtains	12) Window	13) Vent	14) Table	15) Chairs
16) Bed	17) Alligator	18) Dolls	19) Rocker	20) Television

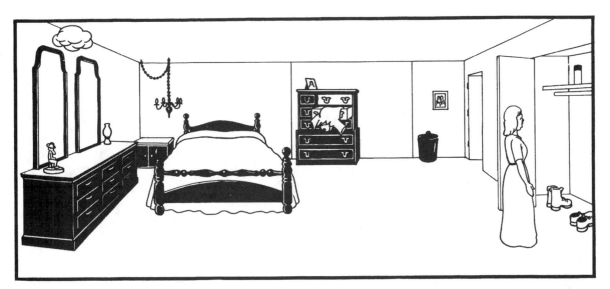

Furniture or Items

1) Chest of Drawers	2) Statue	3) Mirrors	4) Lamp	5) Stuffed Cloud
6) Cedar Chest	7) Hanging Lamp	8) Bed	9) Picture on Chest	10) Chest
11) Shirt	12) Hamper	13) Picture	14) Open Door	15) Woman
16) Closet	17) Boots	18) Shoes	19) Spray Can	

Furniture or Items

1) Door	2) Bag on Door	3) Tile Picture	4) Monkeys	5) Window
6) Drapes	7) Shade	8) Nightstand	9) Lamp	10) Chest Items
11) Needle in Bedpost	12) Bed	13) Stuffed Mouse	14) Pennant	15) Suitcase
16) Stand	17) Camera	18) Chest of Drawers		

Furniture or Items

1) Pumpkin
6) Hobby Horse
11) Writing Set
16) Stool
21) Rolling Toy

2) Baby Carriage
7) Clown Picture
12) Window
17) Doll on Stool
22) Teddy Bear

3) Clown Poster
8) Table
13) Curtains
18) Doll on Rocker
23) Clothes Hamper

4) Footprints
9) Chairs
14) Shade
19) Rocker

5) Closet
10) Purse
15) Animal
20) Horse

Furniture or Items

1) Chair
6) Door
11) Crystal Bowl

2) Buffet
7) Picture of Prayer
12) Candles

3) Grapes in Scale
8) Drapes

4) Scale
9) Windows

5) Bird Cage
10) Table

Furniture or Items

1) Small Blackboard   2) Cabinets   3) Cannister Set   4) Circles   5) Coffee Maker
6) Hanging Pot   7) Hanging Plant   8) Window   9) Containers   10) Sink
11) Hand Lotion   12) Refrigerator   13) Roosters   14) Clock   15) Hole
16) Cloud   17) Hood   18) Light in Hood   19) Chicken in Pot   20) Pot
21) Kids   22) Stovetop   23) Hanging Lamp   24) Table

Furniture or Items

1) Encyclopedias   2) Book Stand   3) Doll House   4) Tray   5) Box
6) Ping Pong Table   7) Cup in Carpet   8) Carpet   9) Bread in Carpet   10) Chair
11) Fan   12) Box   13) Book in Box   14) File Cabinet   15) Pole
16) Lamp   17) Chest of Drawers   18) Desk   19) Television

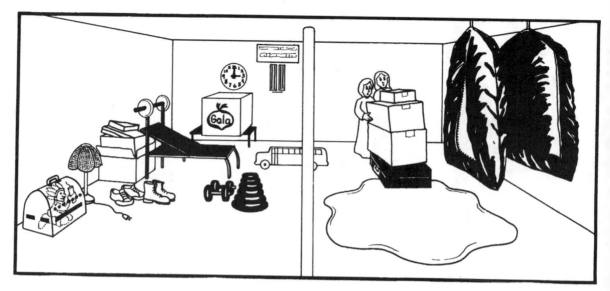

Furniture or Items

1) Doll Case
2) Indian in Case
3) Dynamite in Case
4) Lamp
5) Tennis Shoes
6) Boots
7) Boxes
8) Weights
9) Weight Bench
10) Barbells
11) Stack of Weights
12) Bench
13) Gala Box
14) Clock
15) Plaque
16) Cylinders
17) Toy Bus
18) Pole
19) Stack of Boxes
20) Suitcase
21) Women
22) Water
23) Garment Bags

Alphabetical Animalmania

I have also used what I have come to call **Alphabetical Animalmania** as an associate list. This list is simply a standard listing of **animals in alphabetical order** to use as an associate list. I don't ever change the animals that I use, so the associate list is always the same. It is limited to twenty-six (26) positions, since there are only twenty-six (26) letters in the alphabet, but it is very helpful for certain information. Following is a listing of the animals I use for this application. They may be helpful for you. You can change any animal if you think another one will work better for you.

Ape	Frog	Kangaroo	Porcupine	Unicorn
Buffalo	Giraffe	Lion	Quarter Horse	Vixen
Crocodile	Hyena	Monkey	Rhino	Weasel
Dog	Iguana	Night Owl	Snake	X-ray
Elephant	Jaguar	Octopus	Tiger	Yellow Jacket
Zebra				

Some of these need a little explanation. Vixen is one of Santa Claus's reindeer. I use an X-ray of a dinosaur skeleton, and even though a Yellow Jacket isn't actually an animal, it still works. Remember one of our rules, "**Break any rule if it makes it easier to learn.**" To use this list, you would have to review it to make sure you know it well. Then you could connect any information you needed to learn to each animal in alphabetical order and record the action pictures so you could review them later. You need to be just as **ODD** with animals as well.

Alphabetical Athleticism

I have also used what I have come to call **Alphabetical Athleticism** as an associate list. This list is simply a standard listing of **athletic teams in alphabetical order** to use as an associate list. I don't ever change the athletic teams that I use either, so the associate list is always the same. It is limited to twenty-six (26) positions, since there are only twenty-six (26) letters in the alphabet, but it is very helpful for certain information. Athletic fans especially seem to like this associate list idea. Following is a listing of athletic teams to choose from if you want to develop your own athletic team associate list. There may be others that you would want to use outside of these suggestions.

Astros - Athletics - Angels
Bills - Browns - Bengals - Broncos - Buccaneers - Bears - Braves - Brewers - Bullets - Bucks - Bulls - Bruins - Black Hawks - Blues
Cubs - Colts - Cardinals - Chiefs - Chargers - Cowboys - Clippers - Cavaliers - Celtics - Canadians
Dolphins - Dodgers - Devils - Ducks
Eagles
Falcons - Forty Niners - Flames

Giants
Heat - Hawks - Hornets
Indians
Jets
Knicks - Kings
Lions - Lakers
Magic - Mavericks - Mariners - Mets
Nets - Nuggets
Oilers
Patriots - Pirates - Packers - Pistons - Pacers
Quebec Nordiques
Reds - Raiders - Redskins - Rams - Red Sox - Rockets - Rangers
Steelers - Seahawks - Saints - Super Sonics - Suns - Spurs - Seventy Sixers
Tigers - Timberwolves - Trailblazers
Utah Jazz
Vikings
Warriors - White Sox - Whalers
Xtra Players - Make this a make believe team where you are the world renowned star
Yankees
Zebras - The Referees or Umpires

I didn't have to take too many liberties with this list. The liberties taken were necessary and obvious. You could make up any alphabetical list of anything that you are familiar with. So you can use **Alphabetical Anything** as an associate list.

Parts of the Body

I have also used parts of the body many times for short lists, especially short lists my children needed to learn for school. We simply started at the top of the head and worked to the bottom of the feet. The reason for this is to keep the information in order if it needs to be learned that way. Any of these associate lists can also be used to remember information that doesn't need to be learned in order, though the main use of them is for in-order learning. In that case, you would simply choose the body part that best fit the information being learned and make the connection. We chose body parts that worked best for the information being learned. We didn't always use the same body parts. Sometimes we started with hair on the head or sometimes with the forehead. It all depended on what worked best. Once again, common sense and creativity enter into these selections. I made my children make up more and more of their own association pictures as they got older. They needed to develop their own skills, not just rely on my abilities, although they would have liked that very much. Most people are basically lazy. That is why **ODD** people succeed. All of the information learned with associate lists also must be organized and recorded for later review.

Here is an obvious list of potential body parts to use.

Hair - Forehead - Eyebrows - Eyes - Cheeks - Ears - Mouth - Teeth - Tongue - Chin -

Neck - Adam's Apple - Shoulders - Chest - Arms - Elbows - Wrists - Hands - Fingers -

Stomach - Hips - Legs - Knees - Ankles - Feet - Toes

Parts of a Car or Truck

I have also used the parts of a car or truck many times for an associate list. I simply begin at the front of the car and work my way back. The better one knows the parts of a car the more positions for learning this method provides. Following you will find a picture of a limousine and a list of parts you could use as another associate list. Here is a list of potential car parts to use.

Headlights - Bumper - Grill - Hood Ornament - Hood - Antenna - Radiator - Engine

(You can use individual engine parts if you have the knowledge. I don't.) - Windshield -

Rearview Mirror - Dashboard - Speedometer - Heat and Air Conditioning Controls -

Glove Compartment - Maps in Glove Compartment - Steering Wheel - Horn - Brake

Pedal - Accelerator Pedal - Front Seat - Back Seat - Rear Window - Trunk - Jack in

Trunk - Tools in Trunk - Spare Tire (Other items like ash trays, etc. can also be used.)

Designer Trains

Trains are naturally linked together one car to another, so it only seems natural to use them for the link system. Some trains are very long with many cars while others are much shorter. I have designed different kinds of trains and different kinds of train cars to use as associate lists. You can become a designer of your own trains to use as associate lists. Every train starts with the locomotive engine. Some of my trains start with old steam engines, some with diesel engines, some with gas engines and some with nuclear engines. I can have an engine powered with anything in my mind to start a particular train. After the engine, a simple train could have cars that are in alphabetical order in some way. How they are in alphabetical order is totally up to you. I have short trains in alphabetical by the typical kinds of train cars. Possible cars for this kind of train are coal cars, dining cars, gambling cars, log cars, oil cars, passenger cars, sleeping cars, troop cars and, of course, a caboose. There are many other possible cars as well.

Other trains could be linked together by the types of cars they could transport. The cars should be in alphabetical order. The sky and your imagination are your only limits. After designing your train or trains, make a record of them, and then make the appropriate picture connections to the various cars in order for the information to be learned and record your pictures for later review.

Golf Courses

Some of my students have used golf courses for associate linking. Golfers who play the same courses a lot know those courses intimately. Many of them know the location of every tree, trap, creek, hole, drinking fountain and other obstacle on every hole, because they have hit errant balls there. They can describe almost every blade of grass on every hole in detail. What a great associate list. If you are a golfer, don't overlook this possibility. If your spouse complains about all the golf you play, now you can tell him or her that you are working on your memory skills as you play golf. What a beautiful and legitimate story. Now you have a better reason for playing and paying even more attention to the holes as you play them, and you have an excuse for why you hit the ball all over the place. Naturally you are simply trying to improve your learning skills. I don't know if your playing partners will accept that excuse or not, but give it a shot. It might not be as wild as some of your other golf shots.

You might even become a golf course architect and design your own special golf courses to meet your learning needs. You can develop as many of them as you want. Or you might want to use famous golf courses pictured in golf magazines. With actual pictures, you will have an aid that would work even better. If you are a golfer, use your imagination. You might think of many other clever ways to apply your golf knowledge to learning.

Other Potential Associate Lists

Almost anything you know or can learn in order can be used as an associate list. I have taught mail deliverers who use houses on streets and warehouse employees who use parts in bins. You may have a particular knowledge about something that could serve you well. Think about it and make a list of those things you know that might work. Some people have used articles of clothing that would be worn from head to toe. Other students have used football equipment from head to toe. Use whatever you may be familiar with as an associate list.

CHAPTER 8

Anagrams

As was stated earlier, **The Anagram System** is a tool that develops a word or phrase formed by rearranging the letters of another word, phrase or list of information to provide a trigger or reminder of the original information. These rearranged letters are normally the first letters of the words in the list or information that needs to be learned. The dictionary defines an **acronym** as a word formed from the initial letters of a name or group of words. This tool goes beyond simple acronyms in its application. A simple acronym or anagram is **NCAA**. These letters are the beginning letters in the words National Collegiate Athletic Association. Another is **NASA** which stands for the National Aeronautics Space Administration. As I stated earlier, this is the first memory tool I began to use early in school. Because I was so good at spelling words alphabetically, I would select the beginning letters in a list, alphabetize the letters and make up some silly words or story using the alphabetized letters. It was limited, but it worked for some things and started my creative juices flowing. It is important to note that this tool cannot be used to remember or learn numbers or vocabulary, for instance. You will eventually become competent to know which tool to use for every learning problem.

The first anagram I was taught was a word formed from the beginning letters of the names of the five Great Lakes to help me remember their names. I was actually taught it by a teacher in grade school and always wondered why there weren't more aids like it to help me learn. I was told to imagine **HOMES** floating on the Great Lakes every time I thought of them to be able to remember their names. The letters in the word **HOMES** would later remind me of:

> **H** - Huron
> **O** - Ontario
> **M** - Michigan
> **E** - Erie
> **S** - Superior

This example is a perfect application of this tool, because the beginning letters form an actual tangible word to use as the reminder. It will not always work that perfectly, but very workable anagrams can be developed for any combinations of letters in which anagrams can be applied.

Let's examine another learning problem that can be solved with an anagram. The parts of the intestinal tract in order are the: **D**uodenum - **J**ejunum - **I**leum - **A**ppendix - **C**olon - **S**igmoid **C**olon - **R**ectum. The appendix isn't actually part of the intestinal tract, but it comes in the place where it is listed.

The starting point with this tool is to list the beginning letters of the list. It is important to remember the words in order in this case. In some cases, it isn't important to know a list in order and using the beginning letters in any order would suffice. It also works better if you can relate the information to something you are already familiar with or already know. The beginning letters in this instance are: **D - J - I - A - C - S - R**. These letters fit a fairly well known already existing phrase. How about this: The **D**ow **J**ones **I**ndustrial **A**verage **C**losing **S**tock **R**eport. If you were familiar with this phrase, it would work very well for you, or you could become familiar with this phrase and have it work well for you.

The next step is to connect this phrase to the information you need to learn, in this case, the intestinal tract in order. How about using our imagination to change it to this: The **D**ow **J**ones **I**ntestinal **A**verage **C**losing **S**tock **R**eport. What I have done is change the word "Industrial" to "Intestinal." That little creative change lets me know what information the anagram will trigger, the intestinal tract in order. **Now I must go over the phrase and the names of the intestinal tract in order to make sure I know both**. As always, it is important to make a record of the anagram tool, so it can be used now and any time in the future with a quick review.

Other ideas would work just as well. What about this: **D**id **J**ohn's **I**ntestines **A**ctually **C**lose **S**hut **R**adically? The same letters in the same order have been used in this little phrase. Actually it is a sentence, but I always call them phrases. That phrase would work just as well and perhaps even better for someone who wasn't familiar with the Dow Jones Average. It has the word Intestines in it to help trigger the application of the anagram. Once again, this anagram would need to be recorded for future use.

The method of recording depends upon what you have available to you. If you have a computer at your disposal, **organize** it by class if you are a student and record and save the information appropriately. If you don't have a computer, as I didn't when I was a student, keep a notebook for each class and be **disciplined** to make a record of each memory aid developed in each class. All you will have to do is review your memory aids at test time. What I did was make up my memory aids on a daily basis. Then I was **diligent** to review them on weekends. It only took a few minutes or an hour or so. I didn't think that was too much to do to be successful. Some people may have thought I was **ODD**, but so what!

Developing and using your own imagination will cause the memory aids to work even better for you, because your mind will have to concentrate and think about the anagram as it is developed. This process alone begins the **recognition and registration phase of learning** before the **formal registration process** takes place.

It is important for you to begin to create and use your own imagination, so I want you to think of and record another possibility for learning the parts of the intestinal tract in order. You might think, "He has used the best possibilities already," but who is to say what is best? What will work better for one person may not be the best application for another person. Here is the information and the beginning letters once again.

The parts of the intestinal tract in order are the: **D**uodenum - **J**ejunum - **I**leum - **A**ppendix **C**olon - **S**igmoid **C**olon - **R**ectum. **D - J - I - A - C - S - R**. Work on an anagram of your own and write it on the following lines. I always used a scratch pad when I developed and only recorded the final anagram in my review notebook.

You could accomplish the same end by employing a slightly different application or extension of a pure anagram. You don't have to limit yourself to just the beginning letters if you feel something else might work better. You might find that the beginning sounds sometimes work better than the beginning letters. If that is the case, use the beginning sounds instead of the beginning letters. The mind is a fertile field that can be tilled and plied in many ways. The point is simple - - don't limit yourself by any hard and fast rules. My **Golden Rule of Learning** is: **Use as little as possible to learn as much as possible**. I don't want to develop any more than is necessary when developing my learning and memory aids. If I find that I keep leaving something out during reviews, I will insert an additional aid or reminder at the trouble spot.

I began to help a young man named Jason Cassidy with his learning skills. He was a very good friend of my son J. J. He was a very good student but became a much better student after learning my systems. I want to share a little anagram he developed to learn the periods of the Geologic Time Scale, and he developed it on his own without my help after receiving my instruction. The periods are the Cambrian, Ordovician, Silurian, Devonian, Mississippian, Pennsylvanian, Permian, Triassic, Jurassic, Cretaceous, Tertiary and Quaternary. He had to remember the periods in order, so he couldn't rearrange the beginning letters. The beginning letters are **C - O - S - D - M - P - P - T - J - C - T - Q**. He later told me that he spotted the letters "J" and "C" together which are the initials to his name. It only seemed obvious to use his name for those two letters. Here is the anagram memory aid he developed and recorded. My watch is in my pants, and I **C**an **O**nly **S**ee **D**own **M**y **P**ants **P**ocket. **T**ell **J**ason **C**assidy **T**o **Q**uit asking me what **time** it is. This was a very personal aid for him that worked great. He used my systems with a great deal of success and shared many of his memory aids with me.

Another application of the anagram tool involves using not just the beginning letters in words but the beginning sounds or even a whole word if it works. I will use the periods of the Geologic Time Scale to explain. I will list the periods again, but this time I will put the sounds or words I chose to use in bold. The periods of the Geologic Time Scale are **Cam**brian, **Ord**ovician, **Sil**urian, **Dev**onian, **Mississippi**an, **Pennsylvani**an, **Perm**ian, **Tri**assic, **Jur**assic, **Cre**taceous, **Ter**tiary and **Quat**ernary. Here is the memory aid. Let me tell you about my driving **Time Scale**. I put some overhead **CAM**s in an **ORD**inary, **SIL**ly car and created a **DEV**ilishly fast vehicle. I sped down to **MISSISSIPPI** and then over to **PENNSYLVANIA**. As I drove, my **PERM** straightened out. I was caught for speeding and was **TRI**ed by **JUR**y. It **CRE**ated a **TER**m in jail where I poured **QUAr**Ts of milk on my head to get my perm back. After recording the anagram story, all you need to do is review the story and look at the capitalized letters and relate them to the capitalized letters in the original information. By going over them a couple of times you will easily know the information. You will also have a record of it for future review. If you are a businessperson, simply do the same thing with the information you need to learn. I only use educational material as an example of what to do.

Here is another learning opportunity for an anagram. You will notice that I said learning opportunity instead of learning problem. It is hard for me to think of learning as a problem when there are so many different and creative tools that the **Master Mind Mechanic** can use.

Here is a listing of The Scientific Method:

1)   **C**ollect **A**nd **R**ecord **F**acts **A**ccurately and **S**ystematically.
2)   **A**nalyze and **E**valuate **T**hem.
3)   **S**hare the **F**inal **D**ata and **C**onclusions with **O**thers in the **F**ield.
4)   **A**dd and **R**elate the **N**ew **F**indings to **P**revious **K**nowledge.
5)   **P**rovide **S**ubsequent **R**esearchers with a **B**etter **S**tart.

You will notice that I have capitalized and put into bold type many more than just the beginning letters of the five steps. This is not just a list of five words but a list of five sentences. The five beginning letters of **C** - **A** - **S** - **A** - **P** could work for some people, but some others might need a more detailed reminder. Remember the **Golden Rule of Learning** which is **use as little as possible to learn as much as possible**. The anagram I bought a **CAS**e of **Scientific Methods** at **A** & **P** would work if just the beginning letters would suffice.

A more detailed anagram story using all of the capitalized and bold letters would provide more detail for those who might need it. What about this?

1)   A scientist drives a **CAR** too **FAS**t. Look at the capitalized and bold letters in step number one (1) above, and you will see that the letters in **CAR** and **FAS**t match.

2)   The scientist loves to **EAT** while driving the fast car. Look at the capitalized and bold letters in step number two (2) above, and you will see that the letters in **EAT** are the same letters but don't match the same order. It doesn't really matter if you know to rearrange them in the **AET** order.

3)   The scientist **ShiFteD** the gears and **COF**fed after he ate so quickly. Look at the capitalized and bold letters in step number three (3) above, and you will see that the letters in **ShiFteD** the gears and **COF**fed match even though I misspelled "coughed."

4)   When pedestrians saw the wild driving scientist they **RAN** **F**or **T**heir **ParK**ed cars. Once again the letters match the capitalized and bold letters.

5)   Other **PaSseRByS** also ran for cover as the dangerously driving scientist raced on. Once again the letters match the capitalized and bold letters.

When you look up at the capitalized and bold letters in the **anagram story**, it is easy to relate them to the capitalized and bold letters in the original information. Just by going over the anagram story and the original information a few times, the material will be learned. You would also have a record of the anagram story for future review.

I have given you an example of a **very brief anagram** and a **detailed anagram story** for the same information. How brief or detailed the anagrams need to be may vary with different information. Always remember the **Golden Rule of Learning** which is **use as little as possible to learn as much as possible**. Try to use as little as possible but make sure you use enough to make it work. That decision will need to be made with each new set of information with which you elect to use an anagram.

Anagram Practice

You need to get some experience developing anagrams. Let's review the rules, but remember that memory rules are made to be broken if you can find something that works better.

1) **Use** only the **beginning letters** of the first words in the information to be learned and make up a memory word, phrase or story. Make sure to list these letters on a work sheet as you develop the anagram. I recorded my final version in the appropriate place later. With some anagrams, I doodled a while before deciding on the final version that I felt would work best. The letters cannot be rearranged if the information must be remembered **in order**, but, of course, they can be rearranged if the information doesn't need to be remembered in order. Remember to relate the information to something you already know or are familiar with if possible. I always try to use this beginning letter method first. It will be shorter. Remember that my **Golden Rule of Learning** is **use as little as possible to remember as much as possible**. This procedure may have to be expanded to include the beginning letters in more words than just the first words if the length of the information requires it. You will remember the example of **The Scientific Method** that I developed for this principle earlier.

2) **Use** the **beginning sounds in the words** and make up a memory phrase or story. You will remember the example of the Geologic Time Scale that I developed for this principle earlier. Remember that you can even use whole words if they will work. I used the words Mississippi and Pennsylvania in my example.

3) Use a combination of 1 and 2 above if necessary, or if the information lends itself to it.

4) Remember to connect a sound-alike word or some other memory aid to the anagram, so you know what the anagram information represents.

You could also use sound-alike words for some of the items in the following examples and link them, but this is anagram practice and not linking practice. There will almost always be more than one way to analyze, attack and solve most learning problems, as you will discover.

Practice developing anagrams with the following information. I will say **in order** if the information must be learned **in order**. If that is the case, you must develop an anagram that keeps the information **in order**. If the information doesn't have to be learned in order, the letters or aids can be arranged any way you want as long as the anagram will allow you to retrieve the original information. Apply the three rules using number Rule #1 first if possible. That is one of the beauties of this learning tool. Your own imagination and creativity will cause your memory aid to work best for you, because you create it in your own mind and, of course, as an organized person you record it for review purposes. **Remember that your memory aid must not only contain**

the anagram, but it must also contain a reference to what the anagram information refers to. All learning aids must have this reference, or you may not remember what the information is used for. For instance, when I mentioned the **HOMES** anagram used for remembering the names of the Great Lakes, the picture had **HOMES** floating on the Great Lakes. The anagram **HOMES** wasn't just written down without a good connection to the information being learned. I will list some possible solutions later but, of course, there are many different solutions to each that will all work quite well. Remember to use a good dictionary when developing anagram memory aids. There may be many words that would work well that you might not think of.

1)   The four parts of a quartet are: **S**oprano - **T**enor - **A**lto - **B**ass

     Anagram or memory aid

2)   The colors of the spectrum **in order** are: **R**ed - **O**range - **Y**ellow - **G**reen - **B**lue - **I**ndigo **V**iolet

     Anagram or memory aid

3)   The planets **in order** from the sun are: **M**ercury - **V**enus - **E**arth - **M**ars - **J**upiter - **S**aturn **U**ranus - **N**eptune - **P**luto

     Anagram or memory aid

4)   The cabinet posts for the United States are: **J**ustice - **T**ransportation - **C**ommerce - **H**ealth and **H**uman Services - **E**ducation - **E**nergy - **H**ousing and **U**rban Development - **A**griculture - **I**nterior - **L**abor - **S**ecretary of **S**tate. I have capitalized letters other than just the very beginning letter in some cases where appropriate. Use them only if you think you need them. Since this information is not called upon to be learned in order, write down all of the beginning letters on a scratch pad and begin to put them together in any order you want that will develop words that will work. Your only limit is your imagination, and that should be limitless.

     Anagram or memory aid

5)   The phases of cell division **in order** are: **I**nterphase - **P**rophase - **M**etaphase - **A**naphase **T**elephase

     Anagram or memory aid

6)   The eight parts of speech are: **N**oun - **A**djective - **V**erb - **A**dverb - **P**ronoun - **P**reposition **C**onjunction - **I**nterjection

     Anagram or memory aid

7)   The countries of Central America are: **B**elize - **G**uatemala - **El S**alvador - **H**onduras - **N**icaragua - **C**osta **R**ica - **P**anama - Once again I have capitalized letters other than just the very beginning letter in some cases where appropriate. Use them only if you think you need them.

     Anagram or memory aid

8)   The states bordering the Great Lakes are: **I**ndiana - **M**ichigan - **N**ew **Y**ork - **O**hio - **W**isconsin - **I**llinois - **M**innesota - **P**ennsylvania

     Anagram or memory aid

9)   The elements in protoplasm are: **C**arbon - **H**ydrogen - **O**xygen - **P**hosphorous - **P**otassium **I**odine - **N**itrogen - **S**ulphur - **C**alcium - **I**ron - **M**agnesium

     Anagram or memory aid

10) The four countries in the British Isles are: **I**reland - **E**ngland - **S**cotland - **W**ales

     Anagram or memory aid

11)   The types of open wounds are: **Puncture** - **Incision** - **Abrasion** - **Avulsion** - **Laceration**

Anagram or memory aid

12)   The eight characteristics of life are: **Locomotion** - **Irritability** - **Respiration** - **Reproduction** **Assimilation** - **Mutation** - **Excretion** - **Growth**

Anagram or memory aid

13)   The provinces of Canada are: **British Columbia** - **Alberta** - **Saskatchewan** - **Manitoba** - **Ontario** - **Quebec** - **New Brunswick** - **Nova Scotia** - **Newfoundland** - **Prince Edward Island**

Anagram or memory aid

Possible Solutions

I am listing some possible solutions to increase your exposure to application possibilities. The more you can see and be aware of the more experienced you will become. A **master** always needs to teach an **apprentice** how to apply his trade.

1)   The four parts of a quartet are: Soprano - Tenor - Alto - Bass

Anagram or memory aid - I simply see **BATS** singing in a **quartet** and, of course, would record it for later review as I would for all of the following as well. Imagining **BATS** singing in a **quartet** connects the two pieces of information together. This is a Four-On-One memory problem made easy with this simple anagram.

2)   The colors of the spectrum **in order** are: Red - Orange - Yellow - Green - Blue - Indigo Violet

Anagram or memory aid - My brother **ROY** wore Geeky looking Blue jeans In his Victory race at the **Spectrum**. The **Spectrum** is an arena in Philadelphia, and it reminds me of the colors in the **spectrum**. I also would see him running in **multi-colored** race lanes. This works well for me because I do have a brother named Roy.

3) The planets **in order** from the sun are: **M**ercury - **V**enus - **E**arth - **M**ars - **J**upiter - **S**aturn **U**ranus - **N**eptune - **P**luto

Anagram or memory aid - Please don't **MoVE My JetS** to an **UNP**leasant **planet**. The only potential problem with this memory aid is that there are two letter "M's" that may be learned in the wrong order. If the information didn't need to be learned in order, it would-n't make any difference, but it does in this case. In this and similar kinds of circum-stances, you would have to make sure not to confuse the placements of the two letter "M's." You might think to yourself and later record it for review, "**Mercury comes first,** because he is the fastest."

4) The cabinet posts for the United States are: **J**ustice - **T**ransportation - **C**ommerce - **H**ealth and **H**uman **S**ervices - **E**ducation - **E**nergy - **H**ousing and **U**rban **D**evelopment - **A**griculture - **I**nterior - **L**abor - **S**ecretary of State. I have capitalized letters other than just the very beginning letter in some cases where appropriate. Use them only if you think you need them.

Anagram or memory aid - If I **CATcH HIS JEweL**, he might let me put it in my **cabi-net**. The capitalized letters only stand for the beginning letters of each post. I didn't feel it was necessary to use the "U" and "D" in **H**ousing and **U**rban **D**evelopment or the "H" and "S" in **H**ealth and **H**uman **S**ervices. By recording and reviewing this aid a few times, it will work well without those letters for me. As I have said before, "**Use as little as pos-sible to remember as much as possible.**" If I would happen to have a problem, I could always add more letters later. Look at my aid and see which letters match which posts. I'm sure your aid will work just as well as mine, but I list mine to give you some ideas that may help you in the future.

5) The phases of cell division **in order** are: **I**nterphase - **P**rophase - **M**etaphase - **A**naphase **T**elephase

Anagram or memory aid - A h**IP**py stole my welcome **MAT**, and the police put him into a **divided** jail **cell**. The words **divided cell** easily remind me of cell division and, of course, the **bold** and capitalized letters tell me the five phases of division. I have intro-duced another principle here that I need to discuss. You have already probably noticed that I didn't capitalize the first letter in the word h**IP**py. It doesn't matter. It will still work. No rule says I have to use the beginning letter of a word as has been done up to this point. The words I develop, record and review will allow me to know the informa-tion. I will know which letters are used, because I developed them and reviewed them.

6) The eight parts of speech are: **N**oun - **A**djective - **V**erb - **A**dverb - **P**ronoun - **P**reposition **C**onjunction - **I**nterjection

Anagram or memory aid - A **NAVI CAP**tain taught me the **P**arts **of speech**. I broke another rule here by misspelling "NAVY" and spelling it "**NAVI**." So what! I can do any-thing I want if it will help me learn. This is another idea for you to remember. Don't limit yourself with rules. Make them up as you go.

I have developed full color pictures for my grammar and punctuation curriculum that y teach the names and definitions of the parts of speech.

7)   The countries of Central America are: **B**elize - **G**uatemala - **E**l Salvador - **H**onduras - **N**icaragua - **C**osta **R**ica - **P**anama.   Once again I have capitalized letters other than just the very beginning letter in some cases where appropriate. Use them only if you think you need them.

Anagram or memory aid - **CEN**tral America is just a **B**i**G** **H**o**P** from America. Once again, the capitalized letters only stand for the beginning letters of each country. I didn't feel it was necessary to use the second letters in **E**l Salvador or Costa **R**ica. Since it was-n't necessary to learn the countries in order, I could arrange the letters in any order that seemed to work.

8)   The states bordering the Great Lakes are: **I**ndiana - **M**ichigan - **N**ew **Y**ork - **O**hio - **W**isconsin - **I**llinois - **M**innesota - **P**ennsylvania

Anagram or memory aid - One of the states bordering on the Great Lakes said, "**I'M NO WIMP**." This anagram is absolutely perfect and very unusual. Each of the three words used in the memory aid is capitalized, because each letter in all the words is used to name these states. This very, very rarely happens.

9)   The elements in protoplasm are: **C**arbon - **H**ydrogen - **O**xygen - **P**hosphorous - **P**otassium **I**odine - **N**itrogen - **S**ulphur - **C**alcium - **I**ron - **M**agnesium

Anagram or memory aid - A **pro**fessional karate instructor began to **CHOP** and **SPIN** and **MI**n**C**e and had a **spasm**. A pro having a spasm reminds me of protoplasm. It isn't the exact sound, but so what! It will work just fine for me, and that is what is important.

10)   The four countries in the British Isles are: **I**reland - **E**ngland - **S**cotland - **W**ales

Anagram or memory aid - The **British Isles** are full of **WISE** men.

11)   The types of open wounds are: **P**uncture - **I**ncision - **A**brasion - **A**vulsion - **L**aceration

Anagram or memory aid - I have an **open wound** in my double **AA LIP**.

12)   The eight characteristics of life are: **L**ocomotion - **I**rritability - **R**espiration - **R**eproduction **A**ssimilation - **M**utation - **E**xcretion - **G**rowth

Anagram or memory aid - **MI LEG** is a very **RAR**e **characteristic of life**. Once again, I misspelled the word "MY" by spelling it "**MI**."

13)   The provinces of Canada are: **British Columbia** - **Alberta** - **Saskatchewan** - **Manitoba** - **Ontario** - **Quebec** - **New Brunswick** - **Nova Scotia** - **Newfoundland** - **Prince Edward Island**

Anagram or memory aid - The **Quee**NNN needs a **MAP** for a **Bu**S trip through **Canada**. I really misspelled the word "queen" this time, didn't I? I don't care. When I record and review this memory aid, I will remember how I spelled it.

My answers aren't necessarily any better than yours. Whatever memory aid you think of will work if you record it and review it. I simply wanted to point out a few possible solutions with a couple of different wrinkles that might help you in the future.

I want to provide one more list for practice. I will not make any suggestions on possible solutions for this list. I'm confident that you will develop a very workable solution. The different types of movement of muscles are **F**lexion, **E**xtension, **H**yperextension, **D**orsiflexion, **P**lantar **F**lexion, **A**bduction, **A**dduction, **R**otation, **C**ircumduction, **S**upination, **P**ronation, **I**nversion and **E**version. The beginning letters are listed below, but you can rearrange them if you want to, because they don't have to be learned in order.

F - E - H - D - P - F - A - A - R - C - S - P - I - E

CHAPTER 9

Intangible Lists

Now that you have learned about anagrams, I want to discuss learning lists of intangibles. When you need to learn a simple list of intangible words, you can use more than one tool. I will discuss a few lists I have taught in my Bible learning classes and apply two different learning methods to them. As I have already stated, I am not trying to convert you to a particular religion by using information from the Bible. I am simply working toward making you a **Master Mind Mechanic**, and I need to discuss a variety of information to enable you to reach your goal.

The first list I will discuss is the names of the tribes of Israel from the Old Testament. I will list a sound-alike word for each tribe, and then link the sound-alikes to learn them. The names of the tribes and the sound-alike words for each are:

Judah	Chewed Uh
Reuben	Reuben Sandwich
Gad	E**gad**
Asher	Ashes
Naphtali	Nap Tall He
Manasseh	My NASA (Rocket)
Simeon	San Simeon (California)
Levi	Levi Jeans
Issachar	Is Uh Scar
Zebulum	Zip A Lump
Joseph Multi-Colored Coat	
Benjamin	Benjamin Franklin Stove

I developed a story using the sound-alike words to link these names together. The story begins with the first name and goes to the last like any **Pure Link**. The sound-alike words in the story will be in bold type, so you can easily recognize them.

A man **chewed** on **uh Reuben** sandwich and said, "**Egad**, this thing is full of **ashes**." (**Judah - Reuben - Gad - Asher**)

Then he got sleepy and took a **nap**. Since he was very **tall** he took a nap on **my NASA** rocket. The rocket blasted off and landed in San **Simeon**, California. The first thing the man did after awakening and landing was to check his **Levi** jeans. (**Naphtali - Manasseh - Simeon -**

Levi)

While examining his Levis he said, "There **is a scar** on my leg." His Levis were very fancy and were covered with zippers. He then noticed that one of his **zip**pers had **a lum**p under it. A man in **multi-colored coat** came to his assistance. **Joseph** of the Old Testament wore a **multi-colored coat**. It was a cold, foggy day so the man said, "Come in and sit at my **Benjamin Franklin** Stove to warm yourself up." (**Issachar - Zebulun - Joseph - Benjamin**)

Knowing this story would easily remind a person of the twelve tribes of Israel. If you felt it necessary to associate the word Israel to this list, you could imagine that the man was fishing with a fishing reel as he chewed on his sandwich. That would tie the name of Israel to the story. I never did it because I knew from other study that these were the names of the tribes of Israel. I just needed to learn them. With this application, I learned an intangible list by using both the **Sound-Alike Word System** and the **Pure Link System**.

Since I have taught many Bible memory seminars, I have developed many aids to learn the Bible, and there are many lists throughout the Bible. To learn another application for intangible lists, I will use the list of what comes out of the heart to defile a man as listed in Mark chapter 7. The list below is not the same order in which they appear in the Bible. I rearranged them to make them easier to learn by using the **Anagram System**. They are:

> Adulteries
> Coveting
> Evil Thoughts
>
> Fornications
> Murders
> Thefts
> Slander
>
> Wickedness
> Sensuality
> Pride
>
> Foolishness
> Envy
> Deceit

I have listed them in these groupings, because this is the order in which I decided to use the beginning letters after examining the letters and making up anagram words that would work for me. The words are **ACE FoMiTS** and a **WaSP FLED**. If you examine the beginning letters in the list above and the capitalized and bold letters in the anagram, you will notice that they are the same. I used a capital letter "L" in the word **FLED**, because the word looks funny with a lower case letter "l" as this word shows **FlED**. I imagined that a man named Ace had a sour stomach, and **ACE FoMiTS** instead of vomits. It works for me, and I remembered it with no problem. When this happened, a **WaSP FLED** away from the problem. By going over the anagram, noticing the capitalized and bold letters in it and comparing them with the original list of words a few times, the list will become knowledge.

The real work to develop this list was in arranging the original words in an order that would allow me to develop a workable anagram. This is the part of the application that determines whether you can use an anagram or must use a link of some kind. I like to use anagrams as often as possible. They work very well for me, and I seem to retain the information longer without review when I develop a good anagram.

As you develop ways to learn lists of intangibles, be on the alert for ways to develop good anagrams first and then go to other tools if that becomes burdensome or simply won't work. One of the great qualities of these systems is that you have many choices after you learn the uses of all of the tools.

CHAPTER 10

Combining Systems for Complicated Information

Sometimes it is necessary to combine several systems to solve complicated learning problems. I worked with a student who was a commercial airline pilot and helped him learn information from the 1011 Abnormal Procedure Guide. This particular information was for the **two engine inoperative drift down approach** — whatever that is! The information was numbered, there were a lot of other numbers in it, and he had to learn them in order. He could have used peg words, but it didn't seem to be the best method. I suggested that we design a room to learn the information, because we could create something that would be the closest possible match and provide a better reminder to the information he needed to learn. As it turned out, he was thrilled with how quickly and thoroughly he knew the information. We used a combination of **The Room System**, **The Sound-Alike Word System**, **The Consonant Number System**, **The Peg Word System** and **The Anagram System** to learn this information. The information is as follows.

1) Set .605 EPR, establish 245 IAS, and maintain drift down chart EPR and IAS
2) Jettison fuel if necessary to attain chart gross weight/altitude combination
3) Determine range capability
4) Select rudder limiters to 30 and OVRD.
5) Open all crossfeed valves, use one pump in each tank after fuel jettison
6) If engine #2 is shut down:
   a. Deploy RAT
   b. Place B ATM to auto
   c. Place C ATM to on
7) Start APU below 25,000 feet:
   a. Close operating engine isolation valve
   b. Open APU bleed air shutoff
   c. Select normal mode
   d. Place B ATM to on, if necessary
8) When altitude is stabilized accelerate to 2-engine inoperative MRC speed
9) Complete descent/approach check list
10) Select cabin to final approach altitude
11) With APU generator operating, AC hydraulic pumps on
12) Set BUG to V-ref + 20 knots

13) Flaps 0, BUG + 60 minimum
14) Flaps 4, BUG + 40 minimum
15) Flaps 10, BUG + 20 minimum
16) If go-around required:
    a. Apply go-around thrust
    b. Retract flaps, 10 to 4 - BUG + 20 knots
                 4 to 0 - BUG + 40 knots
    c. Begin climb when reaching 200 knots
17) Intercepting approach slot, extend gear (Landing committed)
18) Pull GND proximity CMPTR AC CB 1B20
19) Turn off pack
20) Complete landing checklist
21) Use normal approach slot, reduce toward BUG + 5 knots on final
22) Extend spoilers manually on touchdown

Since there were twenty-two (22) steps or pieces of information in the process, it was necessary to invent twenty-two (22) pieces of furniture in our make-believe room. We even sketched out the room as we developed it. Obviously, he was familiar with the terms, so that made it easier for him to learn the information. I will list the pieces of furniture we chose to use and make a brief statement about each, so you will understand the process even better. I will not provide a complete picture on each piece of furniture. Look back and forth from the information to the piece of furniture if you don't fully comprehend my explanation.

1) **Chair** - The information starts with the word "set," and you "set" in a chair, so it seemed a natural. Please excuse my grammar. Since he needed to learn the number .605, he imagined he had to **JoStLe** around as he "set" in the chair.

2) **Picture of a jet plane** – We selected that since the procedure called for the pilot to **jetti**son fuel.

3) **Picture of DRaCula** - The capitalized letters in **DRaCula** stood for **D**etermine **R**ange **C**apability.

4) **Boat** - We imagined a boat was in the room to remind him of the word **rudder** and a **MooSe** was captaining the boat for the number 30.

5) **Animal feeder** - The feeder helped with cross**feed**.

6) **Noah's Ark** - Noah represented the number 2, and a **RAT**, **BAT** and **CAT** were on the ark.

7) **Ox** - He wanted to use an ox getting off of Noah's Ark. For some reason of his own, an ox helped remind him of APU. A **NaiL** for the number 25 was its yoke. He associated

the rest of the information at this number to the body parts of the ox. If he hadn't chosen to use the body parts of the ox, he could have used a **Sub Link** at this point.

8) **Horse stable** - We continued the animal theme, and the stable reminded him of the word **stabil**ized.

9) **Checkered tablecloth** on small table - The **checkered** tablecloth helped remind him of the **check**list.

10) **Small toy cabin** - The cabin helped remind him of the word "**cabin**."

11) **Ox** - He imagined another ox walking out of the cabin, which for his purposes, as before, brought APU to mind. He imagined the ox was operating a generator by using a hydraulic pump.

12) **Chair** - Again he "**set**" in the chair wearing a **V**-neck **ref**eree sweater. He also imagined that he hid a big NoSe under **knots** in the sweater.

13, 14 & 15) - **Three stacks of flapjacks** with BUGs on them. He then connected the peg words to the flapjacks to remember the numbers.

16) **Merry-go-round** - This helped remind him of **go-around**. He imagined a **sports car** with lots of **thrust**, a **tractor** with **retracted flaps** and a **fire truck** with **climb**ing ladders as places to ride on the merry-go-round for the other information. If he hadn't chosen to use the special riding pieces, he could have used a **Sub Link** at this point.

17) **Table with slots** - These slots had gears in them to remind him of **slot** and **gear**.

18) **Circuit breaker** - **Pull**ing a **circuit breaker** helped remind him of this information. Of course, he expanded the story to learn the rest of the information. I haven't mentioned that with the rest of the furniture, but you can assume that.

19) **Backpack** - He imagined that he **turn**ed the backpack over and found "**Off**" brand bug spray in the back**pack**.

20) **Picture of landing strip with checkerboard design** - The **landing** strip helped remind him of the word **landing**. The **checkerboard** design reminded him of the **check**list.

21) **Table with slots** - This table had slots with **NAST**y **BUG**s in them. The word **NAST**y reminded him of Normal Approach Slot Toward, and the **BUG**s reminded him of **BUG**.

22) **Goal post** - He imagined that the goal post **extend**ed up out of the floor with **spoilers** on it, and a **man** scored a **touchdown**. The **man** reminded him of the word **manually**.

As I said earlier, he was really excited about this learning tool. He drew the furniture in order on a scratch pad and went over it a few times to learn it in order. Actually, he was a pretty good artist. He did a much better job that I would have. Then he reviewed his pictures a few times until he knew all of the information in order. This may seem like a lot to do to learn this information, but he learned it much faster than he would have with repetition and had a picture of it he could always come back to for review. You'll never really know how well these systems work if you don't apply them. The more practice you get with the systems, the more experience you will acquire, and the more confident you will become in their usefulness.

When you have to learn complicated information like this it would be very difficult without the proper tools. You no doubt will be combining various systems, as you become increasingly adept at applying these tools. This application was particularly helpful, because we chose the pieces of furniture in the room to make the learning problem even easier. That is why I like to become an interior decorator for certain learning problems.

This student went on by himself to develop other rooms for other processes he needed to know. He even used the parts of his body from head to toe to remember the eleven (11) points in the **engine flight start**. He was so very excited because he never before had any tools to make learning fun, easy and creative. He was particularly happy because this whole process made the learning process for him more like a game. He very much enjoyed the process of creating his own rooms and memory aids. This process certainly takes learning out of the mundane, repetitive process and puts a little pizzazz into the process.

I will teach you how to learn an entire issue of a magazine later. That certainly is complicated information, but you will find that it is very easy with these learning tools. You should be feeling very good about your progress as a learning apprentice at this point.

CHAPTER 11

Connecting People with Their Works or Discoveries

Connecting a person with the work or discovery for which they are famous will be quite easy for you now. All you have to do is develop a sound-alike for the person's name, develop a way to picture his or her work and connect them with a memory aid picture. This is a simple **One-On-One** learning problem.

As an example **Hutton** Studied Earth Movements. I will describe a few ways to learn this. First, the rent was paid **SEM**i-monthly **ON** a **HUT**. The beginning letters in **SEM**i are the three beginning letters in Studied Earth Movements. The words **ON** a **HUT** are a sound-alike for the name **Hutton**. How about this idea. When the **EARTH MOVE**d a **MINT** tree fell **ON** a person who **STUDIED** in a **HUT**. I do not really need to explain anything with this example, since it contains all of the information. The important thing is to make up a story that works and record it for later review.

Here are some others with which to practice. Make up picture memory aids for each name and work or discovery combination and write them on the lines provided. After this little practice session, you will feel better about your ability to handle similar information in the future.

Balboa - Discovered the Pacific Ocean

Moliero - Wrote *The Miser*

Rodin - Sculpted The *Thinker*

Whistler - Arrangement of Gray and Black

Curie - Discovered Radium

Magellan - First to sail around the world

Brahm - Wrote *Hungarian Dances*

Hertz - Demonstrated existence of radio waves

Hals - Painted *Laughing Cavalier*

Wren - Designed St. Paul's Cathedral

Dalton - Conceived modern notion of atoms

Chekhov - Wrote *The Cherry Orchard*

Matisse - *The Blue Window*

Bronzio - *Portrait of a Young Man*

Gauguin - *Yellow Canary*

CHAPTER 12

Chemical Symbols

To remember chemical symbols, you simply need to connect the letters that represent the name of the element to the element name. This is a simple **One-On-One** learning problem. Many of them are very easy and don't need a memory aid, because the beginning letters of the element name form the symbol letters. **O**xygen is an example of this. The chemical symbol for **O**xygen is simply the letter "**O**." Other examples of this are Carbon - "**C**," and Hydrogen - "**H**." Other elements start with either the first two letters of the element name or two letters at the beginning of the element name. These don't present a learning problem either. Other symbols are not related to the letters in the element name at all. These are the ones that require special memory aids. **Hg** are the letters that represent the element **mercury**, for instance. Neither of these two letters is even in the element name. **Mercury** is the mythical Greek god of commerce who is supposed to be very fast. Most people know that. Using that knowledge, you could imagine that **Mercury** outran a **H**o**G** in a foot race. You will notice that I not only capitalized the letters I wanted to remember, I also typed them in **bold** type. This makes them stand out in my mind better as my eyes see them. If you record your memory aids in a computer, type them the same way. If you keep written notes, capitalize the appropriate letters. This memory aid easily tells us that the symbol for **mercury** is **Hg**. I could have used any word with the letters "**Hg**" in them as long as I made a good connection to **mercury**. I could have used a **H**a**G** or **H**u**G** with the same results. You could also use two words that begin with these two letters such as, **Mercury** ran so fast he **H**it a **G**ate without opening it. As always, you would record this aid in the chemical symbol section of your notes for later review. An **Apprentice Master Mind Mechanic** must always be organized and disciplined.

I will list a few elements and their chemical symbols for additional practice. As I have said before, the more practice of all kinds you get, the more capable you will become. Simply make up a memory aid for each listed element and record it on the appropriate spaces. Use one word that contains the letters that need to be learned or two words with only the beginning sounds of each word if two letters are necessary.

These applications are similar to the **One Sound** and **One Word Methods** in **The Consonant Number System**. Make sure you use a scratch pad to make up your memory aids. I will list some possible solutions later. This practice will help you add a more experienced tool to your **mental toolbox**. I know I keep repeating this statement. I repeat it, because it is a basic fundamental of becoming an experienced **Master Mind Mechanic**.

1)   Sb = Antimony

      Memory aid

2)   Fe = Iron

      Memory aid

3)   K = Potassium

      Memory aid

4)   Ag = Silver

      Memory aid

5)   Au = Gold

      Memory aid

6)   Pb = Lead

      Memory aid

7)   Na = Sodium

      Memory aid

8)   Cu = Copper

      Memory aid

9)   Sn = Tin

      Memory aid

Possible Solutions

Once again I will offer some possible solutions to expand your awareness of possibilities for solutions. A **master** always needs to teach an **apprentice** how to apply his trade. I want you to become a **Master Mind Mechanic** with a completed and full mental toolbox.

1) Sb = Antimony

Memory aid - An **ant** is **moan**ing in a **SuB**, because it is afraid to be under water.

2) Fe = Iron

Memory aid - I see myself **iron**ing a **FE**nce instead of clothing.

3) K = Potassium

Memory aid - A **po**tato **K**ayoed someone who kidded it about the **tass**els he wore on **him**. A **K**ayo is a knockout in boxing. Here is a prime example of my using the dictionary. As I thought about this element, I thought I might use a girl named **K**ay, but for some reason the aid I made up just didn't seem right to me, so I found the word **K**ayo in the dictionary and liked using it better.

4) Ag = Silver

Memory aid - A secret **AG**ent smuggled **silver** into the country.

5) Au = Gold

Memory aid - The **AU**ctioneer got a huge sum for a **gold AU**stralian **A**ntiq**U**e. There is an obvious new principle in this memory aid that you might like to use when possible. As you can see, I have three references to the element symbol in this memory aid. A triple reminder might work better than a single reminder. This unusual aid required the use of a dictionary to find these three words. I keep mentioning the use of a good dictionary, because it is very helpful.

6) Pb = Lead

Memory aid - The local **PuB** serves heavy drinks loaded with **lead**.

7) Na = Sodium

Memory aid - A **NA**sty woman **sewed him** up.

8)   Cu = Copper

Memory aid - I always drink my hot cocoa out of a **copper CU**p.

9)   Sn = Tin

Memory aid - Rin **Tin** Tin **SN**iffed a **tin** can, **SN**atched it and **SN**eezed after every movie scene. Once again, I have not only put three reminders of the chemical symbol in the memory aid, but I have used the element name twice also.

Once again, my answers aren't necessarily any better than yours. Whatever memory aid you think of will work if you record it and review it.

CHAPTER 13

Associate Peg List

You can develop another peg list, known as an **Associate Peg List,** if you feel that learning a couple of lists at numbered positions at the same time will confuse you. This is a very simple idea. You simply think of something that the basic peg word reminds you of, and that item becomes an associate peg word for that number. For instance, the first thing that pops into your mind when you think of **T**ie might be a **shirt**. **Shirt** then would be your associate peg word for the number one (1), and you could use it as an alternative to **T**ie for another list. It doesn't matter that **SH**i**RT** would translate to 641 in **The Consonant Number System.** It represents the number one (1) with this application. I never felt a need to use associate lists, but some of my students have. I will list possible associates for the basic 100 peg words just in case you would want to use them. Obviously none of these associate words can even come close to causing confusion with any of the basic peg words. If you want to use this idea and don't like some of my choices for associates, simply develop your own. They will work better for you than mine will anyway.

1) **T**ie - Shirt	2) Noah - Flood	3) Ma - Pa	4) Rye - Grain
5) Law - Scales	6) Shoe - Sock	7) Cow - Bull	8) i**V**y - College
9) Bee - Honey	10) ToeS - Foot	11) ToT - Tricycle	12) TiN - Soup
13) ToMb - Skeleton	14) TiRe - Pump	15) ToweL - Beach	16) DiSH - Food
17) TacK - Hammer	18) DiVe - Swan	19) kNoB - Door	20) NoSe - Eyes
21) NeT - Hair	22) NuN - Monk	23) NaMe - Pen	24) NeRo - Fire
25) NaiL - Hammer	26) NotCH - Axe	27) NecK - Bottle	28) kNiFe - Sword
29) NaP - Bed	30) MooSe - Hunter	31) MaT - Porch	32) MooN - Sun
33) MuMMy - Pyramid	34) MoweR - Grass	35) MaiL - Stamp	36) MatCH - Lighter
37) MuG - Coffee	38) MoVie - Ticket	39) MoP - Bucket	40) RoSe - Garden
41) RaT - Mousetrap	42) RaiN - Rainbow	43) RaM - Shepherd	44) RoweR - Lake
45) RaiL - Caboose	46) RoaCH - Spray	47) RuG - Vacuum	48) RooF - Ladder
49) RoPe - Gallows	50) LaCe - Hanky	51) LoT - Weeds	52) LioN - Zoo
53) LaMb - Shears	54) LuRe - Worms	55) LiLy - Swamp	56) LeeCH - Blood
57) LocK - Key	58) LaVa - Soap	59) LiP - Lipstick	60) CHeeSe - Milk
61) JeT - Radar	62) CHaiN - Dungeon	63) JaM - Bread	64) JaR - Glass
65) JaiL - Convict	66) JudGe - Gavel	67) JacK - Top	68) JaVa - Cup

69) SHiP - Ocean   70) CaSe - Loader   71) CaT - Dog   72) CaN - Opener

73) CoMb - Brush   74) CaR - Horse   75) CoaL - Oil   76) CaGe - Bird

77) CaKe - Candle   78) CaVe - Ice   79) CaPe - Magician 80) FaCe - Eyes

81) FaT - Running   82) FaN - Air Cond. 83) FoaM - Rubber 84) FuR - Leather

85) FiLe - Clippers   86) FiSH - Hook   87) FoG - Horn   88) FiFe - Drum

89) FoB - Pocket   90) BuS - Plane   91) BaT - Pitcher   92) BuN - Hot Dog

93) BuM - King   94) BeaR - Nat'l Park 95) BaLL - Glove   96) BuSH - Trimmer

97) BiKe - Traffic   98) PuFF - Wind   99) PiPe - Tobacco 100)DiSeaSe - Medicine

CHAPTER 14

Bible Memory

So very many people have tried to learn facts, verses, chapters or books of the Bible and have given up. It seemed the more they tried to learn, the more frustrated they became, because they kept forgetting what they thought they had learned. At least they had spent enough time on it to feel they should have learned it. This is still the same old problem. With repetition, everything is harder to learn, frustration sets in and people give up. I have used my systems to learn the Bible like I have everything else. As a matter of fact, I used my learning tools to learn the entire New Testament, all 260 chapters. That sounds almost impossible to everyone, but I dedicated myself to it and accomplished it. It took me a whole year of dedication, but you have already learned how **ODD** I am.

You may remember or have heard of the old "$64,000 Question" television program. A few years ago a renewal of that program named the "$128,000 Challenge" began to air. The idea was to have contestants on the program who had knowledge in an area they weren't especially known for. I was a former professional athlete and my subject on the program was the New Testament. I thought I had an agreement with the producers before agreeing to be a contestant. I had not learned the chapters by verse number but by content. I showed you how I did this when I developed the **Room System Associate List**. I knew everything in every chapter, but I hadn't taken the time to learn the verses by number. I agreed to be a contestant only if they did not ask me any verse number questions but only content questions. They agreed, but it didn't turn out that way. The format initially was very similar to the old "$64,000 Question" program. A contestant could win $64,000 by answering all of the questions up to that level. The new wrinkle for this program was to have everyone who won $64,000 come back at the end of the season for a challenge to win an additional $64,000, thus the "$128,000 Challenge." I contended that they wouldn't ask a Shakespeare expert page and line location of a certain fact, so why ask me verse numbers.

I felt confident as I worked my way up toward the $64,000 level. None of the questions were hard, because I had learned every chapter. As the questioning proceeded toward a greater dollar value, there were actually several questions per level. The $64,000 level for me consisted of seven actual questions. Guess what the very last of the seven questions was? They asked me to name the chapter and verse of a particular verse. I immediately knew what chapter it was in, because I had learned the content of every chapter by chapter number, but not having learned it by verse number, I had to guess. First of all, I felt betrayed and flustered, because they had not followed our agreement. My guess was a couple of verses off, and I was unable to enter the challenge stage of the program, because I hadn't won $64,000.

There is no way I could have lost if they had not asked me verse numbers, because I had learned all 260 chapters. I hadn't learned them for the program. I learned them for my own spiritual growth, and the program came along later. Others could learn the whole New Testament or Old Testament as well, but it would take the same kind of **ODD** person for so much information.

I want to discuss something less challenging though. When my children were young, I wanted to teach them basic facts in the Bible initially, such as the names of the books of the Bible, the Ten Commandments, the Fruit of the Spirit and many other facts. I later began to teach them individual verses and even whole chapters. I have published several Bible memory aids including the art work to make learning easy. Like everything else, I changed the words to pictures, so anyone could **see**, **recognize**, **register** and **retrieve** them.

When my children were young, I didn't want to teach them **The Consonant Number System** and **Peg Word System** to picture numbers. They had no burning need for it, and why teach them something ahead of their need or maturity level? I didn't begin to teach them **The Consonant Number System** and **Peg Word System** until they entered middle school. Up until that time I used sound-alikes to have them picture basic numbers. We have already discussed a simple sound-alike peg system elsewhere in this book. I will show you a few examples of what I began to teach them. I used a **gate** to picture the number **eight**. Here is the picture I used to teach them Commandment number **eight**.

The words in commandment number eight are, "Thou shalt not steal," or "You shall not steal," according to which version of the Bible you read. In the picture a large **gate**, number **eight**, is being opened by a large knot in a rope. The **knot** represents the word "**not**." The gate the knot is opening is made of **steel**, for the word "**steal**." The three key ingredients in this picture are the **gate**, **knot** and **steel**. These three words translate into **eight = not steal**.

In my opinion there is no need for the beginning two words of "thou shalt" or "you shall". All ten of the Commandments begin with these words, so it is simple to just say them before each commandment. I simply reviewed this picture with my children a few times, took it away from them and asked if they knew the information.

We made it a habit to study new Bible memory information and review information we had previously gone over before every evening after dinner. I also helped my children with their schoolwork at this evening mealtime. It began to be a time my children anticipated, because it was fun.

I first taught and my children first learned the samples of curricula you have seen throughout this book during these after meal sessions. Making everything my children needed to learn fun to learn helped build a very strong foundation on which to build their skills as Apprentice Master Mind Mechanics. As they got older and needed a tool in school, I taught the tool and how to use it. Gradually they learned all of the tools and how to apply them, just as you are doing.

The words in commandment number nine are, "You shall **not bear false witness**." Here is the picture that teaches those words. Once again, there is no picture for the first two words.

The basic picture for the number **nine** is a **vine**. You see the **vine** in the picture. A bear tied a **knot** in the vine. The **bear** is wearing a **false** face and is standing in a **wet nest**. The words in bold teach the commandment. The key ingredients in this picture are the **vine, knot, bear, false** face and **wet nest**. These words translate into **nine = not bear false witness**. Look back at both of these pictures and review them, and you will easily know the information. A little review from time to time will allow you to keep the information. At a given point in time, the pictures will be branded onto your brain for instant retrieval with just the thought of the commandment number as with a cow, horse or giraffe.

My children and I were not only learning, both Bible and school information during these times, but we were also spending some very special time together as friends. This process drew us closer together, because we were all having fun. I have published a great deal of Bible memory material for facts, verses, chapters and books that might interest you. All of these materials have professional artwork incorporated into them to make the learning process easy.

I began to teach my children so many Bible facts that I eventually developed a board game I named *Around The Table,* because we learned **around the table**. This particular board game has a game board with a picture of a table with chairs on it. Players roll dice and move from chair to chair where we ask questions and learned answers with pictures. Each question goes into a holding area from where we will ask it again during the game. My children, and now others, had a lot of fun as they played and learned.

I developed the picture that you see below to teach my children the books of the Old Testament. It is one of four pictures linked together to learn all of the books of the Old Testament. The books taught in this picture are Genesis, Exodus, Leviticus, Numbers, Deuteronomy, Joshua, Judges, Ruth and Samuel. Read the explanation below this picture to learn the information.

You see a stack of old books in the back of the bus. They represent the books of the Old Testament. I told you that each list should start with a picture illustrating the information, and the rest of the information links to that beginning picture. These old books are another good example of that principle. The boy in the bus owns the old books. He is looking out of the bus toward the girl sipping a **gin**ger ale. She is his **sister** or **sis**. This picture will remind you of the first book, which is **Genesis**. Notice that she is about to **exit** the **bus**, which will remind you of the book of **Exodus**. Her friend in front of her dropped a soda bottle and broke it. She was about to pick it up, but her mother said, "**Leave it, it cuts**," for the book of **Leviticus**. The mother is holding her daughter's math book with **numbers** on it for the book of **Numbers**. Go back and look at the picture to review these first four books before continuing.

A soldier is behind the mother. He is chasing the naughty little boy. Soldiers have duties, and the boy says, "His **duty** is to **run at me**," for the book of **Deuteronomy**. Notice that the soldier is holding his jaw, and the boy is holding a shoe. The boy hit the soldier in the **jaw** with the **shoe** and said it as he ran away. This is the picture for the book **Joshua**. For protection the boy is running to the **judges** to remind you of the book of **Judges**. One of the judges loves candy and is holding a Baby **Ruth** candy bar behind his back for the book of **Ruth**. The mule behind the judges that is tied to the pole by a short rope loves candy too. The mule stretches the rope as far as possible to try to reach the candy, but it can't quite reach it. As a result, it has a tear in its eye, because it is a sad **mule** for the book of **Samuel**. Review the whole picture and explanation one more time before taking the following test.

When you think of the books of the Old Testament, you will think of the **old books** in the back of the bus. What did the boy with the old books see when he looked out of the bus? Of what book does that remind you? What is the girl sipping the ginger ale preparing to do? What book does that remind you of? When her friend dropped her soda bottle, what did her mother say? Of hat book does that remind you? What was on the book her mother was holding? Of what book does that remind you? What did the little boy say about the soldier behind the mother? Of what book does that remind you? Where did the little boy hit the soldier, and what is he holding as he runs away? Of what book does that remind you? Who is the boy running toward for protection? Of what book does that remind you? What was one of the judges holding behind his back? Of what book does that remind you? What wanted to eat the candy? Of hat book does that remind you? The picture works, and if you reviewed it ever so briefly every few weeks you would never forget it.

The next picture begins with the second saddest mule you would have ever seen in your life. This mule represents Second Samuel which means the mule in this picture is actually First Samuel. I didn't say that when I first taught it, because I always do that after I teach the second mule. The picture continues, and the student simply follows it along with my audio taped instructions to learn it.

I also developed pictures to teach my children other facts and Bible information, verses, whole chapters and even whole books. Others began to ask me to help their families, so I began to publish Bible learning material to help other families. All of these publications include audio tapes that interpret and explain each picture in the publication.

CHAPTER 15

Remembering Long-Digit Numbers

Many people need to learn long-digit numbers for one reason or another. You have already learned the systems and tools to do this. You just need some additional applications to make this learning problem easier. There are several ways to attack long digit numbers. The first application is to simply use the One Sound, One Word or Combination Methods for learning phone numbers and extend your method choice to include more numbers. I will give you some examples of these methods before introducing another application.

Speed is not the most important factor as you start to learn these applications. Speed may never need to be a factor for you. When making up **Number Memory Words** for phone numbers, I told you to take your time and develop several possibilities until you find the one that seems to work best for that particular person or company. You should do the same thing with long digit numbers.

To learn long-digit numbers you must begin by listing the potential sounds under each digit the same way you did for phone numbers. Nothing is different in this application except the number is longer than a seven-digit phone number. That means you will have to do a little more work to extend the learning aid than you did for phone numbers. Let's examine a sixteen-digit number to begin this instruction.

```
5  8  1  6  4  2  7  1  2  1  0  8  6  4  3  2
L  F  T  J  R  N  G  T  N  T  Z  F  J  R  M  N
   V  D SH       K  D        D  S  V SH
      CH            C            C     CH
      G                               G
```

The possibilities for forming words for these numbers are almost limitless. Once you form the words, you will be able to apply some sort of linking mechanism to connect **Number Memory Words** together, so you will be using two systems to solve this learning problem. You will apply **The Consonant Number System** first, and after you have developed the **Number Memory Words**, you will need to apply **The Link System** to connect the **Number Memory Words** together. Numbers are simply a listing of digits in order, and you have learned to use **The Pure Link System** to learn information in order.

To begin, you must examine the possibilities, which I have already said are almost limitless. Remember that one of my rules is to **do as little as possible to remember as much as possible**. In this case, that rule means to use as few words as possible to picture this or any number. If you could think of one word that had these sixteen sounds in it in this particular order, of course, that would be ideal, but that isn't going to happen for this or for probably any long digit numbers. That being the case, I always set out to find as few words as possible. That means I will have fewer words to link together later.

The first three digits (581) was as far as I could go for my first word, which is **LoVeD**. I was able to take in the next four digits (6427) for my next word, which is **CHeeRiNG**. You might remember that I have mentioned that I don't use the letter "G" in the "ING" letter combination. I don't use it sometimes when a three-digit number ends in a number two (2), and I can't find a good word without using the "G" in "ING." Even if that were a rule, one of my rules is to break any rule if it helps to make the information more memorable. I was also able to take in the next four digits with the word **DoNuTS**. Herein lies a word-lengthening principle. A digit zero (0) can always be used to pluralize a word if it falls in the right place. I will list several helpful aids like this one that will benefit you after you learn more about this process. I was able to take the last five digits in with only one more word. That word is **FiSHeRMeN**. The numbers along with the four words I developed look like this when aligned with numbers and sounds.

```
5 8 1 6  4 2 7 1 2 1 0 8 6  4 3 2
L V D CH R N G D N T S F SH  R M N
```

LoVeD - CHeeRiNG - DoNuTS - FiSHeRMeN

There are many other words that I could have used to represent this number, but this one will work fine for this teaching segment. After developing the **Number Memory Words**, the next step in the process is to connect or link the **Number Memory Words** to whatever the numbers represent. You would need to develop a sound-alike word for the number's use, and then would have to connect the **Number Memory Words** to that word by linking them together. Since this is only a made up number and not a number that has an application, we will simply link these words together to remember the number. This is the little memory story I would record to be able to review this number later. I **LoVeD CHeeRiNG** and eating **DoNuTS** while watching **FiSHeRMeN**. By knowing **The Consonant Number System**, it is easy to translate the consonant sounds in these four words back to numbers to recall this long sixteen digit number. This is one way to remember long digit numbers. This is the **One Sound Method** taught earlier. One consonant sound was used for each digit in the number to be learned. The **One Word Method** could also be used for long digit numbers, but I prefer not using that method for long digit numbers, because too many words are necessary to remember the number. In this case, I would have needed to use sixteen (16) words to remember this number. The **Combination Method** can be useful for some numbers. The initial exploration of the digit arrangement and the resulting sounds will determine what you do to make it easiest. I will introduce another application for learning long digit numbers soon that will work well, but first I want you to get some practice with other long digit numbers. Remember that the more digits you can take in for each **Number Memory Word**, the fewer words will be in your memory link, so try to extend your words as much as possible. With that in mind, I will list some basic short cuts or standards for forming or lengthening words.

Short Cuts for Forming or Lengthening Number Words

0 - Make the word plural   914(0) - **BuTTeR** becomes **BuTTeRS**

01 - Add "eST" to a word   15(01) - **TaLL** becomes **TaLLeST**

1 - Add "eD" to a word   57(1) - **waLK** becomes **waLKeD**

2 - Add "iN" or "iNg" to a word   85(2) - **FaLL** becomes **FaLL iN** or **FaLLiNg**

27 - Add "iNG" to a word   74(27) - **CaRRy** becomes **CaRRyiNG**

4 - Add "eR" to a word   921(4) - **PaiNT** becomes **PaiNTeR**

5 - Add "Ly" to a word   641(5) - **SHoRT** becomes **SHoRTLy**

8 - Add "oFF" to a word   17(8) - **TaKe** becomes **TaKe oFF**

85 - Add "FuL" to a word   43(85) - **haRM** becomes **haRMFuL**

9 - Add "uP" to a word   61(9) - **SHuT** becomes **SHuT uP**

These standard additions will help extend your **Number Memory Words** when you need to remember long digit numbers. Review them and then look for possible uses of them as you practice the following sets of long digit numbers. I will give you some **Number Memory Words** after your practice is completed. Don't look at my suggestions until you have worked on your own. In any case, there are almost limitless numbers of possibilities.

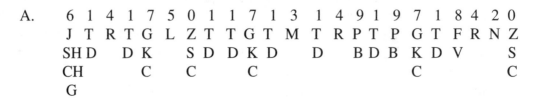

```
A.    6  1  4  1  7  5  0  1  1  7  1  3  1  4  9  1  9  7  1  8  4  2  0
      J  T  R  T  G  L  Z  T  T  G  T  M  T  R  P  T  P  G  T  F  R  N  Z
      SH D     D  K     S  D  D  K  D        D     B  D  B  K  D  V        S
      CH          C     C     C              C                 C
      G
```

```
B.    1  2  7  4  7  1  0  9  5  2  2  7  1  9  5  0
      T  N  T  R  G  T  Z  P  L  N  N  G  T  P  L  Z
      D     D     K  D  S  B  L        K  D  B     S
            C        C              C              C
```

I have listed the sounds for the first two numbers, but I will not list them for the rest of the practice numbers. You need to begin doing everything from scratch, so get some work sheets, list the numbers, write the letter sounds below each digit and form your **Number Memory Words**. This practice will help you add a more experienced number tool to your **mental toolbox**. Develop your own words before looking at my suggestions that follow.

C.   4 0 6 0 9 8 5 9 7 5 4 4 3 9 0 9 4

D.   3 0 1 4 0 9 4 1 0 3 2 2 1 9 7 3 3 4 0 7 5 7

E.   9 0 7 1 9 5 2 3 9 4 9 5 1 0 1 7 8 9 5 0 1 4

F.   0 1 4 9 6 0 0 5 1 0 9 4 1

G.   8 0 0 8 5 1 2 7 9 0 7 1 1 4 8 9 4 2 1

H.   7 5 0 0 1 0 1 7 0 4 2 2 7 0 0 4 0 9 5 2 0 2 7

I.   1 4 3 9 2 0 7 5 1 6 1 8 9 4 1 4 1 4 7 4 3 9

Some Possible Number Memory Words

As I have already said, there are limitless ways of developing Number Memory Words for these number combinations. I have made a suggestion for each number. I'm sure your words would work just as well, but again, the more you see and do, the more talent you will possess.

A.   6 1 4 1 7 5 0 1 1 7 1 3 1 4 9 1 9 7 1 8 4 2 0

6141 -	**SHaTTeReD**
7501 -	**CLoSeT**
171 -	**TicKeT**
31491 -	**MoToRBoaT**
971 -	**BucKeT**
8420 -	**FeRNS**

B.   1 2 7 4 7 1 0 9 5 2 2 7 1 9 5 0

127 -	**TaNK**
4710 -	**RocKeTS**
95227 -	**BaLLoNiNG**
1950 -	**TaBLeS**

C.   4 0 6 0 9 8 5 9 7 5 4 4 3 9 0 9 4

4060 -	hoRSeSHoeS
9785 -	BaG FuLL
9754 -	BuGLeR
4390 -	RaMPS
947 -	PaRK

D.   3 0 1 4 0 9 4 1 0 3 2 2 1 9 7 3 3 4 0 7 5 7

3014 -	MaSTeR
0941032 -	SPoRTSMaN
2197 -	NoTeBooK
3340 -	MeMoRieS
757 -	CLocK

E.   9 0 7 1 9 5 2 3 9 4 9 5 1 0 1 7 8 9 5 0 1 4

907195 -	BaSKeTBaLL
2394 -	NuMBeR
9510 -	BeLTS
178 -	TaKe oFF
95014 -	PLasTeR

F.   0 1 4 9 6 0 0 5 1 0 9 4 1

014 -	SiTTeR
960 -	PuSHeS
0510 -	SaLTS
941 -	BoaRD

G.   8 0 0 8 5 1 2 7 9 0 7 1 1 4 8 9 4 2 1

800 -	FuSeS
85127 -	FieLDiNG
9071 -	BaSKeT
148 -	TRoPHy
9421 -	BuRNeD

H.   7 5 0 0 1 0 1 7 0 4 2 2 7 0 0 4 0 9 5 2 0 2 7

       75001 -   **CLoSeST**
       0170 -   **SuiTCaSe**
       4227 -   **RuNNiNG**
       0040 -   **SciSSoRS**
       952027 -   **BaLaNCiNG**

I.   1 4 3 9 2 0 7 5 1 6 1 8 9 4 1 4 1 4 7 4 3 9

       14392 -   **TRoMBoNe**
       0751 -   **SKiLLeT**
       618 -   **SHuT oFF**
       941 -   **BiRD**
       414 -   **RaDaR**
       7439 -   **CRaMP**

For these or any long digit numbers, the **next step** would be to **make up a memory phrase or story** linking the **Number Memory Words** together with the use for the number. The use for the number would start the link. In these case there are no uses, since they are made up practice numbers. Record the memory phrases or stories for later review as always.

CHAPTER 16

The Adjective Peg Word Method

You will recall that when I was discussing phone numbers I realized some number combinations didn't lend themselves to developing **Number Memory Words**, so I developed and began to use the **One Word Method** for remembering phone numbers. Sometimes long-digit numbers fall into that category as well, and another method to make it easier is necessary. The Adjective Peg Word Method will work very well with this situation. It will also work well for any long digit number. You should have learned all of the peg words by this time. With the Adjective Peg Word Method of remembering numbers, you remember long-digit numbers in combinations of threes. With this method the first of three numbers is an **adjective** that describes the **peg word** that represents the next two numbers in the three number combination. Let's examine the three digit number combination 921 to explain this application.

The **first step** is to **look at the last two digits and recall the peg word for those two digits**. In this case the peg word for 21 is **NeT**.

The **second step** is to **look at the first digit and develop an adjective that will describe the peg word for the last two digits**. In this case the first digit is nine (9). The adjective must begin with a sound that represents the first digit of the three-digit combination, which in this case has to be a "P" or a "B." **Only the beginning sound in the adjective counts** toward the number. This is the same application as the   **One Word Method** where only the first sound in a word is counted.

In this case I could use any word that began with a letter "P" or "B" to describe a **NeT**. It could be a **B**ig **NeT**, a **P**urple **NeT**, a **B**ouncy **NeT** or any other kind of **NeT** described by an adjective beginning with a "P" or "B."

The **third step** is to **continue developing an adjective and peg word for every three digit number combination and link the adjectives and peg words together** to learn the entire long-digit number.

The best way to understand this process is with an example. Let's look at this long-digit number:

$$2\,7\,6 \,-\, 4\,2\,1 \,-\, 5\,4\,9 \,-\, 1\,6\,4 \,-\, 3\,1\,3$$

As you can see, I have separated the numbers into groups of three with the last two digits in each grouping of three digits in bold numbers. Next I will list the peg words for the last two digits in each grouping of three digits in place of the two bold digits.

$$2\,\text{CaGe} \,-\, 4\,\text{NeT} \,-\, 5\,\text{RoPe} \,-\, 1\,\text{JuRy} \,-\, 3\,\text{ToMb}$$

Now I must think of an adjective beginning with the consonant sound for the first number in the grouping of three digits that will describe the peg word in each grouping. The following is just one possible application of this idea for these numbers. I could use any descriptive word beginning with a letter "N," for instance, to describe a **CaGe**, or any descriptive word that begins with a letter "R" to describe a **NeT**. I suggest you use a dictionary when developing these adjectives.

New CaGe - Ragged NeT - Long RoPe - Dirty JuRy - Muddy ToMb

To remember this long digit number, I would need to start a link with a picture for its use and then link the adjectives and peg words to it in order. Since this is just a practice number and it has no use, I might develop this memory link. A **New CaGe** had a **Ragged NeT** over it. I used a **Long RoPe** to pull the net off. I presented the net to a **Dirty JuRy**, but the jury simply used it to cover a **Muddy ToMb**. As always, I record this memory aid so it could be reviewed later.

If the long-digit number ends with one or two digits after you have grouped all the combinations of three digits, use any of the methods you have learned to remember these leftover digits. I don't need to list long digit numbers with which you can practice. Simply write down a string of digits on a piece of scratch paper and practice the **Adjective Peg Word Method** with them. This practice will help you add an even more experienced number tool to your **mental toolbox**.

Other Possible Adjective Peg Word Applications

There are other possible **Adjective Peg Word** applications. Instead of using three digits with only one adjective describing the peg word, you might try using **four digits** and develop **two adjectives** for the first two digits in the four digit groupings that describe a peg word for the last two digits in the four digit groupings. Let's look at the first four digits of the previous long digit number I just used as an example. The first four digits were:

$$2\,7\,6\,4$$

In this case we would use a peg word for the last two digits in this four-digit grouping which are 64. These two digits are bold above. The peg word for 64 is **JuRy**. Two adjectives will be used for the first two digits in this grouping of four digits. What about a **Noisy Crazy JuRy**. These two adjectives begin with the appropriate sounds for the first two digits and complete this application. You might want to experiment with this application. You might find that you like it.

You could also use only one adjective for the first two digits in groupings of four digits with a little different twist. Perhaps only the first and last sounds in each adjective would count toward the number to remember. Or perhaps you could use an adjective with only two sounds. I have never used this idea, but I say it to get you thinking about other possibilities. Don't limit yourself. You may come up with a very applicable new idea if you just use your imagination.

Commonly Used Adjectives

I will list a few possible adjectives for this adjective peg word application. There are hundreds, or even thousands, of possible adjectives. If you plan on using this application regularly, you should extend this list to suit your own needs.

1. Tall, Tiny, Tough, Dopey, Dizzy

2. New, Noisy, Neat, Nasty

3. Messy, Muddy, Mellow

4. Red, Rusty, Rugged, Ripped

5. Lazy, Low, Light, Little, Lousy

6. CHeap, SHy, Giant, Jumpy

7. Grumpy, Green, Crazy, Cold, Quiet, Quick

8. Funny, Fake, Vital, Free, Violet

9. Big, Black, Bold, Purple, Blue, Brown

0. Silly, Sticky, Soapy, Zany

Number Learning Choices

You now have **at least five choices** for learning numbers. All of them are based on **The Consonant Number System**. They are:

1) The Peg Word System

2) The One Sound Method

3) The One Word Method

4) The Combination Method

5) The Adjective Peg Word Method

As I have already said, you may develop some other applications that work well for you in addition to these applications, but these five alternatives provide real choices for different combinations of numbers.

CHAPTER 17

English Vocabulary and Definitions

Some **English vocabulary words** might as well be foreign words if you have no idea what they mean. Of course, every English word falls into this category until you learn it. All English words have no meaning to a youngster before the learning process starts. With this teaching, I will simply teach you how to learn additional English vocabulary words to improve your knowledge and use of words in our language.

Learning **definitions** is almost the same as learning vocabulary except most definitions have more words to describe them. The process and application are the same. You must connect the vocabulary word or term you are defining to its meaning. Sometimes this will be a simple **One-On-One** connection with only one word to connect to one other word, but many times it will involve connecting several words to a vocabulary word or term. This could involve a **Twenty-On-One** or a **Thirty-On-One** application when twenty or thirty words you have to connect to the vocabulary word or term you are defining.

There are several steps to follow when learning vocabulary words or definitions. Those steps are:

1) Read the word or term and its meaning or definition carefully to be as familiar with it as possible.

2) Develop a sound-alike word picture for the vocabulary word or term you are defining, to make it tangible. If it is already tangible this step isn't necessary, but most of the new words you will want to learn certainly won't be tangible or you would already know them.

3) Look at the meaning or definition of the word or term with the intent of making the meaning or definition tangible by using sound-alike words. Sometimes you need only one word to define the word or term, but most of the time several, or even many, words are involved. Many times a picture idea will pop into your mind as you work through this process. The tangible picture for this could be simple or complex depending on the length of the meaning or definition.

4) Analyze the meaning or definition to decide which application method will work best for the material you are learning, knowing that you need to learn this information in order. A

basic **One-On-One** problem doesn't really require any analysis of the material. You would simply connect the two pieces of information together using sound-alike words. A **simple anagram** may work for a limited number of words, or you might need a more **complex anagram** for more lengthy definitions. You may need to develop several sound-alike words and **link** them to solve a complex definition. For some very long definitions, you may even want to use a short **associate list**. This analysis stage is where you need to gain more and more practice and experience.

5)   Develop a memory aid picture and make a record of it. Then you can review it. Always be a very **ODD** person.

I will provide a few vocabulary words and terms and their solutions to get you started. An **anchorite** is a **hermit**. We need to follow the five steps just previously developed. **Step number one (1)** instructs us to **read the word and its meaning** to be familiar with it, which is what we just did. **Step number two (2)** instructs us to **develop a sound-alike word picture for the vocabulary word**. We would need to develop a sound-alike word or words for the word **anchorite**. The sound-alike words I thought of for **anchorite** are **anchor** and **write**. **Step three (3)** instructs us to develop a sound-alike word or words to **make the meaning tangible**. It isn't necessary to develop a sound-alike word for a **hermit**, since we know what a **hermit** is. **Step four (4)** instructs us to **decide which learning method to apply**. This is a simple **One-On-One** problem, so no special analysis is necessary. We simply need to connect the one word to the other word. **Step five (5)** instructs us to **develop a memory aid picture and record it** for later review. It is easy to imagine a **hermit** using an **anchor** to **write** a letter. We then record that memory aid picture for later review. If you think about this silly little connection picture for a while, you will easily know what an **anchorite** is.

I want to list a shorter version of the five steps at this point, since you have been through them with one vocabulary word. This shorter version is all you should need from now on.

1)   Read the word and its meaning to be familiar with it.

2)   Develop a sound-alike word picture for the vocabulary word or term if necessary.

3)   Develop sound-alike word pictures for the meaning to make it tangible.

4)   Analyze the material you are learning to decide which learning method to apply.

5)   Develop a memory aid picture and record it for later review.

Vocabulary Word Practice

I will list a few vocabulary words with which you can practice. I'm purposely not going to list the phonetic pronunciations of the words, so you will get used to using a dictionary more and more. If you aren't sure of the pronunciation of any of the following words, look them up in a good dictionary. You need the proper pronunciation to be able to develop good sound-alike words. Most of the words listed below are quite unusual, as you will find out. As a result, they will provide a good practice session for you. Get out some scratch paper to develop your memory aids. After you develop your memory aid for each word, record it on the space provided below each word. An **apprentice** can never become a **Master Mind Mechanic** without practice and experience. You should never pass up an opportunity for practice. This practice will help you add a more experienced vocabulary tool to your **mental toolbox**. I have developed complete curriculum with pictures to teach vocabulary words at various grade levels. I will also publish a vocabulary book with pictures to teach vocabulary improvement to the general public.

Factotum   **A handyman**

Memory aid -

Bulwark   **A defensive wall**

Memory aid -

Jetty   **A pier or wharf**

Memory aid -

Spoonerism   **An accidental, humorous distortion of words**

Memory aid -

Palindrome   **A word reading the same forward or backward**

Memory aid -

Pedagogy   **The art or profession of teaching**

Memory aid -

Portmanteau word **A word formed by merging the sounds and meanings of two different words**

Memory aid -

Acerose   **Needle-shaped**

Memory aid -

Aduncous   **Hooked**

Memory aid -

Beldam   **An old hag**

Memory aid -

Discommode   **Annoy**

Memory aid -

Gongoozler   **One who stares**

Memory aid -

Incrassate   **Thicken**

Memory aid -

Jactation   **Boasting**

Memory aid -

Nutant   **Drooping**

Memory aid -

Omphalos   **Navel or bellybutton**

Memory aid -

Paraclete   **An advocate**

Memory aid -

Definition Practice

  As I have already stated, definitions have more words with them than simple vocabulary words, but the application is basically the same. You need to connect the term or word to the definition. As an example, the definition of the word **mycology** is **the study of fungi**. For the word **mycology**, I thought of **my college**. It is close enough to work even though it isn't the exact sound. Exact sounds aren't really necessary. For **the study of fungi** I thought that it would be nice to **study** with a **fun guy** instead of a boring guy. It might be nice to study with Jerry Lucas. He is a fun guy who develops all kinds of fun ways for you to learn. To complete the process, I would record this statement for later review. At **my college** I **study** with a **fun guy**. By reviewing this statement a few times I would easily know the definition. Every time I would think of the word **mycology** later, I would automatically be reminded that at **my college** I **study** with a **fun guy**, and I would know that the definition of **mycology** is **the study of fungi**.

  I will list a few terms and their definitions with which you can practice. If you aren't sure of the pronunciation of any of the following terms, look them up in a good dictionary. You need the proper pronunciation to be able to develop good sound-alike words. Get out some scratch paper to develop your memory aids. Your analysis may lead you to determine that an anagram might work best for most of these definitions, or you may feel a simple link will work best. Use the application that catches your fancy for each term. I will put the first letters of key words in the definitions in bold type to help you if you decide to use an anagram. I will then list the key letters following each definition. My bold letters aren't magic. You may find that you need to use more key words than just the ones I have put in bold type, or you may decide to use sound-alike words for key words throughout the definition and link the key words. **Do whatever works for you**. Remember that you don't need to use every word when developing anagrams. A rule is to **use as little as possible to remember as much as possible**. Just because I mention anagrams doesn't mean you have to use anagrams for the following definitions. You should list everything on scratch paper as you develop workable memory aids. I am going to repeat that an **apprentice** can never become a **Master Mind Mechanic** without practice and experience. Don't pass up this opportunity or any opportunity for practice. This practice will help you add a more experienced definition tool to your **mental toolbox**.

Mycelium - A **m**ass of **t**hreadlike **f**ilaments **b**ranched or **c**omposing a **n**etwork which **c**onstitutes the **v**egetative **s**tructure of a **f**ungus. **MTFBCNCVSF**

Accounting - The process of measuring, interpreting and communicating economic information so that informed judgments can be made. **PMICEIIJM**

Sedimentary Rocks - Rocks formed through compaction and cementation of sediment. **RFCCS**

Chattel - Chattel is personal property , such as an automobile, that is sold by a bill of sale if valued over $500. (Since numbers are involved in this definition you will have to incorporate the Consonant Number System along with sound-alike words or an anagram, whichever method you choose to use.) **PPSBSV - 500**

Abyssal plain - A very level area of the deep ocean floor, usually lying at the foot of the continental rise. **LADOFLFCR**

Easement - A right acquired by the owner of one parcel of land to use the land of another for a special purpose. **RAOPLULASP**

Gene - A continuous length of DNA with a single genetic function that controls the development of a hereditary character. **C -DNA - SGFCDHC**

Fascia - A sheet of fibrous connective tissue that encloses a skeletal muscle and separates it from other skeletal muscles. **SFCTESMSSM**

Atomic weight - The average of the atomic masses of isotopes for a given element. **AAMIGE**

Mutation - Any abnormal, heritable change in genetic material. **AHCGM**

Extension - Increasing the angle between two portions of a limb or parts of the body. **IABTPLPB**

Caldera - A large depression typically caused by collapse of the summit area of a volcano following a violent eruption. **LDCCSVFVE**

Geology - The science that examines the earth, its form and composition, and the changes which it has undergone and is undergoing. **SEEFCCUU**

CHAPTER 18

Foreign Vocabulary

As I previously stated, the basic premise is the same as with English vocabulary. You must picture the foreign word using **The Sound-Alike Word System**, and you must connect the English word to it with a memory aid picture. You must make the English word tangible when it is intangible. If you don't know an English word, it might as well be a foreign word. The biggest difference with foreign words is that there may be some different sounds and uses than in English. When that occurs, I find my dictionary and start looking for sounds that will work. I will begin by showing you a few Italian words and how to learn them. The Italian word for **scissors** is **forbici**, pronounced **four-bee-chee**. To learn this word, you need to create a simple connection between a sound-alike for **forbici** and **scissors**. I thought of **four bee**s and **chee**se as a sound-alike. The picture I created to learn is shown below.

As you can see, four bees are using scissors to cut cheese. All of the needed ingredients are incorporated into this picture. Look at it a few times and repeat the two words, and you will know it without any problem. I have told you before that I never drew any pictures when I used my systems for learning. I simply developed a picture and wrote out the words that explained the picture. In this case I would have written, "Four bees are using scissors to cut a piece of cheese." With that simple statement recorded in my foreign language notebook, I could easily review it at any time and create a mental picture of the actual picture you just saw. Later when I thought of **scissors**, the mental picture would pop into my mind, and I would easily know the Italian word **forbici**.

The Italian word for **bed** is **letto**, pronounced **lay-toe**. The following picture ties the two words together very nicely.

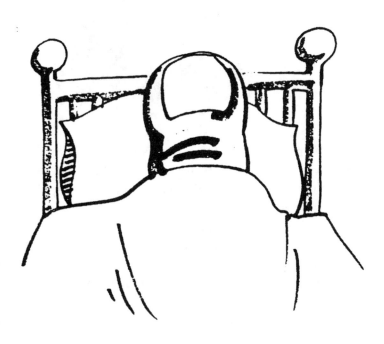

As you can see a big **toe** is **lay**ing in a **bed**. This unusual picture causes the mind to take special note of this information.

The Italian and Spanish word for **beard** is **barba**, pronounced **barb-uh**. I simply use **barb**ed wire for this sound-alike.

As you can see in the picture, this man has a really tough beard. He is actually growing **barb**ed wire as a **beard**. I wouldn't want that daily shaving job. If you felt it necessary to include the last syllable of "uh" in this picture, you might imagine that he says, "Uh, how in the world am I going to be able to cut this wiry beard?"

I will list a few more Italian words, their English meanings and their pronunciations for practice. Think of a connection or association for each and record them. Excuse me if I slightly mispronounce some of these words. I do not know the Italian language. I simply found these words in an Italian dictionary and attempted proper pronunciations.

English Word	Italian Word	Pronunciation
Snow	Neve	Nay-vay

Memory Aid -

Groceries   **Alimentari**   **Ah-li-men-tar-ee**

Memory Aid -

Carpet   **Tappeto**   **Tap-i-toe**

Memory Aid -

Chicken   **Pollo**   **Po-yo**

Memory Aid -

Sea   **Mare**   **More-ay**

Memory Aid -

Bridge   **Ponte**   **Pon-tay**

Memory Aid -

Apple   **Mela**   **May-luh**

Memory Aid -

You would do the same thing for words of any language. If you need to learn words from any foreign language simply develop a sound-alike for the foreign word and connect it to the English word. It may be necessary at times to develop a sound-alike for the English word as well.

I have written an entire 1,600 word vocabulary curriculum for Spanish as well as a book for survival Spanish. These books begin by teaching the student all of the sounds of the letters in the Spanish alphabet. Naturally I use pictures to teach these sounds. I categorize the words and teach them in logical categories to make them more meaningful as they are learned. All of the 1,600 words have the English and Spanish words connected together in a learning picture. It took many years to complete the books. The sound-alikes for the Spanish words not only teach the meaning of the Spanish word in English, but the picture also shows the precise phonetic pronunciation of the Spanish word, to make it visible. I believe this to be a real breakthrough in foreign vocabulary learning. On occasion, my son J. J. learned 20 to 30 Spanish words per hour using these pictures. I always keep striving to make learning easier and easier for all students. That is why I took the time to create this course. I am presently working on a course to teach Spanish speaking people English. This is one of the great challenges facing our nation today. By being able to see the Spanish word in English and see how to precisely pronounce the English word, it will be easier than ever for Spanish-speaking people to learn English.

CHAPTER 19

Knowing the Day of Any Date

Wouldn't it be useful if you could immediately know the day of the week for any date of the current year? For instance, what day of the year will March 30 be? What about June 12, or August 15, or any other date of the year? What if someone called you and asked, "How would you like to go to a ball game with me on the 17th of May?" With the knowledge of what you are about to learn you could reply, "No, I won't be able to go with you. That is a Wednesday, and my biking club rides every Wednesday." It sounds like it would be practically impossible to almost immediately know the day of any date, but actually it is very easy. After you learn how easy it is, you will no doubt wonder why someone didn't tell you about it before this.

To learn how to do this, you must go to a calendar and look up the date of the first Monday of all twelve months for a particular year. Monday is the first day of a business week, and I will also use Monday as the first day of the week later when I teach you how to learn weekly appointments by the day and hour of the day. I'm going to use 1995 in my examples for this application. The dates of the first Mondays in the year 1995 are January 2, February 6, March 6, April 3, May 1, June 5, July 3, August 7, September 4, October 2, November 6 and December 4. The twelve numbers that represent the first Mondays of the year 1995 are:

2 6 6 3 1 5 3 7 4 2 6 4

None of these numbers can exceed the number seven (7). Since there are only seven days in a week, the date of the first particular day in a month can't exceed the number seven (7).

The **first step** in learning how to apply this tool is **to connect the date of the first Monday of every month to that month**. This is a simple **One-On-One** problem of connecting a single digit number to a month. The easiest way to do this is to connect the peg word for the single digit date to a standard way of picturing the month. Here is a list of my standards for picturing the months of the year.

January - A New Year's Eve Party
February - A Valentine
March - Soldiers marching
April - Showers
May - Flowers   (April showers bring May flowers.)

June - A Bride
July - Fireworks
August - Fire   (Typically the hottest month.)
September - School
October - Halloween
November - Turkey   (Thanksgiving)
December - Santa Claus

These standards are quite obvious. Go over them a couple of times and you will know them. Since we now have a way to picture each month, we simply connect that picture to the peg word for the date of the first Monday of each month to continue this process. Here are my suggestions for the year 1995.

January - A New Year's Eve Party - The first Monday in January is the second (2). The peg word for the number 2 is **N**oah, so I simply imagine that **N**oah gave a jubilant **New Year's Eve party** for his family and all of the animals. See that event happening in your mind.

February - A Valentine - The first Monday in February is the sixth (6). The peg word for the number 6 is **SH**oe, so I imagine I put a **valentine** in my **SH**oe, because it has a hole in the sole. Imagine that you are doing the same thing. See that picture right now.

March - Soldiers Marching - The first Monday in March is also the sixth (6). The peg word for the number 6 is **SH**oe, so I imagine I see a regiment of soldiers **marching**. As they march they take their **SH**oes off and toss them in the air to celebrate. They must have just won a great victory. See that picture in your mind right now. It doesn't matter that we had to use a **SH**oe for these two months or any other month. We won't get confused, because the standard picture for each month will pop the appropriate peg word into our minds later.

April - Showers - The first Monday in April is the third (3). The peg word for the number 3 is **M**a, so I imagine I see a **M**a standing out in an April **shower** washing her baby in the clean rain. Imagine that you see that event taking place in your mind right now.

May - Flowers - The first Monday in May is the first (1). The peg word for the number 1 is **T**ie, so I imagine I see **T**ies growing in a flowerbed instead of **flowers**. The flower garden is full of multi-colored **T**ies. See that same picture in your mind right now.

June - A Bride - The first Monday in June is the fifth (5). The peg word for the number 5 is **L**aw, so I imagine I see a **bride** walking down the aisle arm in arm with a **L**aw man she is about to marry. I also imagine that the guests are all **L**awmen. See that unusual marriage taking place right now.

July - Fireworks - The first Monday in July is the third (3). The peg word for the number 3 is **M**a, so I imagine I see a **M**a shooting off all kinds of **fireworks** on July the 4th. The noise is frightening her baby. Imagine that event is taking place right now. See it in your mind.

August - Fire - The first Monday in August is the seventh (7). The peg word for the number 7 is Cow, so I imagine I see a Cow rescuing some people from a **fire**. What a brave Cow. Imagine that you are witnessing that event right now.

September - School - The first Monday in September is the fourth (4). The peg word for the number 4 is **R**ye, so I imagine I see all the children at a school eating **R**ye bread sandwiches for lunch. That's a lot of **R**ye. See that unusual lunch in your mind right now.

October - Halloween - The first Monday in October is the second (2). The peg word for the number 2 is Noah, so I imagine children are **trick or treating** at Noah's ark on **Halloween**. I wonder what kind of treat he will give them? See yourself **trick or treating** at Noah's ark right now.

November - Turkey - The first Monday in November is the sixth (6). The peg word for the number 6 is **SH**oe, so I imagine I see a **turkey** walking around with **SH**oes on its feet to protect them from burrs in the woods. Imagine that you see that same silly picture right now.

December - Santa Claus - The first Monday in December is the fourth (4). The peg word for the number 4 is **R**ye, so I imagine I see **Santa Claus** stuffing stockings with large loaves of **R**ye bread. There may be some unhappy children on **Christmas** morning.

Go over the pictures I just developed one more time before I teach you how to apply this system. As you do, understand that I have solidly connected the peg word for the first Monday of each month to the standard picture for that month, so you can easily retrieve the number at any time or any place.

I want to give you a little test before teaching you how to apply this technique. You can't use it if you don't know what I just taught.

January - A New Year's Eve Party - Who gave the party?
February - A Valentine - Where did you use the valentine?
March - Soldiers Marching - What did the soldiers toss in the air as they marched?
April - Showers - Who washed someone in the rain?
May - Flowers - What was growing in the flower garden?
June - A Bride - Whom did the bride marry, and who were the guests?
July - Fireworks - Who shot off the fireworks?
August - Fire - What rescued people from a fire?
September - School - What did the kids in school eat for lunch?
October - Halloween - Where were the trick or treaters seeking a treat?
November - Turkey - What were the turkeys wearing?
December - Santa Claus - What did Santa Claus stuff in the Christmas stockings?

When you can answer these questions, you are ready to proceed. I'm sure you can answer them. You would keep them in your mind and use them for the entire year, as you will soon find out

Here is how you can use this technique very effectively. Let's assume that someone says to you, "Let's do such and such on March the 7th." The first thing you must do is immediately think of **soldiers marching** which is the standard picture for the month of **March**. Next you will need to recall the picture connection for March. Do you remember what the soldiers tossed up as they marched? Of course you do, **Shoes**. After you recall the peg word association to the month you will know the date of the first Monday of the month. In this case, the first Monday in March is the sixth (6), because the soldiers tossed **Sh**oes up in the air. Since the sixth (6) is a Monday, the seventh (7) has to be a Tuesday, because it is the next day after the sixth (6), which we know is a Monday. It is that simple, and it works just as well for any date of any month of the year. For higher number dates, you will simply need to add multiples of seven (7), the number of days in a week, to the first Monday date until you get close to the date in question. Then you would move forward or backward the correct number of days to arrive at the correct day. You don't have to be a great mathematical genius to apply this system. All you have to be able to do is very simple addition and/or subtraction. You never really have to add more than a few multiples of seven and subtract very low numbers.

The best way to understand this is with a couple of examples. Let's use the same month of March and find what day the thirteenth (13) of March is. Right away we know that the sixth (6) is a Monday, so all we have to do is add multiples of seven, the number of days in a week, to this number to get as close as possible to the date in question. When we add seven (7) to six (6) we arrive at the number thirteen (13). That is the exact date in question, so the thirteenth (13) has to be a Monday. The 20th and the 27th also have to be Mondays, because they are multiples of the number seven (7) from the number six (6) which is the first Monday of the month. That means that the 21st would have to be a Tuesday, since it is one number higher than the number 20. This idea works like a charm. I want to give you several test dates to figure out. Some of them will fall exactly on multiples of seven, but others will not, which is what will happen in actual application. Here are the four simple steps in this process.

1)   When you hear the month, think of the standard picture for the month, so you can see it.

2)   Recall the picture that tells you the peg word that is associated with the month.

3)   Recall the number for the peg word.

4)   Calculate the day of the date in question by applying the simple principle of sevens.

Figure the following dates out by applying these simple steps.

February the 13th is what day of the week?

April the 11th is what day of the week?

March the 5th is what day of the week?

July the 18th is what day of the week?

September the 27th is what day of the week?

January the 12th is what day of the week?

November the 22nd is what day of the week?

May the 22nd is what day of the week?

December the 25th is what day of the week?

To continue to use this system, all you need to do is simply make new month and first Monday connection pictures for each new year. This idea is one of the most simple in this book but one of the most useful and practical as well. I urge you to use it. You will find it most help-ful.

CHAPTER 20

Specific Appointments by Day and Hour

I have already shown you how to remember simple appointments by using the **Pure Link System**, but some people need to remember more detailed information for appointments. The Link System won't work for details such as a specific time on a specific day of the week. To solve this problem, you have to learn how to picture a specific time on any day of the week. Patternized information is always easier to remember, so I have developed a pattern to help you. I put the days of the week into a pattern to start the process. In this pattern, I consider Monday the first day of the week and assign it the number one (1), Tuesday the number two (2), Wednesday the number three (3), and so forth. The days and their corresponding numbers with this pattern look like this:

Monday	Day One (1)	Number **1**
Tuesday	Day Two (2)	Number **2**
Wednesday	Day Three (3)	Number **3**
Thursday	Day Four (4)	Number **4**
Friday	Day Five (5)	Number **5**
Saturday	Day Six (6)	Number **6**
Sunday	Day Seven (7)	Number **7**

According to this pattern, you can now represent each day of the week by a number. Monday equals 1, Tuesday equals 2, and so on. The number representing the day will become the first digit in a two-digit number to represent a day and an hour of that day. The second digit in this pattern will represent the hour of the day. Hours have numbers anyway. With this developing pattern, you can now represent an hour of a day by a two-digit number. For instance, Tuesday at one o'clock could be written as the number 21. How? The digit two (2) would represent Tuesday, day number 2 of the week, and the digit one (1) would represent one o'clock, hour number 1 of the day. With this developing pattern the number 21 could only represent Tuesday at one o'clock, since the first digit will always represent the day, and the second digit will always represent the hour of the day. That means that every number representing Tuesday would have to begin with the digit 2, since it is the second day of the week.

The easiest and quickest way to picture two digit numbers is to use peg words, so the basic peg words will be used to picture any day at any hour. You certainly should have learned all of the peg words by now. If you haven't, there is no way you can become a **Master Mind Mechanic**. I will list the peg words I will use to picture each day and hour of the week. Since there is no zero o'clock we will use the "S" sound to represent 10 o'clock. I will discuss the hours of 11 and 12 o'clock later.

Monday - Day **1**	**Tuesday** - Day **2**	**Wednesday** - Day **3**
1:00 - 11 - **ToT**	1:00 - 21 - **NeT**	1:00 - 31 - **MaT**
2:00 - 12 - **TiN**	2:00 - 22 - **NuN**	2:00 - 32 - **MooN**
3:00 - 13 - **ToMb**	3:00 - 23 - **NaMe**	3:00 - 33 - **MuMMy**
4:00 - 14 - **TiRe**	4:00 - 24 - **NeRo**	4:00 - 34 - **MoweR**
5:00 - 15 - **ToweL**	5:00 - 25 - **NaiL**	5:00 - 35 - **MaiL**
6:00 - 16 - **DiSH**	6:00 - 26 - **NotCH**	6:00 - 36 - **MatCH**
7:00 - 17 - **TacK**	7:00 - 27 - **NecK**	7:00 - 37 - **MuG**
8:00 - 18 - **DiVe**	8:00 - 28 - **kNiFe**	8:00 - 38 - **MoVie**
9:00 - 19 - **TuB**	9:00 - 29 - **kNoB**	9:00 - 39 - **MoP**
10:00 - 10 - **ToeS**	10:00 - 20 - **NoSe**	10:00 - 30 - **MooSe**

The pattern in the above listings is obvious. Every number representing Monday begins with the digit one (1), every number representing Tuesday begins with the digit two (2), and every number representing Wednesday begins with the digit three (3). The two digit number after each hour ends with the digit for that hour as you can see. This same pattern for the rest of the days is below.

Thursday - Day **4**	**Friday** - Day **5**	**Saturday** - Day **6**
1:00 - 41 - **RaT**	1:00 - 51 - **LoT**	1:00 - 61 - **JeT**
2:00 - 42 - **RaiN**	2:00 - 52 - **LioN**	2:00 - 62 - **CHaiN**
3:00 - 43 - **RaM**	3:00 - 53 - **LaMb**	3:00 - 63 - **JaM**
4:00 - 44 - **RoweR**	4:00 - 54 - **LuRe**	4:00 - 64 - **JaR**
5:00 - 45 - **RaiL**	5:00 - 55 - **LiLy**	5:00 - 65 - **JaiL**
6:00 - 46 - **RoaCH**	6:00 - 56 - **LeeCH**	6:00 - 66 - **JudGe**
7:00 - 47 - **RuG**	7:00 - 57 - **LocK**	7:00 - 67 - **JacK**
8:00 - 48 - **RooF**	8:00 - 58 - **LaVa**	8:00 - 68 - **SHaVe**
9:00 - 49 - **RoPe**	9:00 - 59 - **LiP**	9:00 - 69 - **SHiP**
10:00 - 40 - **RoSe**	10:00 - 50 - **LaCe**	10:00 - 60 - **CHeeSe**

2:00 - 72 - **CaN**
3:00 - 73 - **CoMb**
4:00 - 74 - **CaR**
5:00 - 75 - **CoaL**
6:00 - 76 - **CaGe**
7:00 - 77 - **CaKe**
8:00 - 78 - **CaVe**
9:00 - 79 - **CaPe**
10:00 - 70 - **CaSe**

The hours of 11 and 12 o'clock need some special attention since there is no peg word for any three-digit numbers. According to the pattern I have just developed, Monday at 11 o'clock would be represented by the number 111, and Monday at 12 o'clock would be represented by the number 112. I have developed peg words for my own use from 00 to 1,000. These words are listed on page 293 at the back of the book. There is an easier way to handle these double-digit hours. I have developed special words to represent these. I simply use a word with two digits that represent the first and last digit of the three-digit number, but it isn't the basic peg word. For instance, the number according to this pattern that represents Monday at 11 o'clock is 111. I have chosen to use the first and last digits in this number to represent Monday at 11 o'clock which is the number 11. Right away you would probably reply, "Wait a minute. The number 11 represents Monday at 1 o'clock." You would be right, and you could picture that day and hour by seeing the peg word for 11 or a **ToT**, but I have decided to use another word that represents the digit 11 that isn't the basic peg word. The word **DeaD** represents the number 11 and will work very well for Monday at 11 o'clock. Since it isn't the basic peg word, it can't represent Monday at 1 o'clock and must represent Monday at 11 o'clock. Special words to represent the hours of 11 and 12 for each day of the week are listed below.

Monday - Day **1**	**Tuesday** - Day **2**	**Wednesday** - Day **3**
11:00 - 11 - **DeaD**	11:00 - 21 - **NuDe**	11:00 - 31 - **MuD**
12:00 - 12 - **DuNe**	12:00 - 22 - **NiNNy**	12:00 - 32 - **MiNe**
Thursday - Day **4**	**Friday** - Day **5**	**Saturday** - Day **6**
11:00 - 41 - **RooT**	11:00 - 51 - **LiD**	11:00 - 61 - **SHeeT**
12:00 - 42 - **RuiN**	12:00 - 52 - **LoaN**	12:00 - 62 - **JuNe** bug
	Sunday - Day **7**	
	11:00 - 71 - **KiTe**	
	12:00 - 72 – **CoiN**	

When you see how well the application of this process works, you will want to spend some time learning these 11 and 12 o'clock words. You may think of another word that you feel will work better for you at one of these 11 or 12 o'clock positions. If you do, by all means use

When you see how well the application of this process works, you will want to spend some time learning these 11 and 12 o'clock words. You may think of another word that you feel will work better for you at one of these 11 or 12 o'clock positions. If you do, by all means use it.

Appointment Test

The best way for you to understand the application of this appointment tool is to give you a test. Don't you just love tests? This test will assume that all of your appointments are scheduled on the hour. I will discuss minutes such as 3:15, 6:45 or 9:30 a little later. I want you to learn the basic application first.

Let's assume that you make an appointment to meet a **Mr. Harper** on **Thursday at 2:00** o'clock. A.M. and P.M. aren't really much of a concern for many appointments. Your common sense will tell you that you aren't going to meet Mr. Harper at 2:00 A.M. but 2:00 P.M. The number 42 represents Thursday at 2:00 o'clock. The digit 4 represents Thursday, which is day number 4, and the digit two represents the hour of 2. The peg word for the number 42 is **RaiN**. To learn this appointment you would need to connect a sound-alike word for Mr. **Harper** to the peg word **RaiN**. The picture below does that very well. You see a picture of it **RaiNing harps**. **RaiN** represents **Thursday at 2:00** o'clock and **harp** is the sound-alike word for the name **Harper**. Look at the picture and study it for a short while. Even say to yourself, "It is **RaiNing harps**." A mental picture will work just as well, but I like to use real pictures as much as possible when introducing a new concept.

The next assumed appointment that comes up, and appointments do happen randomly, is to meet your **accountant** on **Monday at 4:00**. Appointments don't occur in day and hour order. They can and do occur very randomly. The number that represents **Monday at 4:00** is 14, and the peg word for 14 is **TiRe**. The picture below will teach you this appointment. You see a **TiRe count**ing at a blackboard. The **TiRe** signifies **Monday at 4:00**, and the **count**ing represents your **accountant**. Look at this picture attentively for a short while.

Your next appointment is to **play golf** on **Saturday at 8:00.** . The number that represents **Saturday at 8:00** is 68, and the peg word for 68 is **SHaVe**. The picture below will teach you this appointment. You see a **golf club** being used by a man to **SHaVe**. The **golf club** represents the golf outing, and the **SHaVe** represents **Saturday at 8:00**. Study the picture briefly before continuing.

Your next appointment is to get a **massage** on **Tuesday at 5:00**. The number that represents **Tuesday at 5:00** is 25, and the peg word for 25 is NaiL. The picture below will teach you this appointment. You see a large NaiL giving a person a **massage**. The **massage** represents the appointment, and the NaiL represents **Tuesday at 5:00**. Study the picture briefly before continuing.

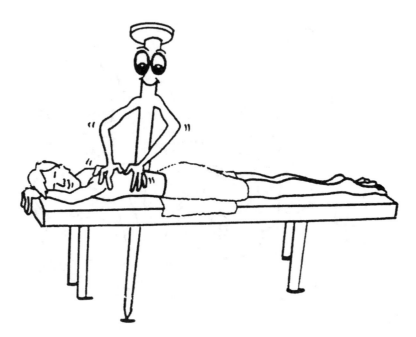

Your next appointment is at the **Roosevelt Hotel** on **Monday at 9:00**. The number that represents **Monday at 9:00** is 19, and the peg word for 19 is TuB. The picture below will teach you this appointment. You see a large **rose**, representing the **Roosevelt Hotel**, taking a bath in a TuB. The **rose** represents the appointment, and the TuB represents **Monday at 9:00**. Study the picture briefly before continuing.

Your next appointment is to **play cards** on **Friday at 7:00**. The number that represents **Friday at 7:00** is 57, and the peg word for 57 is **LocK**. The picture below will teach you this appointment. You see several **LocKs playing cards**. The **card game** represents the appointment, and the **LocKs** represent **Friday at 7:00**. Study the picture briefly before continuing.

Your next appointment is with the **dentist** on **Thursday at 9:00**. The number that represents **Thursday at 9:00** is 49, and the peg word for 49 is **RoPe**. The picture below will teach you this appointment. You see a **dentist** pulling a long **RoPe**, representing **Thursday at 9:00**, out of a person's mouth. The **dentist** represents the appointment, and the **RoPe** represents **Thursday at 9:00**. Study the picture briefly before continuing.

Your next and last appointment for this test is to **fly out of town** on **Sunday at 7:00**. The number that represents **Sunday at 7:00** is 77, and the peg word for 77 is **CaKe**. The picture below will teach you this appointment. You see a **CaKe** that makes up the body of an **airplane** that is **flying out of town**. The **airplane** represents the appointment to **fly out of town**, and the **CaKe** represent **Sunday at 7:00**. Study the picture briefly before continuing.

Go back over each of these eight pictures one more time before taking the following test. To review your appointments for the week, you simply go over the peg words for each day in your mind. I assume that you know the peg words for Monday, Tuesday and Wednesday which are:

Monday - Day **1**	**Tuesday** - Day **2**	**Wednesday** - Day **3**
1:00 - 11 - **ToT**	1:00 - 21 - **NeT**	1:00 - 31 - **MaT**
2:00 - 12 - **TiN**	2:00 - 22 - **NuN**	2:00 - 32 - **MooN**
3:00 - 13 - **ToMb**	3:00 - 23 - **NaMe**	3:00 - 33 - **MuMMy**
4:00 - 14 - **TiRe**	4:00 - 24 - **NeRo**	4:00 - 34 - **MoweR**
5:00 - 15 - **ToweL**	5:00 - 25 - **NaiL**	5:00 - 35 - **MaiL**
6:00 - 16 - **DiSH**	6:00 - 26 - **NotCH**	6:00 - 36 - **MatCH**
7:00 - 17 - **TacK**	7:00 - 27 - **NecK**	7:00 - 37 - **MuG**
8:00 - 18 - **DiVe**	8:00 - 28 - **kNiFe**	8:00 - 38 - **MoVie**
9:00 - 19 - **TuB**	9:00 - 29 - **kNoB**	9:00 - 39 - **MoP**
10:00 - 10 - **ToeS**	10:00 - 20 - **NoSe**	10:00 - 30 - **MooSe**

Go over the peg words for Monday without looking back at the pictures and answer the following questions.

At what hour was your first appointment on Monday?

Who were you to meet at that hour?

Was there another appointment on Monday?

If so, at what hour?

Where were you to have that meeting?

Go over the peg words for Tuesday without looking back at the pictures and answer the following questions.

Did you have an appointment for Tuesday?

If so, at what hour?

What were you supposed to do at that hour?

Go over the peg words for Wednesday without looking back at the pictures and answer the following questions.

Did you have an appointment for Wednesday?

You should have known that you had no appointment on Wednesday!

Listed below are the peg words for Thursday, Friday and Saturday.

Thursday - Day **4**	**Friday** - Day **5**	**Saturday** - Day **6**
1:00 - 41 - **RaT**	1:00 - 51 - **LoT**	1:00 - 61 - **JeT**
2:00 - 42 - **RaiN**	2:00 - 52 - **LioN**	2:00 - 62 - **CHaiN**
3:00 - 43 - **RaM**	3:00 - 53 - **LaMb**	3:00 - 63 - **JaM**
4:00 - 44 - **RoweR**	4:00 - 54 - **LuRe**	4:00 - 64 - **JaR**
5:00 - 45 - **RaiL**	5:00 - 55 - **LiLy**	5:00 - 65 - **JaiL**
6:00 - 46 - **RoaCH**	6:00 - 56 - **NotCH**	6:00 - 66 - **JudGe**
7:00 - 47 - **RuG**	7:00 - 57 - **LocK**	7:00 - 67 - **JacK**
8:00 - 48 - **RooF**	8:00 - 58 - **LaVa**	8:00 - 68 - **SHaVe**
9:00 - 49 - **RoPe**	9:00 - 59 - **LiP**	9:00 - 69 - **SHiP**
10:00 - 40 - **RoSe**	10:00 - 50 - **LaCe**	10:00 - 60 - **CHeeSe**

Go over the peg words for Thursday without looking back at the pictures and answer the following questions.

What was the hour of your first appointment on Thursday?

Who were you to meet?

When was your second appointment on Thursday?

Who were you to meet?

Go over the peg words for Friday without looking back at the pictures and answer the following questions.

When were you to meet on Friday?

For what reason were you meeting?

Go over the peg words for Saturday without looking back at the pictures and answer the following questions.

When was Saturday's appointment?

What were you to do?

Listed below are the peg words for Sunday.

Sunday - Day 7

1:00 - 71 - CaT
2:00 - 72 - CaN
3:00 - 73 - CoMb
4:00 - 74 - CaR
5:00 - 75 - CoaL
6:00 - 76 - CaGe
7:00 - 77 - CaKe
8:00 - 78 - CaVe
9:00 - 79 - CaPe
10:00 - 70 - CaSe

Go over the peg words for Sunday without looking back at the pictures and answer the following questions.

At what hour was your appointment on Sunday?

What were you to do?

I'm sure you were able to answer all of those questions accurately because of the pictures stored in your mind. You may want to use this system on a regular basis if you have many appointments each week. If so, you will want to make sure you know the words used for 11 and 12 o'clock. I assure you that you will not confuse one week's appointments with the next week's appointments. The mind is a wonderful mechanism, and it rejects old pictures and replaces them with the new ones. You should review the peg words for each day on a regular basis anyway, and this review will solidify the appointment pictures. The only way you are going to know how well this system works is to apply it. Try it. You'll like it!

A.M. and P.M. Appointments & Appointments by Minutes

A. M. and P. M. appointments don't normally cause problems. If you plan to have lunch with a friend at 1:00, you know not to show up at 1:00 in the morning; and you normally don't go to the dentist at 9:00 P. M. Sometimes though, it is necessary to make a distinction. My solution is very simple. All of my appointment pictures have no standard for A. M. or P. M. in them unless I know there could be a possibility for confusion. I only use a standard for a P. M. appointment, since most of my appointments are during the A. M. hours. If I do have a P. M. appointment that might be confusing, I simply add a crescent moon to the picture, which is my standard for P. M. or night, and the problem is solved. It isn't necessary to put a standard in every appointment picture for A. M. and P. M. when one may be needed only occasionally.

For appointments by minutes, I would suggest that you get no more specific than 15, 30 or 45 after the hour. If the appointment is 15 minutes or **quarter past the hour** use a **quarter**, the coin, in your picture. If the appointment is 30 minutes or **half past the hour** use a **half of a grapefruit** in your picture. If the appointment is 45 minutes or **three quarters past the hour** use a **pie** in your picture. Of course, I assume that only 3/4 of the pie is left.

These simple additions to your pictures will solve A. M., P. M. and specific minute times if you need them. Personally, I don't use them because the review of my appointment lists is sufficient, but some of my students have wanted these extra aids.

Birthdays and Anniversaries

To remember a person's birthday and/or anniversary you need to know the standards for picturing months that were taught in the chapter on weekly appointments. Since a birthday or anniversary only contains two pieces of information, a month and a day of the month, this isn't a difficult task. I keep my reminders for these dates in my personal file on people which, of course, includes my pictures for phone numbers. Not every one is married and has an anniversary, and it may not be important for you to remember a lot of anniversaries anyway.

I will use my birthday, which is **March 30**, as an example of this application. By now it should be fairly clear what needs to be done. To remember my birthday, you would simply need to associate **soldiers marching**, the standard picture for **March**, and a MooSe, the peg word for the number **30**, to me in some way. Perhaps you would see me **marching** with many MooSe. You would have to record that picture along with my phone number picture in your personal file book. I always file the **phone number picture first**, because I will need to use it far more than the birthday picture. So then, the **birthday picture is second**, and **the anniversary picture is third**, or last, if I feel I need to develop one. My anniversary is **February 25**. A **valentine** and a NaiL are used for this date, so it would be necessary to add some sort of picture with these two pieces of data to your personal file as a reminder. Perhaps I **march** away with many MooSe to deliver a **valentine** with a NaiL stuck through it. The **valentine** and the NaiL would be the third piece of information in my personal file. Occasional review will solidify these pictures in the proper order for all of my friends. Again, in my file the phone number is always first, the birthday second and the anniversary third. You should do the same thing in your personal file to remember these pieces of information for your friends and relatives.

CHAPTER 21

Look-Alike System

I developed the **Look-Alike System** when one of my older sons needed to learn to identify rocks in geology by their appearance. He was having quite a problem until I said, "Son, why don't you just think of something that each rock looks like and connect that to a sound-alike word for the name of the rock." I sat down with him for a little while, and we went over a few rocks. It worked like a charm, and we had a new system and learning tool. This system is quite easy to understand. I have already described its purpose in the discussion above. If you need to recognize and name something by its appearance or what it **looks like**, simply think of something that you are familiar with that **looks like** what you have to learn and connect or associate it to the familiar object. The rocks mentioned above are a good example. Another application is for signs and symbols used in math. I will discuss formulas and equations later.

Another possible use is in recognizing artwork. When students in my seminars have asked me how to connect or associate art to the artist by its appearance, I have told them to use this **Look-Alike System**. I instructed them to find something distinctive in the piece of art that they could easily see and recognize. They were then to think of something familiar that it looked like and connect or associate the look-alike to the name of the artist. They probably needed to develop a sound-alike word for the artist's name. Sometimes you can find something distinctive that is already recognizable like a daisy, for instance, but in some modern art that becomes more difficult, and **The Look-Alike System** is a must. This tool makes it easy to learn whatever you need to recognize by appearance or what it **looks like**.

C H A P T E R **2 2**

Curing Absentmindedness

The dictionary defines an absentminded person as one who is preoccupied or heedless of one's surroundings. If a person is absentminded, it doesn't mean he or she has a bad memory. When something happens that person is simply thinking about something else. Students may be in a classroom, but their minds may be someplace else. One may be daydreaming about scuba diving in the Bahamas, while another may be thinking of snow skiing in Colorado. The mind can only be aware of one thing at a time, and students push aside many lectures as they think of other events.

The same thing occurs, for instance, when a housewife comes home and places her glasses on the television. Instead of paying attention to where she placed her glasses at the time she did so, she may be thinking about what she is going to cook for dinner instead of where she is putting her glasses. As the physical action of placing the glasses took place, her mind wasn't concentrating on that action but was occupied with other thoughts. Later, when she may need her glasses to read the evening paper, she won't remember where she put them, and will accuse herself of having a bad memory. There was no way for her to remember, because no mental registration concerning the glasses took place. Her mind has no knowledge of the event, because it wasn't aware that it ever took place. To her mind it never really happened, so how could she possibly remember it? **If your mind is absent** when an event takes place **no registration is possible** and there is nothing to retrieve or recall. Like so many other people she will have to look every possible place where her glasses might be until she finds them. This happens again and again with glasses, keys and with many other things. People leave home and wonder if they turned off the oven or some other appliance like an iron, or locked the door, for instance.

Believe it or not, these problems can be cured! All you have to do is learn how to keep your mind from being absent. Your mind has to be aware of what you are doing when you are doing it so the information will register. How many times have you said or heard someone else say, "Oh yeah, that reminds me!" Something they saw reminded them of something else. They made some subconscious connection or association between what they saw and of what it reminded them. It's rather like the proverbial string around the finger which you perceive as the ultimate, "Oh yeah, that reminds me!" You place the string around the finger as a reminder to perform or remember a specific task. You can develop mental strings or, "Oh yeah, that reminds me's," that will help cure your absentmindedness.

Let's assume that one of your problems is misplacing your car keys. Every time you reach for your keys to put them down, you must determine that you are going to solve your problem once and for all. The solution is painfully obvious. Your mind must be aware of what you are doing when you do it. Your mind needs an "Oh yeah, that reminds me!" It only takes a couple of seconds to make a quick connection to solve the problem. Let's assume you come home and reach for your keys to place them on the television. At the instant you touch your keys, you must force your mind to make a quick but clear picture connecting them with the television. Perhaps you imagine that you take your keys and throw them through the television screen, breaking it. Of course, you don't actually do it. You just imagine that you do it. What you have done is force your mind to connect your keys to where you put them, on the television. Later, when you think of your keys, you will see the silly little picture in your mind and know that your keys are on the television, because you remember that you imagined breaking the television screen with them. It worked because you took a couple of seconds to lock the two objects together in your mind. Just the thought of your keys brings the whole imaginative picture back to mind, and gives you a mental, "Oh yeah, that reminds me!" You have tugged on the mental string tied around your mind, and you simply walk to the television and find your keys.

A conscious mental connection must take place between the item and where you put it, but you can't run around all day forming silly little picture connections in your mind with everything you do. You must make a decision to solve the problem with those few little annoyances that waste a lot of your time. Perhaps it is the same things for you over and over again. Force yourself to tie mental reminder strings just for the two or three annoyances that cause you continuing problems.

I will discuss a few other annoying problems in this absentminded category before continuing. People often leave umbrellas behind, because umbrellas aren't an item that they normally carry on a daily basis. If you have one with you on a day when it rains hard and never stops raining, you don't have to worry too much about leaving it someplace. The rain itself becomes the perfect, "Oh yeah, that reminds me!" You don't want to get wet, and the rain reminds you that you need the protection of your umbrella. The problem occurs with umbrellas normally in one of two ways. First, you take it with you on a rainy day, but during the day it clears, and the rain is no longer falling to provide the obvious and natural, "Oh yeah, that reminds me!" Your mental string disappeared when the sun began to shine and the rain disappeared. If you took your umbrella to your office, you must make some silly little connection between your umbrella and something that you will have to see or do on your way out of the office, and you must do it when you first enter the office and put your umbrella down. These mental reminders must occur at the same time the event itself occurs. In this case it is the placing of the umbrella. As you put the umbrella down, you could imagine that you are using it to lock the office door as you leave that evening. See that imaginary picture only briefly but quite clearly. It also would be a good idea to briefly reflect on that same picture for just an instant when you pass by that door during the day. This helps to draw the mental string a little tighter around your mind. When you leave it won't matter if the sun is shining brightly and the sky looks like it hasn't held a rain cloud in months. As you reach to lock the door, you will recall that you imagined locking the door with your umbrella, and if you failed to bring it with you, you can go retrieve it. The mental string tugged on your mind to remind you not to forget the umbrella. I used locking a door with the umbrella, but it can be any action or connection that you are sure to have to perform before leaving your office.

Perhaps your wife calls you during the day and says, "Would you please stop and get some milk on your way home tonight?" Has anyone ever made a request like this to you, but ouch, you forgot to stop and————! To make sure you remember, as soon as a person makes the request and you hang up the phone, take an instant and imagine seeing a silly little picture between milk and a couple of things that will remind you to purchase the milk on the way home. You could imagine that your car is full of milk, and when you open the door milk splashes all over you. You could imagine that you must start your car with a bottle of milk instead of keys, or you could imagine that every traffic light is full of milk, and every time one of them changes on the way home, milk flies out of the light onto your car. How much importance your wife placed on the milk might determine how many mental reminders or mental strings you form in your mind. If she says it is crucial, you might want to imagine all of the above suggestions to really solidify the thought.

Many people leave home and then worry for an entire evening if they turned off the iron, oven or some other appliance. If this is one of your problem areas, simply form a silly little picture the instant you turn off the appliance. It is good to get some part of your body involved in appliance pictures. When you turn off the iron, imagine that it fell on your foot. You'll almost remember the pain later when you think of the iron. When you turn off the oven, imagine that a ball of fire singes all of the hair off of your face and you will easily remember that you did it when you think of it later.

Did you ever forget to take the garbage out on the appropriate evening before pickup? When you think of or a family member reminds you about the garbage, perhaps see yourself dumping messy garbage in your bed until it is the last place you would ever want to sleep. If you don't take the garbage out prior to going to bed, when you go to your bedroom you will not only think of the garbage, it might be so clear in your senses that you might actually smell it. This little reminder will keep your home from a weeklong garbage stench and may keep you out of trouble with another family member.

Have you ever gotten a great idea at night and gotten up in the morning and the idea is gone? Who knows, that idea may have changed your life, but now it is gone. The problem with a good idea at night is that you are comfortable, perhaps tired, and you don't want to get up to disturb yourself or some other family member. What I do in that circumstance is to put something in an unusual place that is normally very close to the bed and then associate my idea to it. Perhaps you always wear house slippers to bed and slip them on the first thing in the morning. If so, when you get that great idea, reach down, grab a slipper, toss it across the room and make a little silly mental association between your idea and the house slipper. In the morning when you reach for your slippers and find one of them across the room, you will say to yourself, "Oh yeah, that reminds me," and you will remember your idea. You could turn your clock radio around backwards and make an association between it and your idea. What you use to make the association depends on the layout of your bedroom and your habits. Perhaps you get a great idea while driving and don't have anything with which to write, and you shouldn't write while driving anyway. Simply connect the idea to something you will have to see, touch or do as soon as you exit your car at home. Then you can go inside and write the idea down.

Some people go to an amusement park, ball game or some other similar event where thousands of cars are parked and are so excited to get into the park or event that they don't take time to remember where they parked the car. When the day's festivities are over and they need to go home, they go out to the parking lot and stare at all of the cars because they don't know where there car is. Perhaps even worse situations occur, when people are in a hurry and park in a multi-level, circular parking garage. They may be late, so they jump out of the car and hustle off to the elevator to keep their appointments without even thinking of where they parked the car. When it's time to leave, they don't even know on which floor of the garage to look. It even happens to many people in shopping centers.

Has this ever happened to you? To solve this dilemma, you simply need to take an instant and think of a connection between your car and where you parked it. If you parked in section "A," imagine that you drove to the event with a big **Ape**. When you leave you will remember that you came with a big **Ape** and can walk directly to section "A" to find your car. If you park on level **seven** (**7**) of a parking garage, imagine for an instant that you open the door and milk spills all over the garage, because you had a leaky **Cow** as a passenger. Of course, **Cow** is the peg word for number seven (7). This is a very simple solution, but it will save you a lot of time in the future. If the parking section has a combination of letters and numbers simply use a standard picture for the letter and a peg word for the number and associate them with your car briefly but clearly. I make it a habit to review my little picture in my head as I walk into the event or my appointment, so the picture is clear in my mind.

Many times I get ideas while driving or jogging. There is always a lot of time to think during those activities. When that happens, I make sure to picture the idea. This process usually requires a sound-alike word to picture the idea. I then connect the pictured idea to a **Tie**, the peg word for the number one (1). If I get other ideas, as I usually do, I connect them to the other peg words in sequential order. If a second good idea pops into my mind, I connect it to **Noah** in some funny way. I connect a third idea to a **Ma**. Of course these are the peg words for the numbers two (2) and three (3). As I continue to drive or jog, I mentally review the peg words to solidify the ideas in my mind. When I return from the drive or jog I immediately jot down my ideas so I won't lose them. I do this almost every time I jog. For some reason I seem to get more good ideas when jogging than almost any other time. This process also keeps my mind off a tough run and on something productive.

There are myriads of pesky little problems that cause different people problems in this area of absentmindedness. Some people hide a valuable or special item in a place they know they will always remember, but sometime later they forget where they put it. Some people go to the refrigerator and stare at it, because they forgot what they came to get. Some people forget to take the mail to the post office. Others forget a roast in the oven and burn it. There are many other examples of absentmindedness I could use, but you have gotten the idea. In review, what you need to do is quickly form a silly little picture connecting the item and where you put it, or the event or errand and something you will have to see, touch or with which you will come in contact. These little pictures force you to pay attention to what you are doing when you are doing it. When a sergeant in the Marines calls his men to attention, they obey and respond immediately. You need to call your mind to attention in that same manner. It is somewhat like my using elephant ears to call my mind to attention during introductions. The unusualness of the thought brings your mind to attention. The whole **Lucas Learning System**™ is about bringing your mind to attention and stamping or branding information on it. If you make this process a habit for your own few annoyances, you will save yourself a lot of time and be much less frustrated. Your mind will not confuse a picture from one day for your glasses, or anything else, with another picture you formed with your glasses last week. The mind is an amazing mechanism. It will remember the most recent picture in this process.

I must make one other point before closing this section. So far, I have only discussed using this teaching to correct problems. You can also use it to remind you to better yourself. I do a lot of teaching in churches, and one thing I teach is a ten-point plan to improve family relationships. I also teach people to learn as I teach it by associating each of the ten points to a sound-alike word for the numbers 1 through 10. They are always amazed when they leave the church and have not only remembered but can repeat the ten-point sermon I just gave. I teach them to picture **sticks** for the number **six (6)**. The rhyme peg word idea works well for 10 or 12 numbers as I teach in the chapter on starting children in this book. One of the problems we all have in our family relationships is our **mouth**. We don't always say things to build our family up. Sometimes we say angry words and strike out at family members. Later we are remorseful, but the damage has been done. I teach people to imagine that they have a bundle of **sticks** with them at all times, and when they feel something unproductive welling up inside them to say that they picture opening their **mouth** and inserting **sticks**. It is better to say nothing than to say something that will hurt or harm a family member. That can become a good mental reminder to say good things. I have taken this idea to its logical conclusion. I carry a small bundle of **sticks** wrapped with a rubber band in my car with me when I leave home. Then as I return home at the end of the day, I mentally go through my ten point list by simply counting from 1 to 10 and thinking of the rhyme word every time I stop at a traffic light. These rhyme words easily bring the ten points to mind. When I get to number **six**, I reach and touch my **sticks** and remind myself to be ready to say good things to my family when I arrive home. The other nine remind me to have my mind in the proper frame of mind when I enter my home. We all can use some help in this area, because there can be more friction in our homes than almost any other place. I take this idea one final step. I pick up a real bundle of **sticks** and walk into my home holding them in my hand as a reminder not only to say good things but as a reminder of the other nine points as well. This reminder process has helped me be a better family member, so I have used this reminder technique to remind me and others to think of good habits and not just to correct bad habits that cause absentmindedness.

CHAPTER 23

Picturing the Letters of the Alphabet

Picturing and remembering letters of the alphabet is important for some people. **The Sound-Alike System** is used to picture the letters in the alphabet. I have developed words that begin with a sound that sounds exactly like the letters of the alphabet when they are spoken individually. None of these words can be the same as any of the basic peg words, or confusion might occur in some applications. For instance, we can't use a bee to picture a letter "B," because **Bee** is the peg word for the number nine (9), and they could be confused when remembering formulas or license plates, for instance, since they can contain both letters and numbers. Here are the standard pictures I use to see the letters of the alphabet.

A = **A**pe	B = **B**eetle	C = **C**-clamp
D = **D**eep pocket	E = **E**agle	F = **F**-pole (A **F**lag pole)
G = **G**enie	H = **H**itch	I = **I**ce
J = **J**ay bird	K = **K**ay the cheerleader	L = e**L**ephant
M = e**M**blem	N = i**N**dian	O = **O**-brand **O**veralls
P = **P**eacock	Q = **Q**-tip	R = a**R**cher
S = e**S**kimo	T = **T**-square	U = **U**-bolt
V = **V**-neck sweater	W = **Dubba Ya** brand bubble gum*	
X = e**X**ercise	Y = "**Y**" in a road	Z = **Z**ebra

* With this brand of gum you can **Dubba Ya** or Double Your bubbles.

Letter and Number Combinations

Sometimes we need to remember letters and numbers together. A perfect example of this would be a need to learn license plates on cars or trucks. We can develop no pattern to make it easier, because letters and numbers can and do appear in any order or sequence on license plates. You may have other needs for learning letter and number combinations, but I will use license plates for this instruction. The problem is obvious. We have to change the letters and numbers to pictures in the same order that they appear on the license plates, so we can make them tangible. The main concern in this problem is that we don't think of letters as numbers and numbers as letters. That is one of the main reasons that none of the standard pictures I have developed for the alphabet are the same as any of the peg words. If some were the same a great deal of confusion could result. I will give you a few sample license plates with learning instructions to explain this application.

91 Z 910

There are many ways to change this license plate into pictures. I will give you a couple of examples.

Example # 1 - A **BaD Z**ebra **BiTeS**

Right away I will know that the only letter these words represented is a letter "Z," because it is the only standard alphabet picture included. Of course, the capitalized and bold letters in the other words represent the numbers in the license plate. I used the **One Sound Method** for the numbers in this example.

Example # 2 - **B**ig **T**ough **Z**ebras **B**elong **T**o **Z**oos

Once again I will know that the only letter these words represent is a letter "Z," because it is the only standard alphabet picture included. Of course, the capitalized and bold letters in the other words represent the numbers in the license plate. I used the **One Word Method** for the numbers in this example.

Here is another license plate to use as an example.

XL 448

Example # 1 - e**X**ercising e**L**ephants **R**un **R**eal **F**ast

Example # 2 - e**X**ercising e**L**ephants **ReaRV**iew

With what you already know, you need no explanations.

Here is another license plate to use as an example.

852 PVN

Example # 1 - **FL**yi**Ng** **P**eacocks wear **V**-neck sweaters woven by i**N**dians

This example is also self-explanatory if you know the standards for the alphabet pictures.

Example # 2 - **FL**yi**Ng** and **P**a**Vi**N**g**

This example takes some explanation. You will remember that one of my rules is to break any rule if it will help you learn. I haven't used the standards for the alphabet pictures in this example but have made up an anagram for the letters. I would have to make sure in my review that I knew the second anagram represented the letters PVN, and the first anagram represented the numbers 852. The mind is a great mechanism, and with a little review there should be no confusion.

If you need to learn combinations of letters and numbers, apply these principles and use your imagination to create workable memory aids.

CHAPTER 24

Formulas and Equations

Formulas and equations are actually a sequential listing of symbols, signs, letters and numbers. Since they are in a sequence or are in order, a simple link application can be developed to learn them. The symbols, signs, letters and numbers must be pictured. A standard should be developed for every symbol or sign, and the standard picture should be recorded and never changed. I have already discussed how to picture letters of the alphabet in another section of this book. To picture numbers, **The Consonant Number System** or **The Peg Word System** is used. I will list a few standards for some symbols and signs, so you will know how to picture them. If you have to learn or are interested in formulas and equations, either math or chemical, you should develop your own standards for symbols and signs.

Math Symbols, Signs and Letters

There is more than one way to picture math symbols, but the **Look-Alike System** must be used for some symbols. The requirement, as always, is to make the symbol tangible. That can be done in one of several ways depending on the make-up of the symbol. One way is to simply picture a letter or letters in the formula or equation using the alphabet pictures you learned in the section on picturing letters of the alphabet. Those pictures don't necessarily have to be used though, if you can think of something else in a particular formula or equation that will work better. With some symbols, you can simply use the sound-alike idea to picture them. For the **equal sign** (=), for instance, you might picture an **American flag**, because we are all supposedly **born equal** under our flag. A railroad track could also be used for the **equal sign** (=), because it not only looks like an **equal sign** (=), but the tracks are **equal**, that is, they are **equally** spaced from one another. I will list and discuss a few other common symbols and signs.

- A **minus sign** also has several possibilities for pictures. A **myna bird** would work, because **myna** sounds close enough to **minus**. This, of course, would be an application of **The Sound-Alike System**. You could even use a pencil, since a straight pencil looks like a straight minus sign. This, of course, would be an application of **The Look-Alike System**. There are also any number of other short, straight objects that could be used to picture a minus sign instead of a pencil. Whatever you might choose shouldn't confuse you with any other symbol you might need to picture for formulas and equations. I made that point very clear as I was developing **The Peg**

Word System. One of the great advantages of these systems is that they eliminate confusion.

+ A **plus sign** could be pictured with the word **pulse**. It is close enough, and you could easily see something taking its pulse. You could also use a street **intersection**, because two streets crossing look like a plus sign.

Cotangent - **Cot** are the letters that represent cotangent in formulas. It doesn't take a whole lot of imagination to realize an army type **cot** is a perfect picture to use.

Square Root - For **square root** I use a **tree**, because a tree has **roots**. I didn't even consider using The Look-Alike System to picture what the square root sign looks like, since a tree was an obvious sound-alike choice for me.

Cosine - I simply imagine someone **cosigning** a note or loan.

Degrees - I use a thermometer, because it registers in **degrees**.

If you are interested or if you must learn formulas and equations, you will need to develop standards of your own for the symbols and signs you will be called upon to learn. I have worked far less with math in my applications than I have anything else.

A formula in trigonometry is:

$$\cos 30° = \sqrt{\tfrac{3}{2}}$$

Here is how the various elements are pictured:

Cosine - **Cosign**ing a note

30 - A **MooSe** (The peg word for number 30)

Degrees - A **thermometer** (Tells temperature in degrees)

= - An **American flag**

Square Root - A **tree**

3 = **Ma** and 2 = **Noah**

To learn the formula we must form a link connecting the various elements in the formula together in order from beginning to end. The link should start with a picture for the use or function of the formula. To that we would add a note is being **cosigned** by a MooSe with a **thermometer** in its mouth. The MooSe doesn't feel well, so it wraps itself with an **American flag**. It is sitting under a tree. A Ma in the tree is helped down out of the tree by Noah. The Ma was over Noah. The Ma could also be standing on Noah's shoulders to reach something in the tree. The point is simple. The Ma has to be over or above Noah in some way. Another idea for three (3) over two (2) would be to see a MooN above the tree. The letters "M" and "N" in MooN would tell you three (3) and two (2), but you would have to know from basic knowledge of the formula that the three (3) was over two (2). This little story makes it easy to remember this formula. By recording the story and reviewing it a few times, it can easily be learned. The story will always be available for review for a mid-term or final exam. The **ODD**er the better.

Chemical Formulas

Chemical formulas are somewhat different, but are also somewhat patternized which always makes things easier to learn. Chemical formulas have a combination of letters and numbers in them.

Since chemical formulas themselves are patternized, all we need to do is follow the pattern. The chemical formula for **propane**, for instance, is **CH 3 CH 2 CH 3**. I use a **propane tank** to picture **propane**. To develop words to picture the elements in the letter/number combinations, I start the word with a letter or letters representing the element and the next and only consonant phonetic sound in the word corresponds to the number following the letter or letters. In this case, all of the words must start with the letters "CH," since these are the only letters that come before numbers in this formula. The next and only consonant sound in the first word must represent the sound in **The Consonant Number System** for the number **three (3)**, which is an "M." The word **CHiMe** fits that pattern perfectly. It begins with "CH" and the only other consonant sound in it is an "M" sound. According to the pattern I have developed, the word **CHiMe** could only represent **CH 3**. It couldn't possibly represent anything else. The word **CHaiN** must represent the next letter/number combination, because it begins with the letters "CH," and the only other consonant sound in the word corresponds to the sound for the number **two (2)** in **The Consonant Number System** which is the letter "N." To complete the three words needed to represent this formula, we will simply repeat the word **CHiMe**, since the formula ends with another **CH 3**. According to our pattern this formula can be presented in words as:

CHiMe - CHaiN - CHiMe

Those words have to represent **CH 3 CH 2 CH 3** based on our pattern. To learn the formula, we simply need to connect the picture for the word **propane** to the words **CHiMe - CHaiN - CHiMe**. The picture on the next page does that very well.

You can see a **propane tank** looking up and pointing to a **CHi**Me, a **CHa**i**N and a CHi**Me in that order. I imagine that the **propane tank** lets a little **propane** gas escape, and the gas causes the **CHi**Me, a **CHa**i**N** and a **CHi**Me to make some special music. That is how I get some action into the picture. You could have seen that just as well in a mental picture, but I supplied the tangible picture for you anyway. The words **CHu**M and **CHi**N or any other words that fit the pattern could have been used, but I felt the words I used would work best for this application. Apply this same pattern principle to learn other chemical formulas.

CHAPTER 25

Numerical Positions of the Alphabet

I had a student once who needed to learn the numerical positions of the letters of the alphabet for his job, and I taught him the following idea. If you know the numerical position of the letters in the alphabet you will also have an additional twenty-six position peg list. Some of my students have wanted as many peg lists as possible. To do this, we simply use the same principle that was used with the **Adjective Peg Word Method** for numbers. You will recall that adjectives were used to describe a basic peg word to learn numbers in groups of three. With this application, we will also use an adjective to describe the basic peg words one (1) through twenty-six (26), since there are only twenty-six (26) letters in the alphabet. The adjective will begin with the letter in question, and it will describe the peg word that relates to that letter's numerical position in the alphabet. It is that simple. For instance, the letter "**M**" is the thirteenth letter of the alphabet. An adjective beginning with the letter "**M**" must be connected to the peg word for the number thirteen (13) or **ToMb**, to know that it is the thirteenth letter of the alphabet. By seeing a **Marble ToMb** we will easily know that the letter "**M**" is the thirteenth letter of the alphabet. The adjective **Marble** begins with the letter in question, the letter "**M**," and since it describes **ToMb**, the peg word for number thirteen (13), we know it is the thirteenth letter of the alphabet. A complete listing of the alphabet and the adjectives I developed to learn their numerical positions follows. You may have uses for them.

1) A = **Ascot Tie**

2) B = **Bald Noah**

3) C = **Crabby Ma**

4) D = **Dry Rye**

5) E = **Effective Law**

6) F = **Fragile SHoe** (Glass slipper)

7) G = **Green Cow**

8) H = **High iVy**

9) I = **Infectious Bee**

10) J = **Jointed ToeS**

11) K = **King ToT** (King Tut)

12) L = **Little TiN** can

13) M = **Marble ToMb**

14) N = **Noisy TiRe**

15) O = **Oily ToweL**

16) P = **Porcelain DiSH**

17) Q = **Quacky DucK**

18) R = **Reverse DiVe**

19) S = Sunken Tu**B**   20) T = **T**iny **N**o**S**e   21) U = **U**gly **N**e**T**

22) V = **V**irtuous **N**u**N**   23) W = **W**eird **N**a**M**e   24) X = **X**-rated **N**e**R**o

25) Y = **Y**ellow **N**ai**L**   26) Z = **Z**ig Zag **N**ot**CH**

CHAPTER 26

The Substitute System

What could be more intangible than the Morse code? It is nothing but a bunch of dots and dashes arranged in varying sequences. How in the world could all of these different arrangements of dots and dashes be made tangible and not be confused? **The Substitute System** will solve this problem very nicely. With this system **one thing is substituted for another thing** to make it tangible. To apply this system, a simple pattern or formula is developed to represent the items to be pictured. I have told you before that anything that is patternized is easier to remember. I developed this particular pattern specifically for the Morse code. It has nothing to do with any other system or any other application. It is used for the Morse code and the Morse code only. That application quality makes **The Substitute System** unique. This system is used when none of the other systems will apply, and you must create something unique to, and for, a specific learning problem. In the case of the Morse code, I decided to develop a simple formula. I would **substitute** a letter of the alphabet in place of a dot or dash. The **substitution** is dot (•) = **S**, and dash (-) = **P**. With this pattern only a letter "**S**" and a Letter "**P**" will have any assigned value because of the **substitution formula**. Every letter "**S**" will equal a dot (•), and every letter "**P**" will equal a dash (-). No other letters will have a dot or dash value. As a result, we can make up words to represent the combinations of dots and dashes assigned to each letter of the alphabet. The words have to correspond to the arranged order of dots and dashes that represent the specific letter. For example, the letter "A" is dot-dash or (• -) in the Morse code. With this substitution formula, I have developed the word **SoaP** to represent and picture (• -) which equals the letter "A." To learn this, we simply need to connect the standard picture for the letter "A" learned in an earlier part of this book, which is an Ape, to **SoaP** which is our **substituted picture** for (• -). This is a simple **One-On-One** learning problem, which is a letter connected to a set of symbols, but it requires two different systems to solve it. We use **The Sound-Alike System** for the letters and **The Substitute System** for the dots and dashes. In this case I simply see an Ape taking a bath using a large bar of **SoaP**. The Ape represents the letter "A," and the word **SoaP** represents a dot (•) and a dash (-). Other words would have worked for the letter "A" with this **substitution formula**. The words **SouP, SeeP, SaP, SiP** or **SuP** would have worked according to the **substitution formula**, but I wanted to use something that was easily pictured and that I felt would make a more memorable impression with an Ape. There is no special magic in the letters "S" and "P," but I did want to choose consonant letters with which I can later form many words. I certainly wouldn't have wanted to use the letters "Q" and "X" in my formula. I would have been very limited in my word development. I also don't ever use vowels in these formulas. They are also too confining when developing representative words. Other commonly used consonants would have worked just as well, but for this application a "P" and an "S" worked just fine. Since we aren't trying to remember numbers here, obviously the capitalized letters have nothing to do with the number sounds in **The Consonant Number System**. They relate only to this specially developed **substitution formula** for the Morse code.

I want to show you what I developed for the rest of the letters in the Morse code. A dictionary was an absolute essential tool for developing these words.

B = - • • •   For this we need a word with a letter "P" and three letter "S's" in that order. We must always keep the letters in our picture words in the same order as the dots and dashes representing the letter according to the **substitution formula**. The word I chose to uses is **PreSSeS**. Of course, only the letter "P" and letter "S's" count in this special **substitution formula**, so I won't pay any attention to any other letters when translating the word back into dots and dashes. The word **PreSSeS** could only represent dash-dot-dot-dot according to our predetermined **substitution formula**. To lock this information into our minds, I suggest seeing a Beetle, our picture for the letter "B," that **PreSSeS** clothes. This tells us that B = - • • •.

I won't go through this kind of detailed explanation for the rest of the letters and symbols for the Morse code. I will simply list the letter, the dot and dash combinations, the letter pictures and the little memory picture I developed to learn each letter.

C = - • - •   **ProSPerouS** and C-clamp — A C-clamp is very **ProSPerouS**. It is covered with jewels.

D = - • •   **PoSSe** and a Deep pocket — A **PoSSe** is stuck in a very Deep pocket and can't chase the bad guys.

E = •   Saw and an Eagle — A Saw is used by an Eagle to prepare limbs for a nest.

F = • • - •   **SuSPenSe** and an F-pole — A **SuSPenSe** novel is perched on top of an F-pole.
G = - - •   **PaPooSe** and a Genie — A **PaPooSe** is rubbing a lamp and asking a Genie for its wishes to be granted.

H = • • • •   **SiSSieS** and a Hitch — I see a bunch of **SiSSieS** trying to put a Hitch onto a car or a truck.

I = • •   Sea Shell and Ice — I have introduced a little different principle with these words. Instead of using only one word I chose to use two words to represent the letters in the **substitution formula**. This is like the **One Word Method** rather than the **One Sound Method** in the application of The **Consonant Word System**. It doesn't matter. The words still only have two letter "S's" in them which doesn't break this particular **substitution formula** rule. I see a Sea Shell frozen in Ice.

J = • - - -   Sad **PuPP**et and a **J**ay bird — I see a Sad **PuPP**et being pecked on by a **J**ay bird.

K = - • -   **P**er**SP**ire and **K**ay the cheerleader — **K**ay the cheerleader jumps up and down and begins to Per**SP**ire.

L = • - • •   **SuP**er **S**eed**S** and e**L**bow — Some **SuP**er **S**eed**S** are being stuffed into the ground by an e**L**bow.

M = - -   **PuP** and e**M**blem — A **PuP** is yipping, because someone sewed an e**M**blem on it.
N = - • **P**o**S**t and i**N**dian — A **P**o**S**t has an i**N**dian tied to it.

O = - - -   **P**e**PP**er and **O**-brand **O**veralls — A **P**e**PP**er shaker is wearing **O**-brand **O**veralls.

P = • - - •   **S**oa**P** o**P**era**S** and a **P**eacock — I imagine that the most popular **S**oa**P** o**P**era**S** have **P**eacock as stars.

Q = - - • -   **P**ur**P**le **S**poon and a **Q**-tip — A **P**ur**P**le **S**poon is being cleaned by a **Q**-tip.

R = • - •   **SP**ur**S** and an a**R**cher — I see fancy **SP**ur**S** being worn by the winning a**R**cher in a bow and arrow shooting contest.

S = • • •   **S**au**S**age**S** and an e**S**kimo — I see a string of **S**au**S**age**S** around an e**S**kimo's neck.

T = -   **P**ie and a **T**-square — I see a **P**ie being cut with a **T**-square instead of a knife.

U = • • -   **SuSP**ender and a **U**-bolt — Only one **SuSP**ender is worn by a **U**-bolt. I guess it doesn't need a pair.

V = • • • -   **S**ucce**SS**ful **P**ro and a **V**-neck sweater — I imagine that every **S**ucce**SS**ful **P**ro whom I know wears a **V**-neck sweater.
W = • - -   **S**ki**PP**er and **Dubba Ya** brand bubble gum — I see a **S**ki**PP**er of a boat chewing **Dubba Ya** brand bubble gum and blowing big bubbles.

X = - • - •   **P**a**SSP**ort and e**X**ercise — A **P**a**SSP**ort is being applied for by a person in e**X**ercise clothes. They are even e**X**ercising while waiting in line at the **P**a**SSP**ort office.

Y = - • - -   **P**la**S**tic **P**i**P**e and a "**Y**" in a road — A big **P**la**S**tic **P**i**P**e is laid along a "**Y**" in a road in preparation for a new sewer.

Z = - - • •   **P**ee**P** **S**how**S** and a **Z**ebra — **P**ee**P** **S**how**S** are being watched by a **Z**ebra.

If you need to learn the Morse code, simply review what I have developed and you will know it. Of course, as always, you would record all of these pictures for later review. The **ODDer** you are the closer you will get to your goal of being a **Master Mind Mechanic**. If you ever have to learn something where the same kind of symbols or like items are repeated again and again, use **The Substitute System** and make up a simple little **substitution formula** that will work for your specific needs.

CHAPTER 27

Speeches

Teachers and professors in speech classes tell us to be relaxed, friendly, animated, interesting, flexible, cheerful and so forth when delivering a speech. It is very difficult to portray these tendencies if you aren't comfortable with what you are going to say, because you can't remember it very well. I want to give you my opinion on a couple of "**Do Not's**" before teaching you how to learn speeches. Do not try to learn your speech word for word, because of the following reasons:

1) It takes too much of your valuable time.

2) It won't flow naturally and will seem mechanical.

3) You can get stuck on a word or words and get very flustered.

4) You won't have the best rapport with your audience.

I don't believe you ought to read your speech either. When I am in an audience and someone reads a speech, I think, "I can read as well as he can. Why didn't he just mail that speech to me and I would have read it in my spare time." I don't believe you ought to read a speech for the following reasons:

1) You will have no eye contact with your audience.

2) You won't appear to have any authority and real knowledge about your subject.

3) You won't be able to "**read**" your audience and react appropriately.

4) They can all read as well as you can.

I believe that speeches should be learned in a sequence of thoughts. I mentioned in the chapter on **The Associate List System** how Greek and Roman orators used the furniture in their homes to remember a sequence of thoughts to speak about. They put their thoughts in distinctive "loci" or "places" with which they were familiar. These places were, for the most part, the furniture in their homes. You wouldn't be called upon to speak on a subject if you didn't have any knowledge about it anyway, so all you need is a method of keeping the basic thoughts you want to discuss in the order in which you want to discuss them. A speech is simply a sequence of thoughts delivered in an orderly manner.

Here is a list I believe should be followed when preparing for a speech.

1) **Write out your speech** in the order that you want to deliver it. This can be in as much detail as you want. I normally just list a somewhat detailed sequence of the thoughts I want to get across. This step can be as simple or as detailed as you want it to be. This will depend on your own personality and your personal knowledge of the subject to be discussed.

2) Go over your speech to **become more familiar** with it and to make sure it is in the proper order in which you want to deliver it.

3) **Select the key thoughts or key points** and underline them.

4) **Select the basics** under the key points and underline them.

5) **Select your learning tool**. Since a speech is an orderly presentation of your thoughts, you have to use a tool that allows you to keep the information in order. You have a wide variety of choices for this application. You could use a **Pure Link**. You could use an **Associate Link** such as the furniture in a room, the parts of a car or one of a hundred associate links. You could even use **The Peg Word System**, because the peg words themselves are in numerical order. I have used **The Peg Word System** many times for speeches. This is your choice, and you should use the system with which you feel most comfortable.

6) **Make up your memory stories** or memory aids and connect them to the items in the tool you decided to use and record them. Sound-alike words and memory pictures for numbers may be involved in this process.

7) **Review the stories until you know them**. If you have put your memory stories on the furniture in your home, you will need to be able to take a mental trip through your home and see the pictures you placed on each piece of furniture.

8) **Practice delivering your speech.** These practice deliveries can be an actual speaking of words or just a mental run-through. If you used the furniture in your home, deliver your speech by taking a mental trip through your home and saying all you want to about the thought pictured on each piece of furniture. Simply moving from one piece of furniture to another in your mind moves you from one basic thought to the next. After you have said all you want to about one thought simply move on to the next piece of furniture, see the picture on it and say what you want to about that basic thought. This approach will

make you much more relaxed and confident about what you want to say. Of course, if you have used some other tool, you will be following it in order.

I am going to show you a made-up speech that a person in a somewhat rundown housing project needs to deliver to invoke some action at a residents' meeting. The entire short speech will be written out word for word, so you can better understand the process I have just explained.

Ladies and gentlemen:

You all know why this meeting has been called. I don't need to waste any time convincing any of you that something needs to be done, and done quickly, about **the miserable conditions** of this apartment complex we all call home.

Our leases say that the management is supposed to maintain the apartments in a respectable condition, but the **paint** has peeled or is peeling off of almost every room in every apartment. The **plumbing** in many of the buildings is stopped up much of the time, many people's **appliances** don't work properly, broken **windows** haven't been replaced, and I even heard that one lady's leg went through her **floor** when a floorboard gave way.

The **roofs** of most of the building are beginning to **leak badly**. Most of the apartments on the top floors had a lot of **water damage** this spring and summer, and the water is seeping down to other apartments as well. Cracks are developing in **ceilings** from water damage, and two of the buildings were without **elevator service** when water damaged them.

This leads me to the subject of **wiring** and **fire hazards**. The people living in the buildings where the elevators flooded are very lucky that the water didn't cause fires as it came in contact with wiring in the **elevator shafts**. Have many of you have seen the wires that are exposed in some of the buildings? If we ever have a fire, I'm deathly afraid of what the consequences might be. The **fire escapes** in most of the buildings don't work, and the inside stairs are blocked most of the time by so called maintenance equipment of some kind or another that is never used. It just sits around in everyone's way. To top it all off, on a recent inspection tour, many of the **emergency exits** were found locked from the outside.

Before winter comes, something must also be done about the **boilers** and the **lack of heat** in most of the apartments. You all can easily remember how most of us had to wrap up in **blankets** to keep warm much of last winter. It could be much worse this winter if something isn't done immediately. I don't want to hear of an **elderly** person or a **baby** freezing to death before proper action is taken. **Tragedies** like that have happened in other similar places, and it could happen here too if we don't do something about it.

We are also beginning to have a **garbage** problem, and I'm sure you're all aware of that. All you have to do is take a deep breath on warm days to be very aware of this problem. Not only is the **odor** offensive, but the **disease** possibilities can't be overlooked. The garbage also attracts all kinds of **insects and rodents** that can harm our children and us. Many young **children** have been seen **playing** in or with the garbage itself.

This leads me to the subject of the **manager and assistant managers** of the project. There is no way of getting a straight answer from the **management** if they can be found at all. I think they all have other jobs and show up here once in a while just to make sure the buildings haven't fallen down. The buildings on **35th Street**, **37th Street**, **39th Street**, **42nd Street**, **Argyle Avenue** and **101st Street** are apt to collapse at any time.

What does this all mean? It means, ladies and gentlemen, that we have to take some decisions and fairly **immediate action** to correct our living conditions. I have taken it upon myself to talk to an **attorney** about our problems. He was appalled when he heard about our plight and has agreed to represent us at **no cost**.

I would like to suggest that we form a **committee** this evening to **work** closely **with** the **attorney** to get some immediate and positive action. He suggested a **possible boycott** of rent payments after he meets with us. These conditions have persisted long enough. It's **time for** some decisive and drastic **action** now.

Thank you for your attention.

Here is a listing of the essential thoughts or key points I selected in this speech along with the basic points under the key points that need to be remembered.

1) Miserable Conditions
    Paint
    Plumbing
    Appliances
    Windows
    Floor

2) Water Damage
    Roof
    Ceiling
    Elevator Service

3) Fire Hazards
    Wiring
    Elevator Shafts
    Fire Escapes
    Emergency Exits

4) Cold (Lack of heat)
    Boilers
    Blankets
    Elderly and Babies
    Tragedies

5) Garbage
    Odor

Disease

Insects and Rodents

Children Playing

6) Management

 Managers

  Buildings

   35th Street

   37th Street

   39th Street

   42nd Street

   Argyle Avenue

   101st Street

You can use peg words for these first four numbers and can use **ToaST** for 101.

7) Immediate Action

 Attorney (lawyer)

 No Cost

8) Committee

 Work with Attorney

 Time for Action

After making these lists you would then choose your tool of application. Since they are numbered in order, you could use the **Peg Word System** or an **Associate Link** connected to something you are familiar with or some other tool. I want you to learn the basics in this speech on your own. I use the **Peg Word System** in my seminars when I teach students to learn this speech. Whichever tool you use, you will have to develop **Sub Links** for the more detailed information listed below each key point.

CHAPTER 28

The Directional Link System

As was stated when all of the tools were listed earlier in this book, this tool is used to connect information in a predetermined direction. The preplanned direction determines the order in which the information is learned. This adaptation is especially helpful with maps and other visual information. I developed this application when my daughter Canaan had to learn the location of the states of the United States. To help her, I patternized the map of the United States in some unique ways. A map of the United States is pictured below.

Look at the arrow pointing **up from Louisiana to Minnesota**. This **direction is obviously up**. The memory story I developed to teach her the states in the **direction** of that arrow follows. I said, "A girl named **Louise** found a girl named **Anna** (**Louisiana**) in the first state where this arrow begins, and they started to walk toward the next state following the arrow. They found an **ark an**d a **saw** (**Arkansas**) in the second state. They rode in the ark to the next state along the arrow and found that state full of **misery** (**Missouri**). They walked to the next state where one of the girls found a scale. She weighed herself and said, 'Oh, I weigh too much' (**Iowa**). They got to the next state and forgot about weighing too much, and they sat down at the end of their trip along this arrow and drank **many sodas** (**Minnesota**)." I started her at the bottom of this arrow and reviewed the travel story and what happened at each stop along the **direction** of the arrow. Of course, each stop along the **direction of the arrow** was another state. We went over the travel story a few times stopping at each state along the way and discussed it until she knew the states. This **directional travel story** added some fun to her study. These states were learned in a **straight-line upward directional link**.

Look at the circle in the upper left of the map. It is drawn in a counterclockwise **direction**. This **circular direction** was used to teach her the states along the **counterclockwise direction** of the circle. I started the travel story at **Idaho** and used **The Look-Alike System** to teach her the state where the circle began, so I used two systems for this application. I told her that a girl named **Ida** once told me that the state where the circle began looked something like a **hoe** (**Idaho**). That story helped her start this little travel story with the correct state. I continued that story by saying, "That girl named Ida used her hoe to help with **washing** a **ton** (**Washington**) of clothes in the next state along the path of the circle. All of the water from washing the clothes caused a flood in the next state along the circle, so she used some **oar**s that were actually **guns** (**Oregon**) to row a boat away from all the water. When she got to the next state, there was **no vatah** (water) in that state. **No vatah** represented **Nevada**. I explained to my daughter that some people from certain parts of the world pronounce the letter "w" like the letter "v." We reviewed the travel story along this **circular direction** as we stopped at each state until she knew the states by their appearance. This information was learned in a **circular direction**. You can use any direction with this idea that your imagination can develop. I have used squares, rectangles, triangles and other directional figures to learn and to teach information. Now you have another tool in your **mental toolbox** to help solve even more learning problems.

I used **The Look-Alike System** for the state of California and a **Directional Link** for two states near it. I told her to look at **California** and said, "This state is shaped or looks something like a phone. I could use that phone to **call for you**. The words **call for you** will remind you of the state of **California**, so when you see this state that looks like a phone, you will remember that I could use it to **call for you**, and you will know it is the state of **California**." I continued with a short directional link after drawing a line from California through Arizona to New Mexico by saying, "Imagine that **air** is leaking out of the bottom of California into the next **zone** or state and you will know that the state at the bottom of California is **Arizona**." After reviewing those two states with her for a little while I said, "The air in Arizona was used to pump up a **new Mexi**can **cow** balloon in the next state to the right where the line stops to tell you that that state is New Mexico." This was a short **left to right directional link**. After a little review, she knew those three states well.

I made up several more memory aids to help her with other states. Look back at the state of Maryland on the map. I pointed it out to my daughter Canaan and said, "This state is shaped something like a gun." I continued, "Let's pretend a man is using that gun to make another man marry his daughter. If he doesn't **marry** her, he might **land** in jail. The words **marry** and **land** will tell you that this is the state of **Maryland**." I had to go over this state a few more times, and I especially had to make sure she didn't think this state was Michigan because of the gun sound at the end of Michigan. I added another directional link from Maryland to teach her the states near Maryland. You have probably already realized that I began to use very recognizable states that were easy to identify to begin these directional links.

But I didn't just use directional links for the states. I used several ideas and a combination of systems as well. For the states of **Miss**issippi, Alabama, **G**eorgia and **Flor**ida in the lower right part of the map, I used a combination of the **Sound-Alike**, **Look-Alike** and **Anagram Systems**. You are never limited as to how many systems or tools you can use to solve a learning problem. You simply choose the tools out of your **mental toolbox** that will best solve the problem. First, I told her to notice that those four states looked something like a flag. I also told her that we would start at the left of these four states to begin our story. I said, "A young **Miss**, for the state of **Mississippi**, in the state on the left stuck the pole of what she called **My FLAG** into a **floor**. The pole of what she called **My FLAG** that she stuck into a **floor** is the state of **Flor**ida." You will notice that the letters "**Flor**" in **Flor**ida are bold. I pointed that out to her, to better lock in that the pole in the **floor** was the state of **Flor**ida. I continued by drawing a **zigzag line** from Mississippi down to Florida, back to Alabama and then over to Georgia. The zigzag line is drawn on the map for you to see. This **zigzag line** was the **directional link line** we would follow for this story. I then said, "Let's imagine that this flag falls down a little to the left along the zigzag line and lands in an **alley** in that state and makes the noise '**bam**' when it hits the state. The **alley** and the word '**bam**' will tell you that this is the state of **Alabama**." I stopped to review the story to that point again. I finally said, "A man named **George** in the next state picked the flag up and said, '**Uh**, I wonder whose flag this is.' The name **George** and the word '**uh**' will tell you that this is the state of **Georgia**." After reviewing it a couple more times, I wrote down and pointed out the letters in the words **My FLAG**, and said, "Another way to remember these four states now that you have learned that story is to examine the letters in the words **My FLAG**." I pointed them out to her and continued, "Notice that all of the letters in those two words have been capitalized except the letter "y." The capital letters stand for the beginning letters in these four states. The "**M**" in the word '**My**' will remind you of the state of Mississippi, which starts with the letter "**M**." By the way the young **Miss** who started this story will also help remind you of the state of **Miss**issippi. The capital letters "**FL**" in the word **FLAG** will remind you of the state of **Fl**orida." I took the time to show her the capital letters in **FL**AG and **Fl**orida. I went on to say, "The capital letters "A" and "G" in **FLAG** represent the states of Alabama and Georgia." I combined all kinds of systems, tools and ideas in teaching these four states. Why not? It made it more fun for both of us, and it made it easier to learn. If I wanted to fully describe what I did with these states, I guess I would have to say I used the **Sound-Alike**, **Look-Alike**, **Directional**, **Anagram System**, because all of those tools in one form or another were used with these learning aids.

I want you to practice making up some directional links on the map of the United States by following other arrows I have drawn on the map below. You will notice the arrow that is drawn down from North Dakota to Texas. Make up a directional link and memory story that would enable you or anyone else to learn these states starting from the top and going down in that order. Remember that there are no wrong stories or ideas. Any story or idea that works for you is a good story or idea. Stop and do that now. An apprentice can't become a master without experience.

Now use your imagination and develop a memory aid that would teach someone how to learn the states of Virginia, West Virginia, Kentucky, Tennessee, North Carolina and South Carolina. Use any idea you want that will work for you. Stop, look back at the map and do that now. These practice sessions will help you add a more experienced tool to your **mental toolbox**.

A map of Europe that my son J. J. had to learn is located on the next page. Some of the countries are a bit different today, but I want to teach another idea and will use the memory aid that he and I developed together as a Learning aid for you. I have numbered the countries in a **left to right and top to bottom pattern**. By now you know that anything that is patternized is easier to learn. The countries by number are:

1) **Norway**	4) **Poland**	10) **Corsica**	15) **Wales**
2) **Sweden**	5) **Czechoslovakia**	11) **Sardinia**	16) **Ireland**
3) **Finland**	6) **Hungary**	12) **Sicily**	17) **Scotland**
	7) **Rumania**	13) **Crete**	18) **England**
	8) **Bulgaria**	14) **Cyprus**	
	9) **Istanbul**		

My suggestion would be to learn the countries in the columns listed above. That is countries 1, 2 and 3 together, countries 4 through 9 together, countries 10 through 14 together, and countries 15 through 18 together. Using some of the ideas and tools just previously used with the map of the United States or other ideas of your own, I want you to practice with these countries. After you work on them, I will show you some aids that I developed that may open up even more possibilities to you. Please don't look at my suggestions until you have worked on some of your own for all four groupings of these countries. Get some scratch paper, develop memory aids and write them on the memory aid lines.

Countries 1, 2 and 3 are the northernmost countries and are listed in a left to right direction. Make up your memory aid and record it on the blank lines below. The beginning letters in these countries are **N**, **S** and **F**. You may want to use them in order.

Memory Aid -

Countries 4 through 9 are in order from top to bottom and left to right just below countries 1, 2 and 3. Make up your memory aid and record it on the blank lines below. The beginning letters in these countries in order are **P**, **C**, **H**, **R**, **B** and **I**.

Memory Aid -

Countries 10 through 14 are islands in the Mediterranean Sea from left to right. Make up your memory aid and record it on the blank lines below. The beginning letters in these countries in order are **C, S, S, C** and **C.**

Memory Aid -

Countries 15 through 18 are the four countries of the British Isles discussed earlier when I taught about anagrams. The beginning letters in these countries in are **W, I, S** and **E.** You will notice that countries 16 and 15 are listed out of left to right order, so the **WISE** memory aid used when anagrams were taught could be listed. On the lines below, tell how you would make sure that these two countries would be in the proper order when you remembered the memory aid.

Memory Aid -

My Suggestions for Memory Aids

I will give you several suggestions for each group of countries, so you will gain more experience and ideas for developing memory aids. A **master** always needs to teach an **apprentice** how to apply his trade. You may feel your ideas are better than mine are anyway, and they will be for you because your mind made them up and is more aware of them.

For countries 1, 2 and 3 some possibilities are:

1) It is **N**ot Sa**F**e to go from the top down at the top of Europe. This solves the problem with a **directional anagram**. This solution combined two systems. Any anagram with the correct letters would work just as well as my anagram. You could also imagine that you had **N**on Sufficient **F**unds to travel to the top of Europe. That would work just as well.

2) There is **nor way** I am going to weigh those **sweets** on a fish **fin** in any **land**. These **sound-alikes** will also work.

For countries 4 through 9 some possibilities are:

1) A **PeaCH** colored **RaBbiT** ran from top to bottom and left to right like a letter "L" across Europe following that line on the map. This solves the problem with a **direction-al anagram**.

2) A **pole checked** its belt, because it was **hungry**. It started **roaming** around following that "L-shaped" line looking for food. Its face started **bulging** when it found **itself** stand-ing by a **bull** that looked hungry itself. These **sound-alikes** in the proper order will also work.

For countries 10 through 14 some possibilities are:

1) Could Someone Sail Can Cans along the islands of the Mediterranean Sea from left to right? This **directional anagram** solves the problem.

2) Of Course a Sardine that is Silly could ride a Crate made of Cyprus wood from left to right along the islands of the Mediterranean Sea. This aid would have to be called a **sound-alike, anagram, directional** aid, because all three are used. The letters I have made bold in the memory aid form an anagram. The words that these bold letters begin also are sound-alikes in the proper left to right direction. The word Course represents Corsica, the word Sardine represents Sardinia, the word Silly represents Sicily, the word Crate represents Crete and the word Cyprus represents Cyprus. This is actually a **sound-alike, anagram**, and **directional** aid all in one.

For countries 15 through 18 some possibilities are:

1) A **WISE** person always sails from left to right around the British Isles. The **WISE** ana-gram has been previously discussed when using anagrams was first taught. What is need-ed to get the correct order is to know that **I am selfish and want to come first**. That gives me the proper order of **IWSE** when I think of it later when I remember that **I come first** as a selfish person.

2) **Whales are** terrible on **land**. They don't **scout** out **land** very well. Their whale songs do **sing** throughout the **land** pretty well though. The bold words are sound-alikes that would work just as well when recorded and reviewed with the selfish **I first**.

You will soon learn that the **200 Word Locator** could also be used to solve this problem. It will be another tool in your mental toolbox arsenal.

Directional Anagrams

I have taught students how to learn the placement of letters on a typewriter keyboard by the use of **Directional Anagrams**. To learn anything, you should first analyze it. Look at the typewriter keyboard pictured below and notice what I point out.

You will notice three rows of letters. The top row of letters contains ten (10) letters. The middle row contains nine (9) letters, and the bottom row contains seven (7) letters. Here are the simple **Directional Anagrams** I developed to help students learn the letter placements.

Top Row - Ten (10) letters - Two anagrams are used in a left-to-right direction.

Anagram number one (1). A Q-tip is very **WERTY** instead of being warty. This anagram takes in six (6) of the ten letters. Examine the pictured keyboard, and you will see that the bold letters are in order from left to right.

Anagram number two (2). The Q-tip said to a doctor, "You (U) **I O**we a **P**ea for taking my warts off." Examine the keyboard and you will see that the bold letters are in order from left to right after the letter "Y." It is important to remember that this is not an "IOU" but a "**UIO**."

By going over these **Directional Anagrams** a few times while looking at the letters on the pictured keyboard, a student could easily learn the order of the letters in the top row of letters.

Middle Row - Nine (9) letters - One anagram is used in a left-to-right direction.

Anagram - A **S**a**D** **F**i**G** **H**i**J**ac**K**ed an e**L**ephant. This thought is so stupid it will be very hard to forget. Examine the pictured keyboard once again and you will see that the nine (9) bold letters are in order from left to right.

By going over this silly **Directional Anagram** a few times while looking at the letters on the pictured keyboard, a student could easily learn the order of the letters in the middle row of letters.

Bottom Row - Seven (7) letters - One anagram is used in a left-to-right direction.

Anagram - A **Z**ebra e**X**ercised in a **C**a**V**e while a **B**ee wrote its **NaM**e on the cave. Examine the pictured keyboard once again, and you will see that the seven (7) bold letters are in order from left to right.

By going over this silly **Directional Anagram** a few times while looking at the letters on the pictured keyboard, a student could easily learn the order of the letters in the bottom row of letters.

You may happen upon other learning problems where you could use this **Directional Anagram** application. I have pictured the parts of an eye that are numbered in order. Since they are in order, it provides a great directional anagram opportunity. Develop a **Directional Anagram** for the parts of the eye for practice purposes.

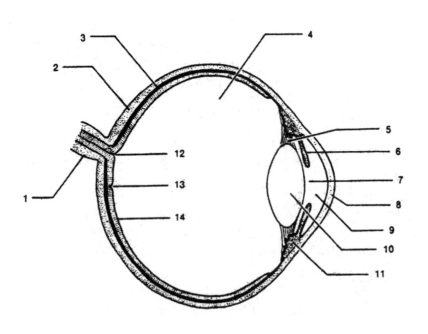

1) Optic Nerve

2) Scleroid Coat

3) Choroid Coat

4) Vitreous Body

5) Suspensory Ligaments

6) Iris

7) Pupil

8) Cornea

9) Aqueous Humor

10) Lens

11) Ciliary Body

12) Optic Disc

13) Macula Lutea

14) Retina

CHAPTER 29

The 200 Word Locator

I have just discussed **The Directional Link** idea that helps with some location problems, but that idea will not permit you to locate or pinpoint specific and separate locations. With it, you can locate a familiar spot and link information from that spot in a predetermined direction. **The 200 Word Locator** is used primarily to help you solve **specific location problems** such as finding a specific city, country or state on a map or a particular bone or muscle in anatomy. It can also be used to learn for purposes other than location as you will become aware, but its main purpose is to pinpoint location problems. I mentioned maps, because the basic learning principle for **this system is built on the location pattern used for maps**. You may recall that there are letters and numbers on the side and top of maps placed in rows and columns. Many maps have an index that has the cities listed in alphabetical order. To find a particular city the index might instruct you to look at **location** "D-6." You simply find the approximate place where row "D" and column "6" meet on the map, and you will find the city in that approximate **location**. This same principle can be used to locate and name information at specific positions, such as locating and naming muscles in anatomy or countries of the world, for example. To be able to do that, you must be able to see a location and make it tangible with the column and row map principle. You already have all of the basic knowledge needed to apply this system, since it also is based on **The Consonant Number System**. I have said several times throughout this book that anything patternized is easier to learn or remember. By lining up columns and rows of letters and numbers, a pattern quickly emerges. Look at this graph or grid on the next page.

	1	2	3	4	5	6	7	8	9	10
A										
B										
C										
D										
E										
F						F-6				
G										
H										
I										
J										

As you can see, **a location or square is formed where each letter and number intersect**. If we could somehow form a tangible picture of each of the **locations or squares**, we would have a very usable learning tool. There is a very simple way to do that. Look across the top of the graph once again, and you will see the numbers 1 through 10 in order from left to right. The vertical columns are announced or headed by these numbers. Now look to the left of the squares, and you will notice that the horizontal rows are announced or headed by the letters one "A" through ten "J." These letters are arranged vertically in alphabetical order from top to bottom. So then, there are ten numbers in numerical order horizontally from left to right across the top, and ten letters in alphabetical order vertically from top to bottom to the left. A pattern has been established, an orderly pattern! Because of this orderly pattern, each of the squares can be identified. You will notice that only one of the squares is identified by using this orderly pattern. That square is square "**F-6**." Why is that square called the "**F-6**" square? Because the horizontal "**F**" row and the vertical "**6**" column meet at that square. As a result, it is a simple procedure to name that location or square or any location or square by this method or pattern. The location name or position begins with the letter heading the horizontal row and ends with the number heading the vertical column. Where any letter and number meet, that position, square or location has a pre-determined identification based on the horizontal letter and vertical number that intersect at that point.

Since each location must begin with a letter and end with a number, a pattern is established. To make each location tangible, we need to create a tangible word for each position or location that begins with the letter heading the row and ends with a letter corresponding to a sound the number would make in **The Consonant Number System**. For the "F-6" position already mentioned, **FudGe** would work, because the word **FudGe** begins with the letter "F" and the only other consonant sound in the word is a six (6), **Soft G**, sound from **The Consonant Number System**. With this simple pattern, it is easy to develop appropriate words for each location. There are only 100 locations on the above graph or grid, but I call this **The 200 Word Locator**. How can that be? Actually this is only half of **The 200 Word Locator**. I will introduce the rest of it after more instruction.

On the next page you will find the identification words for these first 100 locations. Because of the pattern and letter/number combinations, they are fairly easy to learn. You don't necessarily need to know all of them now. Understanding how and why they are developed is the most important point at this juncture. If a word needs an explanation of how to picture it, that explanation will be under the graph. You will notice that none of these words are the same as any of the peg words, because you may want to use **The 200 Word Locator** to learn information for purposes other than just location, and you wouldn't want to confuse it with information learned with **The Peg Word System**. The number ten in this system is equivalent to the zero sound.

	1	2	3	4	5	6	7	8	9	10
A	AiD	AwN	AiM	AiR	ALLey	ASH	ACHe	AVe.	APe	ACe
B	BeaD	BeaN	BeaM	BoaR	BeLL	BadGe	BuG	BeehiVe	BaBy	BuZZ
C	CoT	CoNe	CoMe	CoRe	CooL	CaSH	CoKe	CuFF	CuP	CuSS
D	DaTe	DuNe	DaM	DooR	DiaL	DaSH	DocK	DoVe	DeB	DoZe
E	EaT	EoN	EMMy	EaR	EeL	EtCH	EGG	EVe	EBB	EaSy
F	FooT	FiN	FuMe	FiRe	FoiL	FudGe	FaKe	FiVe	FiB	FuSe
G	GoaT	GowN	GuM	GoRe	GuLL	GaSH	GaG	GaFF	GuPPy	GaS
H	HaT	HeN	HaM	HaiR	HaiL	HatCH	HooK	HooF	HooP	HuFFy
I	ID	INN	I'M	IRe	ILL	ItCH	IcK	IVy*	yIP	Ice
J	JoT	JeaN	JaM*	JuRy	JeweL	JoSH	JoKe	JiFFy	JoB	JawS

Some explanations are in hand for some of these words. I will go through the words in alphabetical order and explain those that may need a clarification as to how they should be pictured. For AiD see a Band-Aid. For AwN see an awning. For AiR see an airplane. For Age I see a birthday cake with many candles. This does not confuse me with CaKe, the basic peg word for 77, because I see a wedding CaKe for the peg word. For ACHe I see sore muscles. Ave. is an abbreviation for Avenue, and I picture a busy Avenue. For Ace I see a playing card.

For BuZZ I see an insect. For CoMe I see an entrance and imagine someone is saying, "Come in." For CaSe you should see a wooden CaSe. For DaTe I see the fruit. For DiaL I use a telephone DiaL. For DeB I picture a young lady, a DeButante. For EoN I picture space. It goes on forever or for EoNs. For EVe I see the sun going down. For EBB I see a tide, an EBB tide. For EaSy I picture a toy slide. What? How in the world did I come to that conclusion. It is far fetched but I think of the well-known phrase, "Take it EaSy Greasey, you have a long way to slide."

For FaKe I picture a magician FaKing people. For FiVe I see a basketball team, because it has FiVe players. For FiB I imagine one of my friends I grew up with who always told FiBs. I won't mention his name. I suggest that you picture someone you know who FiBs a lot too. A GaFF is a large hook on a long handle used to GaFF or snag fish. You won't confuse this with HooK if you see a small fish HooK for HooK.

The letter "I" is very challenging, since the choices are quite limited. For ID I picture an IDentification bracelet, or you might want to see an I.D. card. For I'M I picture myself and think, "I'M going to have to use myself, since I'M limited in the letter "I" category. I see a very angry person for IRe, since IRe is anger. I said I wasn't going to duplicate any peg words in this list, but you see the word IVy with an asterisk next to it. For the peg word iVy I see poison iVy, but for the locator word IVy I picture IVy growing on the side of a college campus building. With those two distinctly different pictures, you shouldn't get confused. I've even used the word yIP in the "I" column even though it doesn't begin with a letter "I." I simply discount the letter "y" and see a yIPPing puppy.

For JoT I picture a person JoTTing information down on paper. JaM* also has an asterisk by it, because it is also a basic peg word. To not confuse these two words and uses, I see myself JaMMing something into a small space for the locator word. For JoSH I personally picture a person I know who is named JoSH. If you don't know a JoSH make one up. For JoKe I see a comedian telling a JoKe to an audience. For JiFFy I picture someone running. They will be there in a JiFFy. For JoB I picture a chore that is the one I hate the most. It is a real JoB for me. You might also picture yourself at work on the JoB.

Using the 200 Word Locator

As I stated earlier, the main use of **The 200 Word Locator** is to pinpoint the location of specific information. Let's assume you needed to learn not only the names of the major bones in the human skeleton, but you also needed to learn where they were located. This problem requires pinpoint placement of the bones. To do this you would first need to superimpose a **200 Word Locator** grid over a drawing of a skeleton. I have supplied various size grids that you can copy on clear acetate sheets for your own use. You will see those later. The size of the grid pattern to use depends upon the detail of the information you need to learn. If not much detail is required, you can use a grid with large sections or squares. If a lot of detail is required, you will need to use a grid with smaller sections or squares. That will become more apparent to you later. First of all, I want you to look at the drawing of the human skeleton on the next page. You will notice that I have drawn a grid structure over the skeleton. That could just as well be a clear sheet of acetate with the grid drawn on it. By scotch taping the acetate over the skeleton, I would have the same appearance that I have drawn. I chose to use grid structure with only three vertical columns and eight horizontal rows, because the skeleton is much taller than it is wide. The squares or sections in the grid are fairly large, because learning the major bones isn't a detailed problem. If I had to pinpoint and name all of the bones in the hand, I would have to use a grid with more and smaller squares because of the detail that would be required.

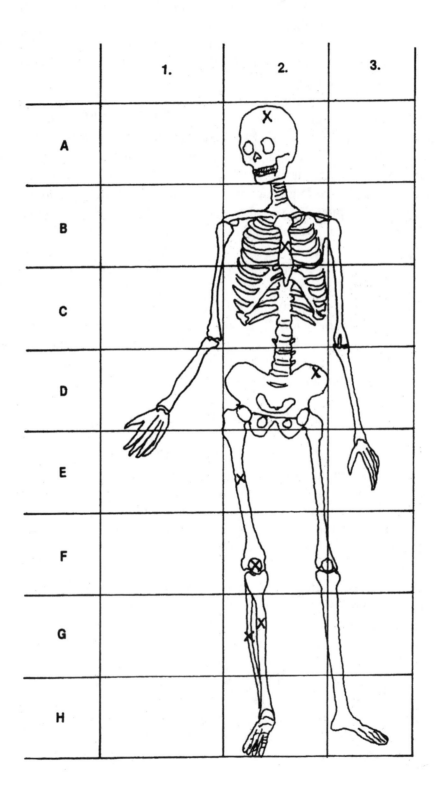

You will notice that I wrote the numbers 1 through 3 across top of the three columns and the letters "A" through "H" to the left of the eight rows. This is important information that would need to be recorded for review purposes. This grid size was chosen and located where it is for a specific, important reason. You will notice that the vertical lines forming column number two (2) basically outline the outside of the entire skeleton. I certainly wouldn't want to locate those lines so they cut through the middle of the skeleton. It wouldn't match the picture very well, and the bones wouldn't be centered in a specific location with that kind of grid. When placing grids over pictures where location is the problem, keep that principle in mind. Place the lines of the grid where you will have the best learning advantage. Don't make your job harder with a nonchalant line placement. If I needed to know more detail, I could use a smaller grid. I could use more letters along the left side and more numbers along the top to provide smaller squares with which I could learn more detail, but it isn't necessary with this skeleton. Remember the **golden rule, which** is **use as little as possible to remember as much as possible**. There are no bones located in the A-1 or A-3 locations or sections. An "X" is on the skull in section **A-2** of this drawing. I put an "X" on a few bones just to identify their locations for teaching purposes. The technical name for the skull is the **cranium**. The identification word for the section where the cranium is located is **AwN**, which is our standard for **A-2**, and we picture an **AwN**ing to make that section tangible. We simply need to connect or associate a sound-alike word for cranium to an **AwN**ing, and we will have learned the location of the cranium bone. I use a **crane** for **cranium**. The picture I thought of to learn this was **that a large crane fell and crushed an AwNing**. That precisely locates the **cranium** in the **A-2** section of this grid. After teaching you a few more bones, I will teach you how to finalize the application of this system.

There is also an "X" on the bone in the middle of section **B-2**, and we picture a **BeaN** for this location. The name of that bone is the **sternum**. To learn it we simply need to connect a **BeaN** to a sound-alike word for **sternum**. I picture a **nun stir**ring something for **sternum**. Although the word **nun** comes before the word **stir**, it will still work. By imagining a picture of a **nun stir**ring a pot of **BeaNs**, the **sternum** bone has been located in the **B-2** location.

You will also notice an "X" on the hip bone at section **D-2**. The technical name for this bone is the **pelvis**. I use **Elvis the Pelvis** referring, of course, to Elvis Presley as the sound-alike to picture the **pelvis** bone. The identification word for the section where the pelvis is located is **DuNe**, which is our standard for **D-2**, and we picture a sand **DuNe** to make that section tangible. I imagine that **Elvis the Pelvis** is singing and grinding his **pelvis** while performing on a sand **DuNe**.

There is also an "X" on the bone in the middle of section **E-2**, and we picture **EoN** for this location. You may recall that I picture **space and the stars** for EoN, because space seems to go on for **EoN**s. The name of that bone is the **femur**. Imagine that you paid a **fee** to buy some **myrrh**, which is perfume. The words **fee** and **myrrh** will remind us of the **femur** bone. Then imagine that you smelled the myrrh, didn't like the aroma and threw it into the **EoN** of space. By doing this, you would make the correct connection and know that the **femur** bone is located in location **E-2**. Although this bone spills over into the F-2 location, it won't cause a problem. The visual "X" is in the E-2 location, and a student studying anatomy will know the difference.

There is also an "X" on the bone near the middle of section **F-2**, and we picture a **FiN** for this location. That is commonly called the knee bone, but its technical name is the **patella**. There is a kind of cigar that is called a **panatela**. By imagining that a **panatela** cigar is stuck on a fish **FiN** we have learned the location of the **patella**. The bold letters in the word **panatela** tell us **patella**, and the **FiN** tells us its location is in the **F-2** spot.

There is more than one "X" in the **G-2** section, so a double connection will have to take place. We picture a **GowN** for this location. The smaller bone to the left is the **fibula**, and the larger bone to the right is the **tibia**. I simply use a **fib** or a lie for **fibula**. I don't need to develop a sound-alike with three syllables because the original intangible word has three syllables when something else much shorter will work. Once again, if I am studying anatomy **fib** should easily remind me of **fibula**. I couldn't think of a word that sounded like or began with the "**tib**" sound, so I looked in a dictionary and the only word I found that even began with "**tib**" was Tibet, and the syllable sounds are different. Therefore, I decided to use the word **tip** as my standard for **tibia**. If I thought of it and made it up, it will work for me. Don't ever forget that a good dictionary is one of your most indispensable tools for developing sound-alike words. Imagine that a girl bought a **GowN** and told her mother a big **fib** about giving a large **tip** to the store clerk. The **GowN** provides the location site as **G-2**, and the words **fib** and **tip** name the bones.

There is one other potential problem in this location. A student doesn't want to learn that both of these bones are located in the **G-2** location but then confuse the bones. Knowledge of the subject and the learning process itself should suffice to eliminate confusion, but if it becomes a problem, a simple standard to identify the bones by their size or left or right placement will totally eliminate the possibility of confusion. The word I used to describe **tip** when I first used it in the last paragraph was **large**. The word **large** will solve any possible confusion, because the **tibia** represented by the word **tip** is the **large bone** in the **G-2** section. A standard to tell us that the fibula is the small bone isn't necessary. If the tibia is the large one, the fibula has to be the small one. You should never do more than is necessary. To know that the tibia is the bone on the right, we could imagine that we are **writ**ing on the **tibia** with the **tip** of a pen. The word **write** will tell us the **tibia** is on the **right** in this view of the bones.

Go back over all of these stories one more time and you will easily know the names and locations of the marked bones. It is vitally important when taking a test to be able to reproduce this grid in you mind. By studying it, you should be able to do it mentally; but if you can't, I have a suggestion. Go to your teacher or professor and tell them about this learning tool and how it is used for location problems. Show them the grid and get permission to bring a clear acetate overlay into a test. Assure your instructor that no answers are on the sheet and that it is simply an aid you used to learn the location of the bones.

I want to mention one more possibility before going on. In some instances, I have found that I needed to learn a great deal more detail in one particular grid location than I did in all other grid locations. If I designed the size of my grid based on the detail needs for the one detailed section, I would need very small grids throughout the entire grid. Instead of doing that, I decided to use one of several ways to solve the problem without having to use a small grid. I could develop a smaller grid within that one grid location and use different letters than were used in the overall grid. I will use the skeleton grid just discussed as an example of what to do. Look back at the skeleton picture again, and you will notice that the left **hand** falls in the **E-3** location. The key word for the **E-3** location is **EMMy**. I realize that there isn't a lot of detail in the picture of the hand in that particular drawing, but let's assume there was lots of detail and you needed to know all of the detailed bones in the hand. You could simply draw smaller grid lines within the E-3 location and head this grid with the numbers 4 through 10, for instance, so no confusion within the larger grid could occur. You would then make your associations on the more detailed bones in the hand within the E-3 grid without having to use the smaller grid line throughout the entire skeleton picture where greater detail wasn't required.

Instead of developing a smaller grid within a larger grid, you could use a Pure Link or an Associate Link within a particular grid to learn more detail. The make-up of the detailed information within a particular grid will determine what tool you would use. One of the points of this discussion is that you should never limit yourself by the formal structure of a particular tool. Just because the 200 Word Locator is used primarily for location problems doesn't mean it can't be used as an Associate Link. The words are in order and can be pictured, so you could use it as an associate list with 200 potential places to put information. I have used it for this purpose. Never limit yourself. You may think of some applications for these tools **within The Lucas Learning System**™ that I have never thought of. Be on the lookout for ways to improve or expand these systems and tools.

I am providing several different size grids that can be used for location problems. Select one of the grid sizes that you think will work best for what you need to learn, get an acetate overlay made, lay it over the pictures and develop learning aids. If you don't want to do that, simply draw a grid over what you have to learn and apply what you have just learned. I will mention an idea a little later when I provide anterior and posterior views of surface muscles that will eliminate any possible confusion if you have to learn similar locations. The size of the grid will depend on how much detail you need to learn. More detail requires a smaller grid.

	1	2	3	4	5	6	7	8	9	10
A										
B										
C										
D										
E										
F										
G										
H										
I										
J										

	1	2	3	4	5	6	7	8	9	10
A										
B										
C										
D										
E										
F										
G										
H										
I										
J										

	1	2	3	4	5	6	7	8	9	10
A										
B										
C										
D										
E										
F										
G										
H										
I										
J										
L										
M										
N										
O										
P										
R										
S										
T										
V										
W										

	1	2	3	4	5
A					
B					
C					
D					
E					
F					
G					
H					
I					
J					

As I said earlier, I have developed 200 words for **The 200 Word Locator**. Different people have varying learning needs. One of my students had so much detailed location problems to solve that he needed more than 100 words for some of his learning requirements. You may never need more than 100 words, but if you do here are an additional 100 words that could be used to expand your detailed coverage possibilities by being able to cover more space with a larger grid.

	1	2	3	4	5	6	7	8	9	10
L	LighT	LawN	LiMb	LyRe	LuLL	LatCH	LucK	LeaF	LeaP	LaZy
M	MeaT	MiNe	MuM	MaRe	MiLL	MuSH	MiKe	MuFF	MaP	MaZe
N	NuT	NiNe	NuMb	NeaR	NeLLy	NaSH	NicK	NaiVe	NaP	NooSe
O	OaT	OwN	OhM	OaR	OiL	OuCH	OaK	OFF	OBey	OoZe
P	PeT	PaN	PaM	PeaR	PoLe	PatCH	PeG	PuFF	PuB	PaCe
R	RoaD	RuiN	RiM	RoaR	RuLe	RaSH	RocK	RouGH	RiB	RaCe
S	SuiT	SuN	SeaM	SeweR	SaiL	SaGe	SacK	SaFe	SaP	SiZe
T	TooT	TaN	TiMe	TaR	TooL	TeaCH	TacK	TaFFy	TaB	ToSS
V	VoiT	VaNe	ViM	VeeR	VeiL	ViG	ViK	ViV	VaP	ViSe
W	WeT	WiN	WhaM	WaR	WaLL	WaSH	WicK	WiFe	WhiP	WiSe

You will notice that the letters "K," "Q," and "U" were left out of this listing. Developing words for these letters is simply too difficult, so I didn't use them. You won't have any difficulty remembering that they aren't used if you need to use this additional grid.

Explanations for some of these words are also necessary to make sure you know how to picture them. For LuLL I picture people resting on a job site. There is a LuLL in the action. For LucK I see a four-leaf clover. It is supposed to bring good LucK. For NiNe I see a baseball team, because there are NiNe players on a baseball team. For NuMb I picture a syringe full of a substance to make you NuMb. For NeaR I picture my shadow. It is always NeaR me. For NeLLy I picture a mule, old NeLLy. A NaSH is an automobile that is no longer manufactured. I remember them well from my boyhood days. For NaiVe I picture a young boy asking a young girl for a date.

For the word OwN I see a deed which proves that you OwN a piece of property. For OhM I picture lightning, because an OhM has to do with electricity. For OuCH I see a scrape on a knee. For OFF I picture a light switch in the OFF position. For Obey I picture a soldier who should always Obey his superiors. For PaM you can picture the cooking product that prevents sticking, or you can picture a friend named PaM. For PuFF I see a giant PuFF of smoke in a forest fire. As a result, there is no confusion with the peg word. For PaCe I picture a PaCe car at an important automobile race.

For RuiN I picture an old building. You might want to picture ancient RuiNs. For RuLe I see a RuLer. For RouGH I picture sandpaper. It is RouGH. For SaGe I see Sagebrush. For SiZe I picture a very, very large SiZe garment of some kind. For TooT I picture a trumpet. For TiMe I see a large clock in a town tower. You might want to imagine Big Ben in London. For TeaCH I picture my favorite TeaCHer from school.

The letter "V" is always a challenge. For VoiT I picture a VoiT brand volleyball. For ViM I see an active person full of ViM and vigor. For VeeR I see a car VeeRing off of a road. For ViG I picture a ViGilante. For ViK I see a ViKing. For ViV I picture a very ViVacious woman. For VaP I see VaPor. For WiN I picture a person WiNNing a race. For WhaM I picture a ping pong paddle WhaMMing against a table. For WiSe I picture the three WiSe men of the Bible.

I am providing pictures of an anterior and posterior view of the surface muscles of a human being for practice purposes. Select one of the grid sizes I provided that you think will work best, get an acetate overlay made, lay it over the pictures and develop learning aids. Even if you don't plan to study anatomy, this will be good practice.

Anterior Surface Muscles

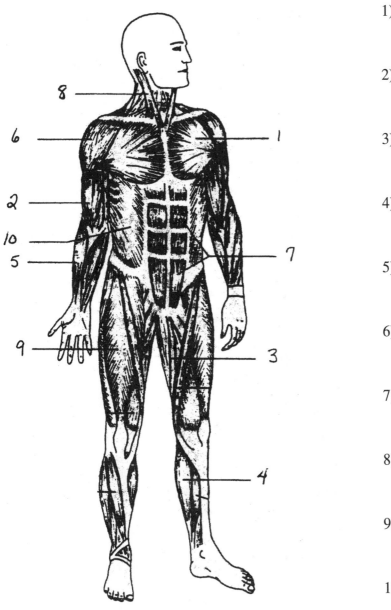

1) Pectoralis Major

2) Biceps Brachii

3) Gracilis

4) Soleus

5) Brachioradialis

6) Deltoideus

7) Rectus Abdominus

8) Sternocleidomastoideus

9) Rectus Femoris

10) External Oblique

It is important to use different letters to start the vertical columns for the posterior view. If you used an overlay grid for the anterior view that was headed by the letters A, B and C, you wouldn't want to use those same letters to head the columns for the posterior view. This might cause confusion. I have provided twenty letters, so you have an abundance of opportunities. You should use D, E and F or some other letters for the posterior view. Don't ever do anything that can possibly lend itself to confusion.

Posterior Surface Muscles

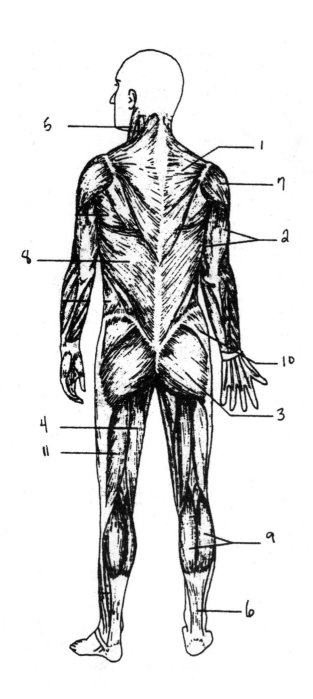

1) Trapezius

2) Triceps Brachii

3) Gluteus Maximus

4) Biceps Femoris

5) Sternocleidomastoideus

6) Achilles Tendon

7) Deltoideus

8) Sternocleicomastoiceus

9) Soleus

10) Gluteus Maximus

11) Semitendinosus

Since the last few pages have had a medical connotation, I want to discuss a couple more categories in medicine. Although you may never have to study medicine, the material may give you some ideas you can apply to other learning problems. I never studied it myself, but I had one of my students ask me how to learn it.

The make-up of white blood cells is listed on the left below. You will also notice that I have listed the sound-alikes and pegs for the numbers to the right. This is certainly more than a One-on-One learning problem, and it requires more than one tool, since there are words and numbers involved.

Leucocytes	**Loco Sites** - A **loco**motive on a **site**
1) Neutrophil - 60 - 70 %	1) **Neutral fill** (Truck) - **CH**ee**S**e **CaS**e
2) Eosinophil - 2 - 4 %	2) **Leo sin fill** - **NeRo**
3) Basophil - .15 %	3) **Base fill** - **ToweL**
4) Lymphocytes - 20 - 25 %	4) **Limp off site** - **NoSe NaiL**
5) Monocytes - 3 - 8 %	5) **Mono site** - **MoVie**

I made up a story that began with a sound-alike for the word **Leucocytes**. You can see that the sound-alike words I chose were **Loco Sites**, and I pictured a **loco**motive dump**site**. I imagined it was a site where old locomotives were dumped, and the site was a big hole in the ground that looked terrible. To learn **neutrophil 60 - 70 %,** I imagined that a dump truck backed up to the site to begin to fill it in. The driver put the truck in **neutra**l and began to dump the contents of the truck to **fill** in the hole. **Neutral fill** reminds us of **neutrophil**. I also imagined that the driver dumped **CHeeSe** into the hole. Actually, he dumped **CaSe** after **CaSe** after **CaSe** into the hole. These peg words tell us that the percentages of neutrophil are **60 to 70**.

It only made sense to continue the story with the same theme. I don't change the theme of a story unless I think the change will make the information easier to remember. Changing horses in midstream is difficult. Next I imagined that **Leo** the lion was driving the truck, and he said, "It is a **sin** to **fill** up this old locomotive site." The bold letters in **Leo sin fill** remind us of **eosinophil**. They don't represent the exact pronunciation, but it is close enough to work. I should know how to pronounce these words properly if I am studying them anyway. By imagining that **NeRo** is his passenger in the truck, the percentages of **2 to 4** are remembered. Although **NeRo** represents the number twenty-four (24), it will still work for the numbers **2 to 4**. Your mind won't let you make this 24 % since you are looking at and developing the learning aids. It will be obvious.

I imagined that a **base**ball field was built over the site after it was **fill**ed up. The bold letters in **base**ball **fill**ed easily remind us of the word **basophil**. I then imagined that **ToweL**s were used as bases. This is actually **.15 %** or point fifteen percent and not fifteen percent. If you feel you might think of 15 % instead of .15 %, you could imagine that something **point**ed was used to fasten the bases down. **Point**ed and **ToweL** can only translate to **.15 %**.

The story continues with a boy sliding into the bases. As he slid, he got hurt and had to **limp** off of the **site**. The bold letters in the words **limp off** of the **site** easily remind us of the word **lymphocytes**. He was hurt even more, because his **NoSe** got a **NaiL** stuck in it as he slid. The

NaiL must have been the pointed item used to affix the bases. The peg words NoSe and NaiL remind us of the percentages **20 to 25**.

The boy went home, got patched up and asked his mother to go back to the same site to play some more. His **ma** said. "**No**, you are not going back to that **site**." The bold words **ma no site** will remind us of the word **monocytes**. The boy then said, "Mom, I'm bored, and I want to do something." She said, "Here is some money. Go to a good **MoVie**." The peg word **MoVie** will remind us of the percentages **3 to 8**. Again, common sense will tell the student that the percentage is not 38 %.

This unusual story will easily remind us of this information. Not only will it remind me of it, but I have also had fun making it up. The process of making up learning stories is a lot more fun than boring repetition, and obviously, it makes the information much easier to remember. When it is recorded and reviewed, it will be known, but it will also be available for later review for a mid-term or final exam. Being **ODD** saves a lot of time in the long run.

The anterior and posterior views of surface muscles were just pictured for a practice drill. In addition to location, anatomy students are also asked to learn a muscle name, its origin, its insertion and its action. I will discuss one particular muscle and how this information could be learned. The name, the origin, the insertion and the action of the muscle are always in that same order, so it isn't necessary to develop special reminders of those words. The order of the memory stories will provide that knowledge, since each muscle would follow that order as it is learned. Listed below is the information for the trapezius muscle.

> Name - Trapezius
> Origin - Occipital bone
> Insertion - Spine and accromin of the scapula
> Action - Adduction of the scapula

The story begins with a sound-alike word for the name of the muscle. A **trapeze** works very for **trapezius**. The first part of the story must contain the information for the origin of the muscle. By seeing a man flying on a trapeze, the story has started. I imagine there is an **ox** down under the trapeze artist watching him perform. As he watches, he is **sip**ping a drink through **a tall bone**. The bold letters in the words **ox sip**ping **a tall bone** easily remind us of the words **occipital bone** and, since this is the **first part of the story**, it has to tell us that this bone is the **origin** of this muscle, because the **origin** information **comes first**.

Unfortunately the trapeze artist fell off the trapeze. He fell on his **spine** and hurt himself. **A crow** and some **men** came in and scooped him up on a large **spatula**. The bold letters in the words **spine**, **a crow men** and **spatula** easily remind us of the words spine and accromin of the scapula. The word **spatula** would simply become a standard for the **scapula** and would be used for it every time it was mentioned. This part of the story is silly, but so what! It works! Since this is the **second part of the story**, it has to tell us that this is the **insertion** of this muscle, because the **insertion** information **comes second**.

A duck that **shine**s then ran out with another **spatula** to help give more support to he injured trapeze artist who is a friend of his. The bold letters in the words **a duck shine**s and **spatula** remind us of the words **adduction of the scapula**. Since this is the **third part of the story**

it has to tell us that this is the **action** of this muscle, because the **action** information **comes third**.

The next step, as always, would be to record this story for later review. Later when the student thought of the **trapezius** muscle, he or she would immediately think of a **trapeze**, see the story mentally and know the information.

Go back and review this story a couple of times until you remember it, and you will easily know this information in the proper order.

CHAPTER 30

Word for Word Learning

When learning information word for word, I still apply the **golden rule** of **use as little as possible to learn as much as possible**. Of course, you have to be much more precise and include far more detail with word for word learning than you do with general learning. I handle word for word learning the same basic way I do speeches. Word for word learning and speeches have to be learned in order. When I discussed speeches, I told you not to learn them word for word, but in this instance word for word is mandatory. I told you to learn speeches in a sequence of thoughts. Word for word memory should be accomplished in the same way, but you will have to include more detail in your sequence. You must also choose a tool that will allow you to learn the material in sequence. Since the information must be learned in order, you have a variety of application choices. According to the content of the material and its complexity, you could use a **Pure Link**, an **Associate Link** such as the **Room System**, an **Anagram**, or even the **Peg Word System**, since peg words are in number order. You could even use the words in the **200 Word Locator** since the location words are in order. The complexity of the information will determine which tool you should use. An **Associate Link** such as the **Room System** is much more applicable for lengthy, complicated material than an **Anagram**, for instance.

The first thing I do for word for word learning is to find the basics in the material and begin to develop a **skeleton** of the basics. It is necessary to learn the basic **skeleton** information in order with the tool that was chosen to solve the problem. I only add **meat** to the skeleton as needed to fill in details that the **skeleton** might not allow me to recall. If a **skeleton** would suffice, that is all I would use, but invariably I have to add **meat'** to the **skeleton** in various places when, in review, details are left out or forgotten.

Our language contains some built-in memory aids, because there are definite ways of expressing ourselves. Examine this sentence.

The boy walked home with his dog.

You would never express that sentence as follows.

Home the boy with his dog walked.

There are only certain acceptable ways grammatically to express one's self. If you can learn the **basics** of the information, the **if's, and's and but's**, as I call them, should fall in place rather nicely. The **if's, and's and but's** to me are the other words that **wrap around the basics**. In the above sample sentence, I consider the words "**boy walked dog**" to be the **basics** of that sentence. If I can learn those basic words, the rest of the words should fall into the proper sequence without too much of a problem. The grammatical make-up of the words, along with a little common sense, should be all that is needed. If you had a problem later with the word "home," that is, knowing where the boy walked, you could incorporate that word into your memory aid, but I don't think that would be necessary. By going over the words once the tool was being applied, the correct words would pop into your mind.

Here are the steps involved in word for word learning:

1) **Read the material** over to be familiar with it.

2) Go back and **underline the basics** to begin to **develop a skeleton**. These basics are the **key words** around which everything else will revolve. As you become more adept, you will find that you need fewer key words. Just make sure you don't leave out any important thoughts.

3) **Decide which tool you will use** to learn the information. As I stated earlier, the complexity of the information might determine this step. Short material might be linked with the Pure Link. More complicated information might require an Associate Link or some other application. You will find that you will develop favorites among the tools and will use those more than others.

4) Begin to **make up your sound-alike words** and record them.

5) **Begin to associate** or connect the sound-alike words within the confines of the tool you have chosen.

6) **Go over your developing story** enough to make sure the basics have been learned.

7) **Concentrate on your story** to see if you can recall all of the words from your skeleton outline.

8) If some words are continually left out or forgotten, stick them into the proper place and change your story accordingly. Continue to do this until you **put enough meat on the bones** of the skeleton to remember everything word for word.

9) As always, **keep a record** of your learning aids for future reference and review.

The best way to explain it is by application. I will use part of the Gettysburg Address as a teaching aid for this instruction. The Gettysburg Address is as follows:

Fourscore and **seven** years ago, our **fathers** brought forth on this **continent** a new nation, conceived in **liberty** and dedicated to the **proposition** that all men are **created equal**. Now we are **engaged** in a great civil **war**, **testing** whether that **nation**, or any nation **so c**onceived and so dedicated, can **long endure**.

We are **met** on a great **battlefield** of that war. We have come to **dedicate** a **portion** of that **field** as a final **resting place** for those who here **gave their lives** that that nation might live. It is **altogether fitting** and **proper** that we should **do this**. But, in a **larger sense**, we **c**annot dedicate -we **c**annot **c**onsecrate - we **c**annot **h**allow - this **ground**.

The brave men, living and dead, who struggled here have consecrated it far above our poor power to add or to detract. The world will little note nor long remember what we say here, but it can never forget what we did here.

It is for us, the living, rather to be dedicated here to the unfinished work, which they who fought here have thus far so nobly advanced. It is rather for us to be here dedicated to the great task remaining before us - that from these honored dead we take increased devotion to that cause for which they gave the last full measure of devotion; that we here highly resolve that these dead shall not have died in vain; that this nation, under God, shall have a new birth of freedom; and that government of the people, for the people, shall not perish from the earth.

By examining the address again you will see that I have put what I believe the **basics** or **key words** of the address in the **skeleton** in **bold type**. You will notice that I have also put the beginning letters of some words in bold type. I plan to use those words in anagrams. I have only done this with about half of this address, because I want you to go on to select the key words and develop learning aids for the rest after I teach you what to do with the first half.

I must use or develop something for this teaching process with which all readers can be familiar, so I am far more limited than I would be if I could call upon my own knowledge of rooms or other data to learn this. I have developed a **skeleton** and will add or mention about adding **meat** along the way at various points, so you fully understand this instruction.

Since this address begins with the word "**Fore**" I will assume that Abraham Lincoln, who gave the Gettysburg Address, was a golfer. I will make up a golf story and develop a **Pure Link** as the game is played and my story develops. I could just as easily use furniture in a room or anything else that would allow me to learn it in order. I must use all of the words and letters in bold in the same order they appear in the address, since it must be learned in order. Look back and forth from the actual address to my suggestions as I proceed. Don't get in a hurry; stop from time to time to learn the pictures and review the word for word information in the address.

I imagine Abraham Lincoln said "**four** was my **score**" on hole **seven**. I assume that he started to play on hole number seven. All four of the people in his foursome were **fathers**. As he teed off on the next hole, he saw a **continent**al car drive by and drove his ball into a replica of the **liberty** bell that was on a wooden **prop**. If you felt you might need to add something to remind you of the word "conceived" prior to the word "**liberty**," you could associate a convict and sleeves to the bell in some way. These kind of additions can be added anyplace they are needed to remind you of other words that weren't selected as key words but are troublesome. Imagine that the wooden prop was actually a **crate** of **Equal**, the sugar substitute. On the next tee an **engaged** couple begin to have a **war** as Mr. Lincoln begins **testing** his driver with a picture of our **nation** on it. He uses his influence to calm them down and presents them with a **CD** of his Gettysburg Address. The letters **CD** will remind you of the words **c**onceived and **d**edicated. After making the peace, he stepped up and hit a very **long** drive that landed **in a door** of a home on the course. This takes us through the first paragraph. Go back and review the story and the words until you know them word for word. If you need extra aids, add them in appropriate places.

Mr. Lincoln walked up and **met** the people whose door he hit. He looked into the house and saw a **battlefield** board game. The man of the house said, "Mr. Lincoln, I am going to **dedicate** a **portion** of this **field** to you and, if you are tired, come on in for a **resting place**." He went in and they **gave** him **their life**savers for refreshment. His pants seemed to be too short, so they **all** stood **together** while the lady of the house gave him a **fitting** for his pants. She said, "Put your foot on this **prop**, and I will **do this** for you." He paid for the alterations with larger cents than they had ever seen and headed back to the course. As he left, he gave them a **CD** and noticed a **Ca**C**tus** in their yard with a **Ca**H**ing** crow on it. The **CD** will tell you "**c**annot **d**edicate," the **CC** in **Ca**C**tus** will tell you "**c**annot **c**onsecrate" and the **CH** in **Ca**H**ing** will tell you "**c**annot **h**allow." He noticed the cactus fell to the ground as the crow flew away. As you have just seen, I took him totally off of the golf course for a while, because it fit the words that needed to be learned so well. I have simply created a Sub Link connected to the house that Mr. Lincoln entered to supply more detail.

Some people might say, "It will take longer to make up the story and learn it than it will to just learn the original material. It certainly doesn't for me, because I have experience, which you need. I absolutely love the creative process involved in making up the stories anyway. I probably would make them up even if it took longer, but it doesn't. It is far easier to remember a tangible story than intangible words with no method of keeping them in order. You will only be convinced if it works for you. Please, for your own sake, take the time to review this complete story and learn these first two paragraphs. After doing that, I want you to select what you believe to be the basics or key words in the last two paragraphs and learn them word for word using your continuing story. Just pick up the story where Mr. Lincoln saw the cactus fall and go on with it. You will get much needed practice and will be happy with yourself for having made the effort. It will draw you ever closer to your goal of becoming a **Master Mind Mechanic**.

For further practice you could learn the Preamble to the Constitution word for word. Here it is:

We the people of the United States, in order to form a more perfect union, establish justice, promote the general welfare and secure the blessing of liberty to ourselves and our posterity, do ordain and establish this constitution for the United States of America.

CHAPTER 31

Learning Textbooks

The thought of trying to learn a textbook is more than most minds could possibly begin to grasp, but I developed a way to learn the basics in most of my textbooks as a college student. If you begin to think of the structure of textbooks, they are fairly predictable. Almost all textbooks are divided into chapter headings and sub-headings within chapters. There are normally brief explanations under the headings and sub-headings that give more detailed information about the headings. When you think about this structure, it is somewhat patternized, and I have stated before that anything that is patternized is easier to remember. What I did was really quite simple. There certainly was no special genius connected with it. I simply developed sound-alike words for the headings and sub-headings and wrote them next to the headings in my textbook. Then I read the material under the heading or sub-heading and underlined the basics. I did a little creative thinking and wrote my memory aid pictures that connected the heading to the basics in the margin of the book. I didn't draw any pictures but simply described in words what the picture entailed. I was disciplined to keep up with this on a regular basis. I was also diligent to review my pictures on weekends. I kept a record of the headings and sub-headings on a separate sheet of paper, so I could look at them as another review. Hopefully when I read one of the headings, the sound-alike word or words for it would pop into my mind, and along with it would come the picture for the basics if I had reviewed well enough to lock the pictures securely into my mind.

When I first began to try this, I got a little discouraged because I wasn't very good, but I realized the only way to improve was to get more experience. I got better and better as my experience increased. Many people would simply give up and jump back to repetition. Don't be one of them. If you need to learn material in textbooks, give this idea a chance. It may seem burdensome at first, but with experience you will be pleased. Of course, this idea can't be applied to all textbooks, but it works well with some. A full and complete knowledge of all of my systems and tools is required for this application to work properly. It will get easier and easier if you really apply yourself, and you will begin to spend less and less time developing your memory aids. You will also know the material better and better.

A great advantage of this idea is that you are making a record of your picture aids in your textbook. They will always be there for review time for mid-term or final exams. As a result, you won't have to go through the long honored, if you want to call it an honor, process of repetitive cramming into the late hours of many nights without adequate sleep.

CHAPTER 32

Learning Magazines and Manuals

Many times, I have learned an entire 100-page issue of a current magazine to demonstrate my knowledge of the magazine on radio and television talk shows. I don't actually learn it word for word but in enough detail to amaze people. You now have the ability to do the same thing if you have fully learned all of the fundamentals of my tools. I want you to learn about twenty pages of a magazine and demonstrate to your friends. When you learn how easy it is, you may want to learn more pages to make your demonstration even more impressive. You should do this for a couple of reasons. It will provide you with more practice and experience, and it will also enable you to perform under pressure and increase your confidence in your newly acquired skills.

The application is really quite simple. Page numbers identify pages in a magazine. To see a page in your mind all you have to do is think of the peg word for the page number. For page number thirty (30) you would simply picture a MooSe, the peg word for number 30. To learn what was on page 30, you would simply associate the information on page 30 to a MooSe. The best way to teach you is by actual application. On the next two pages you will find reproductions of two pages from a Time magazine. These pages are part of a much longer story about genetically engineered crops. You will need to turn back and forth from the pages to my instructions as I teach you the process. These two pages have a great deal of detailed information on them. Most magazine pages are far easier, but you will be impressed with how easy it is.

THE GLOBAL FOOD FIGHT

① BRUSSELS, 1998
France, Italy, Greece, Denmark and Luxembourg team up to block introduction of all new GM products in the European Union— including those approved by E.U. scientific advisory committees and even a few developed in these five countries. Several E.U. countries have also banned the importation and use of 18 GM crops and foods approved before the blockade went into effect. New safety rules could eventually break this logjam.

② SEATTLE, NOVEMBER 1999
Taking to the streets to protest the spread of "Frankenfoods," among other issues, demonstrators trying to disrupt the World Trade Organization summit are tear-gassed and beaten by police.

③ MIDWESTERN U.S., 1999
A coalition of agricultural groups calls for a freeze on government approval of new GM seeds in light of dwindling markets in anti-GM European countries. Planting of GM corn drops from 25 million acres (10 million hectares) in 1999 to 19.9 million acres (8 million hectares) in 2000.

④ MONTREAL, JANUARY 2000
130 nations, including Mexico, Australia and Japan, sign the Cartagena Protocol on Biosafety, which requires an exporting country to obtain permission from an importing country before shipping GM seeds and organisms and to label such shipments with warnings that they "may contain" GM products.

Key
Strongly in favor of GM foods

Somewhat in favor of GM foods

Opposed to GM foods

Canada
POPULATION 31,147,000
ATTITUDE Generally pro, though consumers are wary
REASON Second biggest producer of GM products, after the U.S., and a major food exporter.

Grains make up 24.8% of diet

–By Michael D. Lemonick. With reporting by Yudhijit Bhattacharjee and Max Rust/New York, with other bureaus

U.S.
POPULATION 278,357,000
ATTITUDE Cautiously pro
REASON As a major food exporter and home to giant agribiotech businesses, led by Monsanto, the country stands to reap huge profits from GM foods.

Grains make up 23.6% of diet

Argentina
POPULATION 37,031,000
ATTITUDE Pro
REASON Third largest producer of biotech crops in the world, after the U.S. and Canada.

Grains make up 29.5% of diet

Brazil
POPULATION 170,116,000
ATTITUDE Very cautiously pro
REASON The country is eager to participate in the potentially profitable biotech revolution but is worried about alienating anti-GM customers in Europe.

Grains make up 30.9% of diet

Britain
POPULATION 58,830,000
ATTITUDE Strongly anti
REASON "Mad cow" disease in beef and a report that GM potatoes caused immune-system damage in rats have alarmed most Brits. Markets ban GM foods, and experiments are tightly controlled.

Grains make up 22.8% of diet

France
POPULATION 59,079,000
ATTITUDE Strongly anti
REASON Like Britain, France has been stung by incidents with tainted food. Its attitude is also colored by hostility to U.S. imports and a desire to protect French farmers.

Grains make up 24.3% of diet

⑤ COLOMBO, SRI LANKA, FEBRUARY 2000
The government bans GM foods pending further research.

⑥ RIO DE JANEIRO, FEBRUARY 2000
A U.S. ship suspected of carrying GM corn is turned away by a Brazilian meat producer. The nation as a whole prohibits the importation

of GM foods unless they've been proved safe; earlier this month, a federal court upheld that policy despite a statement from the Cabinet that Brazil "cannot be left out of this technology."

⑦ NEW DELHI, MAY 2000
The government approves large-scale field trials of Bollgard,

Monsanto's pest-resistant GM cotton. Two years earlier, activists and angry farmers had burned fields planted with transgenic cotton.

⑧ BEIJING, JULY 2000
While still receptive to GM foods, the government passes a law requiring the labeling of GM seeds.

⑨ TOKYO, 2001
New rules will go into effect requiring GM foods to be labeled as such and tested for safety—although the government is also promoting the export of Japanese GM expertise and technology to Third-World nations. Meanwhile, a small anti-GM movement is growing stronger.

India		
POPULATION		
1,013,661,000		
ATTITUDE		
Cautiously pro	*Grains make up*	
REASON	*62.6%*	
Needs to find the most efficient ways to feed and clothe its enormous, rapidly growing population.	*of diet*	

China		
POPULATION		
1,277,558,000		
ATTITUDE		
Pro	*Grains make up*	
REASON	*54.7%*	
Needs to feed and clothe a large population; rural hunger brought about a revolution 50 years ago, and leaders don't want another one.	*of diet*	

Japan		
POPULATION		
126,714,000		
ATTITUDE		
Cautiously pro, but heading toward anti	*Grains make up*	
REASON	*40.7%*	
Japan has a national obsession with food quality, enhanced by several recent food-poisoning incidents, and a tradition of protectionism for Japanese farmers.	*of diet*	

tion International, an advocacy group based in Winnipeg, Canada. "Asian farmers get (unproved) genetically modified rice, and AstraZeneca gets the 'gold.'" Potrykus was dismayed by such negative reaction. "It would be irresponsible," he exclaimed, "not to say immoral, *not* to use biotechnology to try to solve this problem!" But such expressions of good intentions would not be enough to allay his opponents' fears.

WEIGHING THE PERILS

BENEATH THE HYPERBOLIC TALK OF Frankenfoods and Superweeds, even proponents of agricultural biotechnology agree, lie a number of real concerns. To begin with, all foods, including the transgenic foods created through genetic engineering, are potential sources of allergens. That's because the transferred genes contain instructions for making proteins, and not all proteins are equal. Some—those in peanuts, for example—are well known for causing allergic reactions. To many, the possibility that golden rice might cause such a problem seems farfetched, but it nonetheless needs to be considered.

Then there is the problem of "genetic pollution," as opponents of biotechnology term it. Pollen grains from such wind-pollinated plants as corn and canola, for instance, are carried far and wide. To farmers, this mainly poses a nuisance. Transgenic canola grown in one field, for example, can very easily pollinate nontransgenic plants grown in the next. Indeed this is the reason behind the furor that recently erupted in Europe when it was discovered that canola seeds from Canada—unwittingly planted by farmers in England, France, Germany and Sweden—contained transgenic contaminants.

The continuing flap over Bt corn and cotton—now grown not only in the U.S. but also in Argentina and China—has provided more fodder for debate. Bt stands for a common soil bacteria, *Bacillus thuringiensis,* different strains of which produce toxins that target specific insects. By transferring to corn and cotton the bacterial gene responsible for making this toxin, Monsanto and other companies have produced crops that are resistant to the European corn borer and the cotton bollworm. An immediate concern, raised by a number of ecologists, is whether or not widespread planting of these crops will spur the development of resistance to Bt among crop pests. That would be unfortunate, they point out,

These are pages number 44 and 45 and are opposite of each other in the magazine. I will start with page 44. The number 44 is pictured by seeing a RoweR, which is the peg word for number 44. You simply connect the information on the page to the peg word, which identifies the page. The page begins with the words, "The global food fight." Imagine two people rowing boats around a globe of the earth while having a food fight. The word "rowing" is enough to remind you of RoweR for page 44, and the rest of the picture will easily let you recall the introductory words on the page. Later when you think of page 44, or are tested on page 44, simply think of a RoweR, and the picture of the RoweR having a food fight on a globe of the earth will pop into your mind, and you will easily remember the headline that introduces that page.

When I am learning a magazine, I learn the basic introduction of eight or ten pages and then go back and fill in detail. Let's do that for page 45. The number 45 is pictured by seeing a RaiL, which is the peg word for number 45. You will recall that a RaiLroad track is used to picture the number 45. The key words on page 45 are, "Weighing the perils." Imagine seeing a large scale on a RaiLroad car that is weighing a pair of oil cans to picture this information. A pair of oil cans is a simple sound-alike to picture the word "peril." Later when you think of page 45, or are tested on page 45, the picture of the RaiLroad car that is weighing a pair of oil cans will pop into your mind, and you will easily remember the headline that introduces that page.

After I learn the basic introductory information, I go back and begin to add more detail to my pictures. I will discuss page 44 first. Since the numbers 1, 2, 3 and 4 are on page 44, there could be some confusion if peg words were used to picture the information in these four sections. When you think of the peg words, you might think of the basic information on pages 1, 2, 3 and 4 instead of the additional detailed information on page 44. To eliminate any confusion I use sound-alikes to picture these numbers. To picture number one (1), I use the word run. Since the information in that section relates to Brussels, I would see Brussel sprouts running in a race. See that picture in your mind now, and you will know that section number one (1) relates to Brussels. To picture number two (2), I use the word shoe. Since the information in that section relates to Seattle, I would see myself trying on shoes in Seattle. See a picture of yourself trying on shoes in Seattle in your mind now, and you will know that section number two (2) relates to Seattle. To picture number three (3), I use the word tree. Since the information in that section relates to the Midwestern U. S., I would trees growing only in the Midwestern part of the U. S. See that picture clearly in your mind now, and you will know that section number three (3) relates to the Midwestern U. S. To picture number four (4), I use the word door. Since the information in that section relates to the Montreal, I would see myself opening a door and walking into Montreal. See that picture clearly in your mind now, and you will know that section number four (4) relates to Montreal.

Now review the words run, shoe, tree and door in your mind to make sure these four areas come to mind. If for some reason one doesn't review it until you know it for sure. I always do a great deal of review before any demonstration.

It is easy to remember the pictures that are on pages, because they are already visual. You simply need to be able to describe each picture and its location on the page. Page 44 has an eyedropper and part of a world map formed from pieces of grain. The portion of the world is all of North and South America, Africa and Europe. Your common sense tells you that the rest of the world map as well as another eyedropper are on page 45. To feel more secure about these pictures and their page numbers I would see the RoweR and the RaiLroad extending into grain after the initial information already discussed.

To remember the nations discussed in more detail on page 44 I developed an anagram. I imagine that I am CUSsing in alphabetical order. The alphabetical order is ABBF. The letters "CUS" in CUSsing tells me Canada and the U. S. The letters "ABBF" tell me Argentina, Brazil, Britain and France. I can then learn as much detail about each country that I want to learn. For instance, the population of Canada is 31,147, 000. I'm not concerned with the three ending zeros, because the population of all the countries is given with three ending zeros. All I have to remember is 31,147 and add the three zeros to these numbers. To remember 31,147 I simple make up a way to picture these numbers and associate the picture to Canada. How about this! See yourself driving through MuD in Canada in a TRucK. MuD TRucK will tell you 31,147. If you remember the MuD TRucK you can't forget 31,147 based on the Consonant Number System which you already know. To remember that grains make up 24.8% of the diet in Canada I would simply continue the story picture. I would imagine that I lost my NeRVe while driving through all of that mud. NeRVe translates back to 24.8% based on the Consonant Number System. Remembering that there is a percentage in the number is no problem at all, because all of the percentages of grains in the diet of each country end with point something. After reviewing this little story a few times the information would become knowledge.

I have combined several learning tools so far to learn this information on pages 44 and 45. I used the Peg Word System to picture the page number. I then used the Sound-Alike Word System to learn the key words, or headings, on each page. I used the Anagram System to learn the list of countries. I used the Consonant Number System to learn the numbers, and I used a Rhyming Peg List to picture the numbers 1, 2,3 and 4 on page 44. I discuss this simple rhyming peg list in more detail in the Starting Children section of this book.

To learn the rest of the information on these two pages I would continue to do the same thing that I demonstrated for Canada. For instance, the population of Britain is 58,830,000. By imagining that LoVe FuMeS were rising up from Britain I would easily know the population is 58,830,000. It will take a lot longer to learn pages with detailed information like this than it will a full-page ad for a product. For instance, if a full-page ad for a Cadillac automobile appeared on page 30 of a magazine, I would simply imagine that a MooSe was driving a Cadillac. Later during a review when I thought of page 30 I would think of what a MooSe was doing, and I would know it was driving a Cadillac. That would tell me that page 30 was a full-page ad for a Cadillac automobile. I could add other information on the page like I just discussed for pages 44 and 45 of the Time magazine. I simply use the proper tool of learning needed to learn information on any page and make it part of the ongoing story. Many times I use the Link System or some variety of the Link System to learn more detailed information on a particular page. The information on each page dictates the tools that will be used. Obviously, some pages are much easier than other pages. By going over the picture stories for each page a few times you would have no problem remembering it. A little bit of discipline solves a lot of problems.

If there is an article or long story on a particular page I pick out some of the highlights or basics to remember. I certainly don't attempt to learn the articles word for word. I write the highlights on a separate piece of paper and highlight the basic information I will be learning with a highlighter. I want the magazine to look as normal as possible except for the highlighted areas.

When be tested these highlighted areas stand out dramatically.

Only after a great deal of review do I feel comfortable placing the magazine in a friend's hands. I would then say, "Open the magazine without me being able to see it, call out a page number, and I will tell you what is on that page." When the person calls out a page number, think of the peg word and simply tell them what you see associated with the peg word. You will amaze them.

I used to learn entire 100 page issues of current magazines and demonstrate on television shows. When I did it with Johnny Carson, he finally tossed the magazine over his head in disbelief after I correctly named great detail on several pages he had called out randomly.

When doing this, you will find that some pages aren't numbered. Simply take a marker and write the appropriate page number at the bottom.

This demonstration is impressive enough with just the basics, but I began to put more and more detail into my stories, so the demonstration would be more impressive. You should start with the basics and add detail after you become more experienced. A very impressive demonstration is the contents page. The contents page contains a synopsis of each section of the magazine. If that page wasn't called out, I normally asked the person to turn to that page so I could tell them what was on it. I usually began with the contents page anyway. For instance, it might say that the world section began on page twenty-eight (28) with an article about the Philippines. When I learned the contents page, I already had a pretty good outline of the magazine locked into my mind. As I got to each section, I simply added detail.

Now that you have learned how to do this, get a current issue of a magazine like Time or Newsweek and learn at least twenty (20) pages for practice and demonstration to your friends and family. You should do more pages of the same magazine as your experience, positive results and enthusiasm grow. They will be impressed no matter how old the magazine may be. I use current issues in my demonstrations, because it is more impressive if it is a brand new issue. People know I couldn't have had weeks or months to learn it. Don't get in a hurry when developing your stories. I will list some steps for you to follow shortly. Your ability to do this will amaze your friends and family members, and it will give you practice under fire. As a result, your experience and confidence will increase. Here are the basic steps involved in this process.

1) You, of course, must use the basic peg words to identify each page. The Peg Word System is the basic foundation of this application.

2) Begin to create your memory aid pictures. Simple pages with large ads and pictures won't be much more than a One-On-One learning problem. You will simply connect the peg word for the page to whatever you chose to picture on that page. More complicated pages will require a more detailed memory aid. They may require a Pure Link and even a Sub Link within the Pure Link. You can use Sub Links or Associate Links for very detailed information on detailed pages. You could see a MooSe walking around your living room, for instance, to learn detailed information on page 30. By connecting the information to the furniture, you could learn as much detailed information as you wanted. You would have to use the Consonant Number System if numbers are involved. Remember that you don't have to learn the magazine word for word. Telling your friends you have learned the basics is impressive enough. Take your time while making up your

memory aids, and make them as vivid and unusual as possible.

3) Make sure you record your memory aids.

4) Review your learning or memory aids in depth until you are sure you know them well.

5) Test yourself by thinking of different pages and seeing if you can recall everything that you are supposed to on each page.

6) Don't demonstrate until you are absolutely positive you know everything well. When you feel confident, hand the magazine to a friend and ask them to call out some of the pages you have learned at random. Make sure you are in control of the situation. When they call out a page number, begin immediately to explain what is on the page as you have learned it. If they ask you some detail you haven't yet learned, reply with something like this, "I am still learning detail on the pages and haven't learned that yet. Why don't you call out another page, and I will tell you what is on it." After a few pages they will be amazed at your ability.

7) I am going to suggest that you keep learning more pages from the rest of the magazine until hopefully you have learned the basics of the entire issue. This not only will be an incredible demonstration but, more importantly, it will have improved your abilities, which is what this whole demonstration process is all about.

You apply the same principles to learn manuals as for magazines. It is no different. Simply use peg words to picture the pages and make the associations in the same fashion as with magazines. You will be very pleased with the results.

CHAPTER 33

Spelling Demons

Spelling is another subject to which I have devoted an entire curriculum. The beginning part of this curriculum is built on the fundamentals taught in my reading curriculum, so I won't be able to give this subject proper justice in this publication. One of the aids in my curriculum involves pictures I have developed for all of the rules of spelling. When those are learned, and students know how to tangibly picture the letters of the alphabet, as well as all of the sounds made by the English language, spelling becomes a fun adventure. A thorough knowledge of phonetics is required for good spelling. As I just said, I teach students how to tangibly see every sound made in the English language. Since that requires a complete work of its own, all I can do now is give you some ideas of how to handle what are commonly called **Spelling Demons**. These ideas will help you with words that are normally troublesome for you. The best way to correct a word that is troublesome for you is to make a tangible correction that can be pictured in your mind. Simply seeing the intangible letters isn't good enough. I have already taught you how to picture the letters of the alphabet in an earlier chapter. That is about all you need to know to be able to apply methods to solving **Spelling Demons**.

The problem with some words is an incorrect single letter. It is relatively easy to correct these problems. Some people misspell the word insurance as insur**e**nce. The bold letters represent the problem. Some people use a letter "**e**" instead of a letter "**a**" before the "nce" in this word. I use an Ape to picture the letter "A." As a result, you can imagine that an Ape is your insurance agent, and you would know that a letter "**a**" is used instead of a letter "**e**" in this word. Use this idea when one letter causes you a problem in words. You must connect the standard picture for the troublesome letter to the word in some unique way. As always, you should record your learning aid.

Sometimes there is a problem of omitting one of a set of double letters in a word. I will give an example using the word "sleep" first. Almost everyone knows how to spell this word, but some youngsters have a problem with it and spell it "slep." I use an **E**agle to picture the letter "**e**." Knowing this, you could tell a child to imagine that he or she always went to "sleep" with **two E**agles. By explaining that this picture would remind the child that the word "sleep" has **two** letter "**e's**" in it, the problem will be solved. This idea can be applied with any troublesome double letter words. The word s**upp**re**ss** has two sets of double letters in it. A **P**eacock and an e**S**kimo are used to picture the letters "**p**" and "**s**." If you imagined and recorded for review that **two P**eacocks were s**upp**ressing **two** e**S**kimos you would have the problem solved. Use this idea for any troublesome double letters. There is another way to solve a misspelling of the word "suppress," as you will soon find out.

You can also use this idea for words that sound exactly alike but are spelled differently. The words "stationary" and "stationery" are often used incorrectly. The only differences in these two words are the letter "**a**" and the letter "**e**" before the letters "ry." By knowing the definition of these two words, the spelling problem is easily solved by using the application idea just discussed above. You already know that an Ape is used to picture the letter "**A**." An Eagle is used to picture the letter "**E**." The word stationary" with the letter "**a**" means to **not move**, and the word "stationery" with a letter "**e**" is **writing paper**. The solution to this problem involves a connection between the definition and the appropriate letter. See the picture below, and you will never again misspell these two words.

STATIONARY
STATIONERY

You see an Ape in the army that is standing at attention. He is stationary and **not moving**. This easily reminds you that the stationary that means to **not move** is spelled with a letter "**a**," since an Ape for the letter "**a**" is stationary. You also see an Eagle that is writing on stationery. This easily reminds you that the stationery that is **writing paper** is spelled with a letter "**e**," since an Eagle for the letter "**e**" is writing on the stationery. This is an example of some of the pictures that appear in my spelling curriculum.

You can also correct problems with some words by finding a word within a word that you already know how to spell and making a proper connection or association. The word "guidance" is sometimes misspelled "guidence." A letter "**e**" is used instead of a letter "**a**." You could imagine that an Ape was a guidance counselor to solve this problem as has already been explained, but there is another principle that will help with this and other similar words. You will notice that the word "**dance**" is part of the word "gui**dance**." By imagining that you are going to **dance** with a gui**dance** counselor you would easily solve this problem. This aid assumes, of course, that the person having the problem already knows how to spell the word "dance." In the same manner, the word "sup**press**" that has already been discussed could be corrected with this idea. You could imagine that you were being sup**press**ed at **sup**per because you were **press**ing clothes while eating. This idea assumes that you would already know how to spell the words "supper" and "press." An additional aid exists with this aid as well. The word su**pp**er has **two** letter "**p's**" which will help lock in the double letter "p's" even better.

Another application of this idea will work with the names Franc**is** and Franc**es**. There is a very simple solution for this problem. Franc**is** with an "**i**" is h**is** name, and Franc**es** with an "**e**" is h**er** name. H**is** has an "**i**" in it, and the word "h**is**" is masculine. H**er** has an "**e**" in it, and the word "h**er**" is feminine. Look for similar solutions.

Many people misspell the word penicillin. I have seen all kinds of screwy spellings for this word. A close examination of **pen**ic**ill**in reveals two three letter words within this word. The following aid will help lock in the proper spelling. If you imagine that a doctor gave you a shot of **pen**ic**ill**in with a **pen** so you wouldn't get **ill**, you have solved the problem.

The word "acquire' is often spelled "aquire" with the letter "**c**" omitted. If a person having problems with this word knew how to spell the word "**act**or," the following memory aid would suffice to solve the problem. An **act**or must **ac**quire good speaking skills. Since **ac**tor and **ac**quire both begin with "**ac**" the problem is solved. Look for words within troublesome words or parts of words known how to spell and apply these ideas.

Similarly the word "calen**dar**" is often misspelled "calender" with an "e" in place of the letter "a." Imagine that you are throwing a **dar**t at a calen**dar**, and you won't misspell it again, that is if you know how to spell the word "**dar**t."

Sometimes your cleverness and imagination can help with spelling problems. The word "develop" is often spelled "develop**e**" with an **extra** "**e**" on the end of the word. To solve this problem, I thought that someone needed to **lop** off the letter "e" to deve**lop** the best way to spell the word "deve**lop**." If someone is told to **lop** off the "**e**," they know that the word "deve**lop**" not only doesn't have a letter "e" on the end of it, but it also ends with the word "**lop**."

The words "stalag**m**ite" and "stala**ct**ite" are similar to "stationary" and "stationery" as to their spelling problem. A stalagmite is a deposit that projects upward from the floor or bot**to**m of a cave or cavern. A stalactite is a deposit that projects downward from the roof or **top** of a cave or cavern. The letter "**t**" in the word "**top**" tells you that a "stala**ct**ite" projects from the **top**. The letter "**m**" in the word "bo**tt**o**m**" tells you that a "stalag**m**ite" projects from the botto**m**. Problem solved! However, the letters "g" and "c" could also cause a problem with these words. If you imagine you have to use a C-clamp to hold a "stala**c**tite" to the **top** of a cave, you will not have a problem.

The word "cemetery" causes a problem for some people who spell it "cemetary" with a letter "a." A close examination of the word "c**e**m**e**t**e**ry" reveals **three** letter "e's" in the word. By imagining that **three** **E**agles are digging a grave in a c**e**m**e**t**e**ry, the problem is solved.

I could use many more examples but I think you have gotten the idea. Until my spelling curriculum is published, use pictures for letters and your cleverness, imagination and observation to develop helpful spelling aids for troublesome words.

CHAPTER 34

Starting Children

You have read a great deal about how I began to teach my own children to make the learning experience enjoyable. All children reach the point of "**hitting the wall**" at some time in their lives. The longer that point can be delayed, the better off the child will be. I started my children with some form of my systems when they were about three years old. I introduced my pictures to learn states and capitals to my son J. J. at three and taught him one or two pictures at a time. I didn't want to burden him or continue with the session if he seemed bored. Very young children don't have very good concentration skills, so I never extended my children past what they wanted to do. It is quite obvious when they wanted to go on to something else and the session ended abruptly. Later that day or the next day, I would review a previous picture and discuss a new one. The most important aspect of this process was **FUN**! I always tried to make it a fun procedure and not burdensome. If it was fun, they would want to do it repeatedly, and they did. I gradually introduced more pictures with more detail as they got older.

I taught J. J. a simple rhyming peg list of ten items at a very young age, so he could help with the shopping when I went to a supermarket or grocery store. The list was:

One - Run	Two - Shoe	Three - Tree	Four - Door
Five - Dive	Six - Sticks	Seven - Heaven	Eight - Gate
	Nine - Vine	Ten – Hen	

Before going to a store, we would make up our pictures. Notice that I said "we" and not "I." I asked J. J. to begin making up his own pictures at a very young age. The sooner he could get experience, the better he would be able to apply these systems. I always made up the list in and out of order. The procedure went something like this, "J. J. we need to buy some bread. Let's put it at number three. What picture should we see?" Of course, J. J. knew all of the rhymes for the numbers very well. J. J. might respond, "Let's see a tree growing loaves of bread instead of leaves." In this case I might have said, "That is a great picture. We will review it in a moment." If I didn't think he created a very good picture, I would make another suggestion. I might continue, "We also need to purchase some milk. Let's put it at number seven." J. J. might say, "I want to see milk pouring down out of the clouds in heaven instead of rain." I would have encouraged him for making up such a good picture. The associations would continue with a brief review after every three or four were learned. In the car on the way to the store another review took place. When we got to the store, he was ready and very eager to help with the shopping. Not only was he getting some experience with my systems, but he was also occupied during the shopping time and wasn't interested in pulling items off the shelves and getting into other mischief. He was responsible for making sure we didn't forget any items we needed to bring home.

As I have previously told you, I began to develop actual pictures to help J. J. and my daughter Canaan learn their schoolwork. Matt, Jeff and Julie, my older children, weren't helped as much, because I was still playing professional basketball and was away from home a lot when they were young. They learned my systems later though and used them effectively. I kept the learning process as fun as possible for J. J. and Canaan, but my plan was to have them begin to develop their own learning aids as soon as possible. I gradually put more and more of the onus for learning on them as they became increasingly experienced. As early as the second grade, I had them developing pictures to learn their vocabulary words. We didn't draw pictures. We simply made them up, recorded them and reviewed them.

You have seen some of the pictures I developed to make the process of learning fun for my children. I showed you examples of a state and its capital, the presidents and what to capitalize among other things. I have also written books under the authorship of Dr. Memory™ that teach the alphabet, numbers and colors with tangible pictures. These publications will make learning these basics fun and easy for all children.

I have written an entire curriculum on reading and writing that accomplishes what no other course has ever done. In the first part of this curriculum, known as *Dr. Memory's™ Alphabet Friends*, students are taught a tangible picture for every letter of the alphabet. This tangible picture not only looks exactly like the letter in upper case and lower case, but it also sounds exactly like the letter when saying the letters of the alphabet. That is not all that is accomplished by this picture. It also allows students to see every sound made by the letter and tells the students if the letter is reliable or unreliable. That is, can it be relied upon to always make the same sound, or does it require special notice because it can make more than one sound. Students actually see a sound and see what to say as sounds are put together. Students are also taught how to act out the sounds made by every letter. They learn how to read each other as they act out these sounds to form words. They love this activity. The course goes on to lay very strong foundations in all aspects of reading and writing using the photographic mind. In the second phase of this curriculum, known as *Dr. Memory's™ See and Know Picture Words*, students are taught revolutionary principles that enable them to learn the 240 basic sight words. These words make up more than 75 % of all the reading students will do in the elementary grades and over 50 % of all the reading students will do the rest of their lives. These words have been taught primarily by repetition in the past. Dr. Memory™ teaches how to learn these words with fun pictures and characters. When students finish this course, they know 94 % of everything they will ever need to know to be able to analyze and read any word in the English language and, most importantly, they understand it, because they can see it.

A character known as Silly Bull, representing a syllable, helps lead students through the course. He and his friends, who are all tangible characters, teach everything about syllables, the basic building blocks of words, and how to understand them. Students learn how to picture all vowels including long and short vowels and how to understand them. They learn about silent vowels and what I call disguised vowels. Disguised vowels don't make the normal vowel sound the students learned in *Dr. Memory's*™ *Alphabet Friends*™ course, but they disguise themselves to make a new and different sound. The students actually see this process take place tangibly and fully understand it. They learn about what Dr. Memory™ calls Vowel Pals and Foul Vowels and fully understand them. They learn how to picture consonants and their uses.

There is some terribly difficult terminology in reading that some teachers don't even fully understand, so it is brutally difficult for most students. A **digraph**, for instance, is one of those terms. Do you remember what a **digraph** is? Probably not! The dictionary gives the following definitions. A **digraph** is a pair of letters representing a single speech sound, as the "ph" in phone. Another definition is two letters run together to represent a special sound. My definition is two letters appearing next to each other that combine to change their sound to a new sound. When these letters are consonants, Dr. Memory™ calls them **Consonant Changers**. They are pictured holding **coin changers**, so the student can see that a **change of sound takes place**. In my pictures, the coins fall down on the new sound so the student can tangibly see it and understand it. This course is full of other pictured principles that very clearly teach what reading is all about. This curriculum will be published soon for school and in-home use.

I have also developed full curriculum with detailed pictures for adding and subtracting, the times tables, grammar and punctuation, spelling, vocabulary, and I have even done a beginning dictionary entitled *See What I Mean*. The meaning to the words is in a picture, so the student can **see what the word means**. I have also written many other fun, adventure books for children to add enjoyment to the learning process.

In addition I have written animated computer programs for many of my curriculum and developed ideas for changing my learning pictures into video games. Can you imagine a clever, fast-paced video baseball game, for example, that teaches the student what to capitalize as the game is played?

My books for children will be published soon. Be looking for them in the Dr. Memory™ series. They will make the learning process fun and rewarding for you and your children.

Learning Disabilities

Countless thousands of young people and adults have been labeled as LD's or people who have learning disabilities for one reason or another. My experience has shown me that many of these individuals are suffering from what others are also suffering from which is not a learning disability at all but teaching limitations. Since we have never been able to use the greatest learning gift of all in school, some people have difficulties. I have received countless letters from parents of children who supposedly had learning disabilities. These children were able to learn quickly and easily with my books and, for a change, the children enjoyed it. One specific problem is dyslexia, which is a tendency to see letters backwards or upside down, causing reading problems. In my experience people who are dyslexic do not turn my pictures around. When they are taught the baseball team to learn what to capitalize, for instance, they have no problem with the pictures and learn as well as others. Dyslexics have no problem with pictures. Even though my tangible reading system has been tested very successfully, it hasn't yet been used with dyslexics. I am very anxious to see what will happen. It is my fervent hope that dyslexics will not have a problem with the letters and sounds in my curriculum, because all of these have been transformed into tangibles. If the same thing holds true with these pictures as has with my other pictures, one of the great learning disability problems could be solved. I am always very gratified to know that my efforts have been beneficial for others.

CHAPTER 35

How to Analyze, Attack and Solve Learning Problems

I have given you samples of learning problems for practice throughout this book. I'm confident I have given you enough samples to teach you what to do. There is no way I can sit by your shoulder and say, "No, don't do that but do this," or "Yes, that was a great application. As a matter of fact it was a better idea than I would have used." You should be more than ready to continue this great learning adventure throughout the rest of your life. I know it will work as well for you as it has for me if you just apply the tools consistently. There is a logical procedure to follow as you approach learning problems. Those steps are:

1) You must **analyze the information** to be learned. This process will involve the following kinds of questions:

a) Does the information contain only words, only numbers, a combination of words and numbers, symbols, formulas, maps, etc. Once the content is   analyzed, the proper system or systems to be used can be ascertained.

b) Does the information have to be learned in order or in any order?

c) Is this a simple One-On-One problem, or is it more complicated?

These are the kinds of questions that must be involved in this analysis process. All aspects must be thought of. This process isn't burdensome or complex, but it is absolutely vital. Remember to always look for patterns in the material to be learned. Anything that can be patternized is always easier to learn. Once these kinds of questions have been ascertained, you can go on to the next step.

2) **Determine which system or systems are required to attack and solve the learning problem**. If the information must be learned in order, you have a variety of application choices. According to the content of the material and its complexity, you could use a **Pure Link**, an **Associate Link**, a **Directional Link**, an **Anagram**, the **Room System** or even some sort of **Peg System**, since Peg Systems are also in number order. You could even use the words in the **200 Word Locator** since they are in order. If you have to know infor-

mation at numbered positions, you will have to use the **Peg Word System**. I make my choice based solely on the content of the information to be learned at this point. The more you use the systems, the better prepared you will be to make these kinds of choices, and most exciting of all, you have many options from which to choose. You aren't corralled in with only repetition or just one tool. You will no doubt use a **Sub Link** within the system chosen for the main application if you need to learn more detail at a particular point within the information.

If the information is numbers, you will have a choice of **The Consonant Number System**. Within that system, you can choose the **One Sound Method**, the **One Word Method**, the **Combination Method**, the **Adjective Peg Word Method** or the **Peg Word System**. The arrangement and complexity of the numbers will determine this choice. I don't know which application I might use until I begin to list or think of the sounds for the numbers and see if picturable words will be obvious or will take a little manipulation. Once again though, you have a variety of options at your disposal. With my systems you always have a wide selection of possibilities. You simply select the system and tools that best fit your needs for a particular problem.

If location is important, you could use the **200 Word Locator** or perhaps a **Directional Link** in less complicated information. These are the kinds of decisions that must be made during the analyzation and attacking processes.

3) Use **your imagination and creativity and make up your memory aids**. Don't get in a hurry. A little more thought may develop a better application.

4) **Record your memory aid**.

5) **Review your memory aid** from time to time to make sure you know it.

This has proven to be a foolproof method for me when I apply it. I am no different than anyone else. If I leave out the recording and reviewing process, I will eventually lose the information. If I record it and don't review it regularly, I still have it for review at any time in the future when I might need it.

For your edification, I will lead you through this process and tell you what I did when I developed the baseball picture to learn what to capitalize earlier in this book. Here were the steps involved.

1) **Analyze the information** to be learned. This wasn't really very difficult. Only words were involved, it could be learned in any order, and it was much more than a simple One-On-One problem. I realized my first step was to develop a sound-alike word for the word "capitalize." You know that I chose a **cap** with **tall eyes**. This choice somewhat determined what my next thought process had to be.

2) **Determine which system or systems are required to attack and solve the learning problem**. I had to accomplish at least two things for my young son. First, all of the rules

needed to be in a central location, so they could easily be retrieved from his mind as a group. A baseball field became my choice because of the **cap** with **tall eyes**. That was one basic location. Second, he had to be able to distinguish one rule from another and not confuse them. I accomplished this by using individual players at the various baseball positions. My idea came down to placing a rule or rules at the nine baseball positions as well as in the outfield stands. The next step in this process became the most important as far as I was concerned. I had to examine the rules.

3) Use **your imagination and creativity and make up your memory aids**. This step in this particular learning problem became the most important as far as I was concerned. I had to examine the rules and determine which rule or rules would be at which position. This was made somewhat easier, because my son was only called on to learn a few rules in his first exposure to capitalization. I wanted to develop a full baseball team, although he only had to learn a few rules to start with. I decided to look ahead in his textbook and find future rules he would need to learn to make this creative process more meaningful for me. Next I began to develop the sound-alike words to picture the various rules and record them for even more analyzation. I had to decide which rules seemed to fit best at which positions. I felt the most complicated picture needed to be in center field where it wouldn't be crowded. Simpler pictures needed to be used in the infield where players were closer together. I began to draw stick figures on scratch paper to see how my baseball team might look. I thoroughly enjoyed this process. Creating and developing learning aids is a delightful pleasure for me. But more than that, I knew the end result would make learning these burdensome rules much more enjoyable and much easier for my son and hopefully millions of others in the future.

4) **Record your memory aid**. For this process I went to an artist, showed him my stick figure drawing, explained it to him and asked him to draw a detailed pencil drawing that we could examine and critique. This, as you no doubt realize, became a lengthy process, because I wanted to develop something that would last for generations and possibly help millions of people in the long run. My son J. J. was my first concern at this point though, because he had asked me to help him learn the material in the first place.

5) **Review your memory aid** from time to time to make sure you know it. To review this picture, I played baseball with my son and taught him each player and the rule he or she represented. In no time he had learned the twenty (20) rules portrayed by that very special **Capitalize Baseball Team**. To continue the review, as I stated earlier in the book, I became an announcer and J. J. was my play-by-play associate. We played imaginary baseball games as we drove in the family car, and the picture became knowledge to him in a very short time. As a result, he didn't have to lose, cram again, lose again, cram again, lose again, etc. He learned it, kept it and could use it. So could every other child or adult who would study the picture.

I already somewhat led you through a similar five-step development process with complicated information when I described what the commercial airline pilot did to learn his material. This process is fun and necessary. For some material it will be quick and simple, but for more complicated information it will take a little longer, but the rewards are outstanding.

The ODDer the Better

Now that you have learned all of my systems and how to apply them to become a full-fledged qualified **Master Mind Mechanic**, you have to become a very **ODD** person. Without being **ODD**, you will never be as good as you could be. My hope for you is that you become one of the **ODD**est people in the world. In that regard, assume that your doorbell just rang and a gift arrived, a gift from me. After opening it, you find a basketball. The ball doesn't have a brand name of a manufacturer on it, but it simply reads **Learning Tools**. I have stated earlier that I became a good basketball player because I practiced a lot. I also have stated that I became a **Master Mind Mechanic** because I practiced with my learning tools as well. You have everything it takes to succeed. You even have a ball with which to practice, although it is imaginary. What are you going to do with it? If you practice with it, the sky is the limit. If you don't practice with it, you will never reach your potential. You will always be much better at learning than you ever before dreamed possible by just knowing about and being able to apply these systems. The really great players, the Hall of Famer's, are **ODD** enough to work harder than others. Here's hoping you become very **ODD**. Good luck!

CHAPTER 36

The Consonant Number Dictionary

The Consonant Number Dictionary is a super list of peg words from 00 to 1,000. This dictionary can be used very effectively when sounds are needed to remember numbers of all kinds. It is really only necessary to know the 100 basic peg words for most people, though some of you who work regulary with numbers may find this dictionary extremely helpful.

00	·	SeeSaw	017	·	STeaK	034	·	SMeaR
01	·	SeeD	018	·	SToVe	035	·	SMiLe
02	·	SNow	019	·	STeP	036	·	SMooCH
03	·	SwiM	020	·	SiNuS	037	·	SMoKe
04	·	SeweR	021	·	CeNT	038	·	Saw MaFia
05	·	SaiL	022	·	SNowiNg	039	·	ZoMBie
06	·	SewaGe	023	·	CiNeMa	040	·	Sea hoRSe
07	·	SKi	024	·	SNoRe	041	·	SwoRD
08	·	SoFa	025	·	SNaiL	042	·	SiReN
09	·	SoaP	026	·	SNowSHoe	043	·	SeRuM
010	·	CiTieS	027	·	SNaKe	044	·	SouReR
011	·	STuDio	028	·	SNiFF	045	·	CeReaL
012	·	SaTiN	029	·	SuNuP	046	·	SeaRCH
013	·	STeaM	030	·	SeaMS	047	·	Sea wRecK
014	·	STaR	031	·	SuMMiT	048	·	SuRF
015	·	SaDDLe	032	·	SeaMaN	049	·	SyRuP
016	·	STaGe	033	·	See MayheM	050	·	SoLoS

051	·	SaLaD	075 ·	SKiLL
052	·	SaLooN	076 ·	SQuaSH
053	·	SLiMe	077 ·	SQuawK
054	·	CeLeRy	078 ·	SCuFF
055	·	SLyLy (fox)	079 ·	SKiP
056	·	SLuSH	080 ·	SaFeS
057	·	SiLK	081 ·	SiFT
058	·	SLaVe	082 ·	SiPHoN (f sound)
059	·	SLeeP	083 ·	SaVe Me (swimmer)
060	·	SaSHeS	084 ·	SapPHiRe (f sound)
061	·	SwitCH hiT (silent t)	085 ·	SouFFLe
062	·	SeSSioN (sh sound)	086 ·	SaVaGe
063	·	Sea CHiMe	087 ·	CiViC
064	·	SeaSHoRe	088 ·	SaFe View
065	·	SeaSHeLL	089 ·	SaFe Pie
066	·	wiSe JudGe (silent d)	090 ·	SPiCe
067	·	SaGe Key	091 ·	SPaDe
068	·	Sea SHaVe	092 ·	SPooN
069	·	Sea JeeP	093 ·	Sea BuM
070	·	SQueeZe	094 ·	SPRay
071	·	SQuiD	095 ·	SPooL
072	·	SKiN	096 ·	SPeeCH
073	·	eSKiMo	097 ·	iCe PicK
074	·	SCaR	098 ·	SPooF

099	-	SoaP uP	23	-	NaMe	47	-	RuG
0	-	Saw	24	-	NeRo	48	-	Roof
1	-	Tie	25	-	NaiL	49	-	RoPe
2	-	Noah	26	-	NotCH (silent t)	50	-	LaCe
3	-	Ma	27	-	NecK	51	-	LoT
4	-	Rye	28	-	kNiFe	52	-	LioN
5	-	Law	29	-	kNoB	53	-	LaMb (silent b)
6	-	SHoe	30	-	MooSe	54	-	LuRe
7	-	Cow	31	-	MaT	55	-	LiLy
8	-	iVy	32	-	MooN	56	-	LeeCH
9	-	Bee	33	-	MuMMy	57	-	LocK
10	-	ToeS	34	-	MoweR	58	-	LaVa
11	-	ToT	35	-	MaiL	59	-	LiP
12	-	TiN	36	-	MatCH (silent t)	60	-	CHeeSe
13	-	ToMb (silent b)	37	-	MuG	61	-	JeT
14	-	TiRe	38	-	MoVie	62	-	CHaiN
15	-	ToweL	39	-	MoP	63	-	JaM
16	-	DiSH	40	-	RoSe	64	-	JaR
17	-	TacK	41	-	RaT	65	-	JaiL
18	-	DiVe	42	-	RaiN	66	-	JudGe (silent d)
19	-	TuB	43	-	RaM	67	-	JacK
20	-	NoSe	44	-	RoweR	68	-	SHaVe
21	-	NeT	45	-	RaiL	69	-	SHiP
22	-	NuN	46	-	RoaCH	70	-	CaSe

71 ·	CaT	95 ·	BaLL	119 ·	Tea TaP
72 ·	CaN	96 ·	BuSH	120 ·	DuNCe
73 ·	CoMb (silent b)	97 ·	BiKe	121 ·	TeNT
74 ·	CaR	98 ·	PuFF	122 ·	TeeNy-weeNy
75 ·	CoaL	99 ·	PiPe	123 ·	Too NuMb (silent b)
76 ·	CaGe	100 ·	DiSeaSe	124 ·	DiNNeR
77 ·	CaKe	101 ·	ToaST	125 ·	ToeNaiL
78 ·	CaVe	102 ·	DoZeN (donuts)	126 ·	TeeNaGe
79 ·	CaP	103 ·	DiCe eM	127 ·	TaNK
80 ·	FaCe	104 ·	TeaSeR	128 ·	TuNe oFF (bad music)
81 ·	FaT	105 ·	TaSSeL	129 ·	TuNe uP
82 ·	FiN	106 ·	DoSaGe	130 ·	DiMS
83 ·	FoaM	107 ·	DeSK	131 ·	ToMaTo
84 ·	FuR	108 ·	DeCeiVe	132 ·	DeMoN
85 ·	FiLe	109 ·	ToSS-uP	133 ·	TiMe Me
86 ·	FiSH	110 ·	TooTS	134 ·	TaMeR (circus)
87 ·	FoG	111 ·	DoTTeD	135 ·	TaMaLe
88 ·	FiFe	112 ·	DeaDeN	136 ·	aToM aGe
89 ·	FoB	113 ·	ToTeM (pole)	137 ·	ToMahawK
90 ·	BuS	114 ·	TuToR	138 ·	hiT MoVie
91 ·	BaT	115 ·	TiDaL	139 ·	ToMBoy
92 ·	BuN	116 ·	DeTaCH	140 ·	DReSS
93 ·	BuM	117 ·	hoT DoG	141 ·	DiRT
94 ·	Bear	118 ·	aDDiTiVe	142 ·	TRaiN

143	·	DRuM	167	·	haT SHacK
144	·	DRyeR	168	·	DutCH wiFe (silent t)
145	·	TRoLLey	169	·	Toy SHoP
146	·	TRaSH	170	·	DoG houSe
147	·	TRucK	171	·	TicKeT
148	·	TRoPHy (f sound)	172	·	TyCooN
149	·	TRaP	173	·	DoGMa
150	·	TooLS	174	·	TiGeR
151	·	ToiLeT	175	·	TicKLe
152	·	TaLoN	176	·	DoG SHow
153	·	TeLL Me (a secret)	177	·	hoT CaKe
154	·	TaiLoR	178	·	hoT CoFFee
155	·	DoLL iLL	179	·	TeaCuP
156	·	DeLuGe	180	·	whiTe FaCe
157	·	weDLocK	181	·	ouTFiT
158	·	TeLL oFF	182	·	TyPHooN (f sound)
159	·	TuLiP	183	·	DeFaMe
160	·	DuCHeSS	184	·	DiVeR
161	·	hoTSHoT	185	·	DeFiLe
162	·	aDDiTioN (sh sound)	186	·	hoT FudGe (silent d)
163	·	TouCH Me	187	·	TouGH Guy (f sound)
164	·	TeaCHeR	188	·	T.V.Fee
165	·	DitCH oiL (silent t)	189	·	hoT FiB
166	·	heaD JudGe (silent d)	190	·	TuBeS

191 ·	TiPToe	215 ·	NooDLe
192 ·	TiePiN	216 ·	NighT watCH (silent t)
193 ·	wiDe BeaM	217 ·	iNDiGo
194 ·	DiaPeR	218 ·	NaTiVe
195 ·	TaBLe	219 ·	NighT Pay
196 ·	whiTe BeaCH	220 ·	oNioNS
197 ·	Tea BaG	221 ·	uNkNiT (silent k)
198 ·	ToP heaVy	222 ·	uNkNowN
199 ·	whiTe PoPPy	223 ·	No NaMe
200 ·	NooSeS	224 ·	No hoNoR
201 ·	NaSTy	225 ·	soN-iN-Law
202 ·	iNSaNe	226 ·	kNee hiNGe (silent k)
203 ·	eNZyMe	227 ·	No NaG
204 ·	NoSieR	228 ·	NiNeVeh
205 ·	NoZZLe	229 ·	uNioN Pay
205 ·	NiCe SHoe	230 ·	eNeMieS
207 ·	No SacK	231 ·	iNMaTe
208 ·	uNSaFe	232 ·	NoMiNee
209 ·	NewSBoy	233 ·	New MoMMy
210 ·	NuTS	234 ·	New haMMeR
211 ·	hauNTeD	235 ·	aNiMaL
212 ·	iNDiaN	236 ·	No MeSH
213 ·	aNaToMy	237 ·	aNeMiC
214 ·	wiNTeR	238 ·	NyMPH (f sound)

239	·	No MaP	263 ·	No GeM
240	·	NuRSe	264 ·	iNJuRy
241	·	NaRaTe	265 ·	iNiTiaL (sh sound)
242	·	uNwoRN	266 ·	hyeNa CHa CHa
243	·	No RooM	267 ·	No CHecK
244	·	NaRRoweR	268 ·	aNCHoVy
245	·	uNReaL	269 ·	wiNeSHoP
246	·	eNeRGy	270 ·	yaNKeeS
247	·	New yoRK (city)	271 ·	NuGGeT
248	·	NeRVe	272 ·	kNocK-kNee
249	·	uNRiPe	273 ·	iNCoMe
250	·	iN LawS	274 ·	aNCHoR (k sound)
251	·	NewLyweD	275 ·	aNKLe
252	·	NyLoN	276 ·	eNGaGe
253	·	New LiMb (silent b)	277 ·	syNaGoGue
254	·	iNhaLeR	278 ·	kNocK oFF
255	·	hoNoLuLu	279 ·	kNeeCaP
256	·	uNLeaSH	280 ·	iNVoiCe
257	·	uNLucKy	281 ·	iNVaDe
258	·	iN LoVe	282 ·	No FuN
259	·	No heLP	283 ·	No FaMe
260	·	hiNGeS	284 ·	uNFaiR
261	·	uNwaSHeD	285 ·	NaVeL
262	·	eNGiNe	286 ·	wiNe FudGe (silent d)

287	·	iNVoKe	311	·	iMiTaTe	335	·	MaMMaL
288	·	NaVy wiFe	312	·	MuTiNy	336	·	haM MuSH
289	·	No FiB	313	·	MeDiuM	337	·	MiMiC
290	·	NaPS	314	·	MeTeoR	338	·	hoMe MoVie
291	·	NoBoDy	315	·	MoTeL	339	·	MaMBa
292	·	oNe·By·oNe	316	·	MoD SHow	340	·	MaRS
293	·	No BeaM	317	·	My DucK	341	·	MaRRieD
294	·	NeighBoR	318	·	MoTiVe	342	·	MaRiNe
295	·	NiBBLe	319	·	MuD Pie	343	·	hoMeRooM
296	·	oNe·PaGe	320	·	MiNeS	344	·	MiRRoR
297	·	uNPacK	321	·	MiNT	345	·	MuRaL
298	·	uNBehaVe	322	·	hoMe NeoN	346	·	MaRSH
299	·	NiP uP	323	·	My eNeMy	347	·	hoMewoRK
300	·	MoSSeS	324	·	MiNeR	348	·	aMMo whaRF
301	·	MaST	325	·	MaNhoLe	349	·	MaRaBou
302	·	MoiSteN (silent t)	326	·	MuNCH	350	·	MiLLs
303	·	MuSeuM	327	·	MaNiaC	351	·	MaLLeT
304	·	MiSeR	328	·	My NaVy	352	·	MeLoN
305	·	MuScLe	329	·	MaN aPe	353	·	My LiMe
306	·	MaSSaGe	330	·	MuMS	354	·	MiLeR
307	·	MuSiC	331	·	hoMe·MaDe	355	·	MoLehiLL
308	·	MaSsiVe	332	·	MaMMoN	356	·	MiLeaGe
309	·	MiShaP	333	·	MaMMa Mia	357	·	MiLK
310	·	MaiDS	334	·	MeMoRy	358	·	hoMeLiFe

359	·	MeLBa	383	·	My FaMe	407 ·	ReSCue
360	·	iMaGeS	384	·	MoVeR	408 ·	ReCeiVe
361	·	MaSHeD	385	·	MuFFLe	409 ·	ReCiPe
362	·	MoTioN (sh sound)	386	·	hoMe VoyaGe	410 ·	RoaDS
363	·	hoMe GyM	387	·	huM FiG	411 ·	ReD-hoT
364	·	MooCHeR	388	·	MoVe oFF	412 ·	RoTTeN
365	·	MuTuaL (ch sound)	389	·	My FiB	413 ·	ReDeeM
366	·	MuCHaCHa	390	·	MaPS	414 ·	RiDeR
367	·	MaGiC	391	·	MoPPeT	415 ·	RaTTLe
368	·	hoMe CheF	392	·	haMBoNe	416 ·	RaDiSH
369	·	heM SHoP	393	·	waMPuM	417 ·	ReTaKe
370	·	MiKeS	394	·	eMBeR	418 ·	RaDio waVe
371	·	MaGGoT	395	·	MayPoLe	419 ·	ReTaPe
372	·	aMMo CaNoe	396	·	aMBuSH	420 ·	iRoNS
373	·	hoMe GaMe	397	·	hyMnBooK (silent n)	421 ·	RuNT
374	·	MaKeR	398	·	My BeehiVe	422 ·	ReuNioN
375	·	MoGuL	399	·	My PuPPy	423 ·	ReNaMe
376	·	My CaSH	400	·	hoRSeS	424 ·	RaiNweaR
377	·	My CoKe	401	·	RuST	425 ·	uNReaL
378	·	MaKe oFF	402	·	ReSiN	426 ·	RaNCH
379	·	MaKeuP	403	·	heRoiSM	427 ·	RiNK
380	·	MuFFS	404	·	RaCeR	428 ·	RuN oFF
381	·	MiFFeD	405	·	wReStLe (silent t)	429 ·	RaiNBow
382	·	MuFFiN	406	·	RoSe itCH (silent t)	430 ·	aRMieS

431	·	heRMiT	455	·	RoyaL Law	479	·	RuGBy
432	·	aiRMaN	456	·	ReLiSH	480	·	ReFuSe
433	·	heaR MaMa	457	·	ReLiC	481	·	RiVeT
434	·	aRMoR	458	·	weRewoLF	482	·	RaViNe
435	·	aiRMaiL	459	·	eaRLoBe	483	·	waR FaMe
436	·	RuMMaGe	460	·	aRCHeS	484	·	ReFeRee
437	·	ReMaKe	461	·	RatCheT (silent t)	485	·	RiFLe
438	·	ReMoVe	462	·	uRCHiN	486	·	RaVaGe
439	·	RaMP	463	·	Raw CHaMois (silent s)	487	·	Raw FiG
440	·	hoRRoRS	464	·	RiCHeR	488	·	ReViVe
441	·	RewaRD	465	·	RiTuaL (ch sound)	489	·	RouGH uP
442	·	ReRuN	466	·	ReJudGe (silent d)	490	·	RoBeS
443	·	RewaRM	467	·	ReSHaKe	491	·	RaBBiT
444	·	RewiReR	468	·	aRCH Foe	492	·	ReoPeN
445	·	RuRaL	469	·	waRSHiP	493	·	aiR BooM
446	·	ReRuSH	470	·	RaGS	494	·	RePaiR
447	·	RewoRK	471	·	RacKeT	495	·	RiPPLe
448	·	ReaRView	472	·	RaCCooN	496	·	wiRe hiBaCHi
449	·	wiRe RoPe	473	·	waR GaMe	497	·	RePacK
450	·	haiRLeSS	474	·	RaKeR	498	·	RePaVe
451	·	RoyaLTy	475	·	ReCoiL	499	·	RiP uP
452	·	aiRLiNe	476	·	RicK SHaw	500	·	LaSSoeS
453	·	heiRLooM	477	·	ReCooK	501	·	LoST
454	·	RuLeR	478	·	aRChiVe	502	·	LeSSoN

503	LeaSe Me	527	LiNK	551	weLL-heeLeD
504	LaSeR	528	LiNe oFF	552	aLoha haLLoweeN
505	Low SaiL	529	LiNe uP	553	hauL heLiuM
506	aLLey SaGe	530	LiMbS (silent b)	554	LowLieR
507	iLL SoCK	531	a La MoDe	555	aLL LoyaL
508	aLoha houSewiFe	532	LeMoN	556	whaLe LodGe
509	LiSP	533	yeLLow MeMo	557	LiLaC
510	LeTTuCe	534	iLL MayoR	558	Low LiFe
511	Low TiDe	535	aLL-MaLe	559	LuLLaBy
512	LighTeN	536	LiMe-waSH	560	LodGeS (silent d)
513	yuLeTiMe	537	wooL haMMocK	561	wooLSHeD
514	LaDDeR	538	LyMPH (f sound)	562	LoTioN (sh sound)
515	LaDLe	539	LaMP	563	haLL CHiMe
516	LaTe CHow	540	waLRuS	564	wheeL CHaiR
517	iLL DoG	541	LaRD	565	LuSHLy
518	LeaDoFF	542	LeaRN	566	Lei CHa-CHa
519	hiLLToP	543	aLaRM	567	LoGiC
520	LeNS	544	hoLLeReR	568	aLLey CHeF
521	LiNT	545	LauReL	569	oiL JoB
522	LiNeN	546	LaRGe	570	LeGS
523	hoLy NaMe	547	LaRK	571	LiQuiD
524	LuNaR	548	LaRVa	572	LaGooN
525	LiNeaL	549	LayeR-uP	573	LeGuMe (vegetable)
526	LauNCH	550	oiL weLLS	574	LoGGeR

575 ·	aLCohoL	599 ·	LaP uP	623 ·	CHow aNeMia
576 ·	LuGGaGe	600 ·	JuiCeS	624 ·	CHiNa waRe
577 ·	oiL CaKe	601 ·	CHeST	624 ·	CHaNNeL
578 ·	aLCoVe	602 ·	CHoSeN	626 ·	CHaNGe
579 ·	LooK uP	603 ·	ChooSe Me	627 ·	JuNK
580 ·	LoaVeS	604 ·	CHaSeR	628 ·	SHy NePHew
581 ·	LoFT	605 ·	CHiSeL	629 ·	CHiN-uP
582 ·	LiVe iN	606 ·	CHewS SHoe	630 ·	CHiMeS
583 ·	iLL FaMe	607 ·	CHeeSe Cow	631 ·	SHaMeD
584 ·	LiVeR	608 ·	CHaSe oFF	632 ·	CHiMNey
585 ·	LeVeL	609 ·	JuiCe uP	633 ·	witCH MeMo
586 ·	LaViSH	610 ·	SHeeTS	634 ·	SHiMMeR
587 ·	LiVe oaK	611 ·	SHaDeD	635 ·	SHe MuLe
588 ·	LeaVe oFF	612 ·	SHowDowN	636 ·	GyM SHoe
589 ·	LiFe Buoy	613 ·	SHow TiMe	637 ·	haSH MucK
590 ·	aLPS	614 ·	CHeaTeR	638 ·	huGe MuFF
591 ·	LeaPeD	615 ·	SHuTTLe	639 ·	JuMP
592 ·	aLBiNo	616 ·	JeT SHoe	640 ·	CHeRRieS
593 ·	aLBuM	617 ·	watCH DoG (silent t)	641 ·	CHaRioT
594 ·	LaBoR	618 ·	SHuToFF	642 ·	CHuRN
595 ·	LaBeL	619 ·	SHuT uP	643 ·	GeRM
596 ·	Law BadGe	620 ·	oCeaNS (sh sound)	644 ·	CHeeReR
597 ·	Law BooK	621 ·	SHaNTy	645 ·	SHRiLL (whistle)
598 ·	aLL BeeF	622 ·	GeNuiNe	646 ·	CHuRCH

647	SHaRK	679	CHicK-Pea	703	ChaSM (k sound)
648	SHeRiFF	680	CHieFS	704	GeySeR
649	SHuRB	681	SHaFT	705	CaStLe (silent t)
650	SHeLLS	682	CHiFFoN	706	oaK SaSH
651	CHiLD	683	CHieF haM	707	GooSe eGG
652	CHow LiNe	684	SHiVeR	708	KiSS oFF
653	SHaLoM	685	SHoVeL	709	GaZeBo
654	JeweLRy	686	CHew FudGe	710	KiTeS
655	JeLLy oiL	687	eaCH FaKe	711	CaDeT
656	GeoLoGy	688	SHoVe oFF	712	CoTToN
657	SHeLLaC	689	SHoVe uP	713	KiD Me
658	SHeLF	690	GyPSey	714	CaTeR
659	JaLoPy	691	aSHPiT	715	CuDDLe
660	CHa-CHaS	692	wiSHBoNe	716	CoTTaGe
661	JoSHeD	693	huGe BoMb	717	heCTiC
662	SHoeSHiNe	694	SHoPPeR	718	oCTaVe (music)
663	huGe CHiMe	695	CHaPeL	719	CuTuP
664	CHeSHiRe	696	CHew PeaCH	720	CoiNS
665	CHew CHiLi	697	SHoePacK	721	CaNDy
666	CHoo-CHoo waSH	698	CHoP oFF	722	CaNNoN
667	huGe CHicK	699	SHaPe-uP	723	eCoNoMy
668	SHy CHeF	700	KiSSeS	724	CaNaRy
669	SHe SHeeP	701	CaSSeTTe	725	CaNaL
678	SHocK waVe	702	CaSiNo	726	GuN-SHy

727 ·	eGGNoG	751 ·	CLeaT	775 ·	GoGGLe
728 ·	CoNVoy	752 ·	CLowN	776 ·	eGG CaSH
729 ·	CaNoPy	753 ·	CoLuMn (silent n)	777 ·	wicK CaKe
730 ·	GaMeS	754 ·	CoLLaR	778 ·	KicKoFF
731 ·	CoMeT	755 ·	CoaL oiL	779 ·	eGGCuP
732 ·	KiMoNo	756 ·	CoLLeGe	780 ·	CaFeS
733 ·	Key MeMo	757 ·	CLocK	781 ·	GiFT
734 ·	CaMeRa	758 ·	GLoVe	782 ·	CoFFiN
735 ·	CaMeL	759 ·	CLuB	783 ·	eGG FoaM
736 ·	weaK iMaGe	760 ·	GauGeS	784 ·	GoPHer (f sound)
737 ·	CoMiC	761 ·	GadGeT (silent d)	785 ·	GaVeL
738 ·	KeyMoVe	762 ·	CuSHioN	786 ·	hoGFiSH
739 ·	CaMP	763 ·	hooKy CHuM	787 ·	Key FaKe
740 ·	CRoSS	764 ·	CaSHieR	788 ·	GooF oFF
741 ·	CaRRoT	765 ·	eGGSHeLL	789 ·	CouGH uP (f sound)
742 ·	CoRN	766 ·	Go SHuSH	790 ·	CaBS
743 ·	CReaM	767 ·	hoG JocKey	791 ·	CuPiD
744 ·	CRieR	768 ·	hocK CHeVy	792 ·	CaBiN
745 ·	CoRRaL	769 ·	CaSHBoy	793 ·	hicK PoeM
746 ·	CRaSH	770 ·	KicKS	794 ·	CoPieR
747 ·	CoRK	771 ·	CocKaToo	795 ·	Cue BaLL
748 ·	GRaVe	772 ·	CoCooN	796 ·	CaBBaGe
749 ·	CRiB	773 ·	hocKey GaMe	797 ·	hocKey PucK
750 ·	CLawS	774 ·	CouGaR	798 ·	KeeP oFF

799 · CoBweB		823 · VeNoM		847 · FoRK	
800 · VaSeS		824 · VeNeeR		848 · FaR-oFF	
801 · VeST		825 · FuNNeL		849 · oVeRPay	
802 · ViSiNe (eye drops)		826 · VaNiSH		850 · FLeaS	
803 · FuSSy Ma		827 · V-NecK		851 · FLuTe	
804 · ViSoR		828 · heaVy NaVy		852 · VioLiN	
805 · FiZZLe		829 · eVeN uP		853 · FiLM	
806 · FiSH itCH (silent t)		830 · FaMouS		854 · FLaRe	
807 · PHySiC (f sound)		831 · VoMiT		855 · FueL oiL	
808 · FaCe-oFF		832 · FaMiNe		856 · FLuSH	
809 · oFFiCe Boy		833 · heaVy MaMa		857 · FLocK	
810 · VaTS		834 · FeMuR		858 · FLuFF	
811 · VoTeD		835 · FaMiLy		859 · FLiP	
812 · FaTTeN		836 · heaVy MeSH		860 · VoyaGeS	
813 · halF TiMe (silent l)		837 · heaVy MiKe		861 · oFFSHooT	
814 · FighTeR		838 · waVe MoVe		862 · FaSHioN	
815 · FiDDLe		839 · VaMP		863 · halF GeM (silent l)	
816 · FooD SHow		840 · FiReS		864 · oFFSHoRe	
817 · FaTiGue		841 · FoRT		865 · FaCiaL (sh sound)	
818 · PHoTo Fee		842 · FeRN		866 · halF JewiSH (silent l)	
819 · FeD uP		843 · FaRM		867 · FiSHhooK	
820 · FeNCe		844 · FRyeR		868 · hiVe JiVe	
821 · FaiNT		845 · FRiLL		869 · halFway CHuBBy	
822 · FuN heN		846 · FoRGe		870 · FiGS	

871 ·	aVoCaDo	895 ·	FeeBLe	919 ·	PuT uP
872 ·	aFGhaN	896 ·	halF PaGe	920 ·	BuNNieS
873 ·	VaCuuM	897 ·	halFBacK	921 ·	PaiNT
874 ·	FiGuRe	898 ·	halF PayoFF	922 ·	BuNioN
875 ·	VehiCLe	899 ·	halF·BiB	923 ·	PaNaMa
876 ·	heaVy CouCH	900 ·	BaSeS	924 ·	PioNeeR
877 ·	hi·Fi KayaK	901 ·	PoST	925 ·	PiNwheeL
878 ·	heaVy CouGH (f sound)	902 ·	PoiSoN	926 ·	BeNCH
879 ·	Fee CoPy	903 ·	BoSoM	927 ·	BuNK
880 ·	huFFy VoiCe	904 ·	PaSSeR	928 ·	haPPy NaVy
881 ·	ViViD	905 ·	PuZZLe	929 ·	PiN uP
882 ·	iVy ViNe	906 ·	PaSSaGe	930 ·	PoeMS
883 ·	hi·Fi FaMe	907 ·	BaSK	931 ·	BoMbeD (silent b)
884 ·	FeVeR	908 ·	PaSSiVe	932 ·	BowMaN
885 ·	halF VoLLey	909 ·	Pea SouP	933 ·	oBey MaMa
886 ·	waVe eFFiGy	910 ·	BooTS	934 ·	BeaMeR
887 ·	heaVy FiG	911 ·	PoTaTo	935 ·	PuMMeL
888 ·	weaVe FiVe	912 ·	BuTToN	936 ·	hoP MuCH
889 ·	halF FiB (silent l)	913 ·	BoTToM	937 ·	wiPe haMMocK
890 ·	V.i.P.'S	914 ·	BuTTeR	938 ·	hiP MoVie
891 ·	hooFBeaT	915 ·	BoTTLe	939 ·	PuMP
892 ·	halF oPeN	916 ·	PoTaSH	940 ·	PuRSe
893 ·	oFF BeaM	917 ·	PaDDocK	941 ·	PaRaDe
894 ·	VaPoR	918 ·	PaiD oFF	942 ·	BRaiN

943	-	BRooM	967	-	Pay CHecK	983	-	Pie FoaM
944	-	BRiaR	968	-	haPPy JayVee	984	-	BeaVeR
945	-	PeaRL	969	-	hoBBy SHoP	985	-	BuFFaLo
946	-	PoRCH	970	-	BooKS	986	-	Bay VoyaGe
947	-	PoRK	971	-	BucKeT	987	-	BiVouaC
948	-	BRieF	972	-	PeCaN	988	-	PuFF oFF
949	-	BuRP	973	-	PyGMy	989	-	PuFF uP
950	-	PiLLS	974	-	PucKeR	990	-	PaPooSe
951	-	BeLT	975	-	PicKLe	991	-	PuPPeT
952	-	PLaNe	976	-	PacKaGe	992	-	BaBooN
953	-	BLooM	977	-	PeaCocK	993	-	hiP PoeM
954	-	BowLeR	978	-	PicK oFF	994	-	PePPeR
955	-	PooL haLL	979	-	PeeKaBoo	995	-	BuBBLe
956	-	PoLiSH	980	-	PaVeS	996	-	Pea PatCH (silent t)
957	-	PLaGue	981	-	PiVoT	997	-	PayBooK
958	-	BLuFF	982	-	BuFFooN	998	-	PoP oFF
959	-	BuLB	963	-	PaJaMa	999	-	PoP-UP
960	-	aPaCHeS	964	-	ButCHeR (silent t)	1000	-	DiSeaSeS
961	-	PoaCHeD	965	-	BuSHeL			
962	-	PiGeoN	966	-	BeaCH SHoe			

Doctor Memory™ Web Site

To enter the Doctor Memory™ web site go to:

http://www.doctormemory.com

Doctor Memory™ Products

All Dr. Memory™ products use the Lucas Learning System™ where visually reinforced association models make learning fun and easy. Dr. Memory™ teaches Learning That Lasts™. Please visit the web site at www.doctormemory.com for up-to-date information on the complete product line. Included are descriptions of the complete Learning That Lasts™ product line, as well as actual demonstrations. Excerpts of many of the products are available free of charge also. These revolutionary products available at doctormemory.com include the following:

Adult - Young Adult General Interest

Doctor Memory's™
Picture Perfect Spanish
A Survival Guide to Speaking Spanish

Doctor Memory's™ Learning That Lasts™ methodology is adapted to learn more than 600 "Survival" words required for basic communication of the Spanish language. Careful attention has been paid to insure that the most critical words are taught and that each word is associated with the English equivalent in a way that guarantees accurate pronunciation. In this course, the Spanish language is explored primarily through commonly used words. The addition of basic sentence structure, common phrases and sentences complete the materials; which are designed to prepare the reader to speak the Spanish language more thoroughly than that which is typically covered in a one-year Spanish foreign language course. In addition to teaching over 600 words this book teaches phrases, sentences and basic rules of sentence structure required to speak Spanish.

Doctor Memory's™
Comprehensive Picture Perfect Spanish
Your Reference to the Spanish Language

Doctor Memory's™ Learning That Lasts™ methodology is adapted to aid in the memorization of over 1,600 of the most commonly used Spanish words in this four-volume set. Careful attention has been paid to insure that each word is associated with the English equivalent in a way that guarantees accurate pronunciation. This comprehensive reference teaches words, more detailed grammar, basic sentence structure, conjugation of verbs and more while also exploring common phrases and sentences typical of the Spanish language.

Doctor Memory's™
Names and Faces Made Easy
The Fun and Easy Way to Remember People

The Jerry Lucas technique for remembering names and faces revealed! This unique product tailors Doctor Memory's™ Learning That Lasts™ methodology to aid in remembering the first and last names of those you meet. This method has enabled Mr. Lucas to meet, remember, and correctly pronounce the names of more than 500 people at a time in live studio audience environments. The technique has been successfully taught to hundreds of thousands of people, including numerous Fortune 500 companies. While based on teachings in the best selling The Memory Book, the material covered here is far more detailed and comprehensive. Previously available only through exclusive guest appearances and live seminars, this fun and easy technique can now be purchased in either a book or videotape format.

Doctor Memory's™
Learning How to Learn

Doctor Memory's™ unique learning methodology is taught in detail in this comprehensive follow-up to the best selling The Memory Book that was co-authored by Mr. Lucas in 1973. Learning How to Learn teaches the reader how to apply the Learning That Lasts™ methodology to any subject matter. All eight tools of learning developed by Jerry Lucas are taught in detail. Hundreds of applications are discussed and illustrated. Taking almost 30 years to compile, this is the most innovative and comprehensive learning instruction book ever written!

Childrens' Educational Products

Doctor Memory's™
Ready Set Remember
States & Capitals and The Presidents

Doctor Memory's™ unique Learning That Lasts™ methodology is adapted to children's social studies to instruct the memorization of the states, their capitals, and the presidents of the United States. This book with accompanying audio cassettes will guide the learning process and is ideal for either self-directed students or for use in a more traditional classroom environment. An interactive computer based training version is currently under development and will include animation to assist in learning the geographic location of each state as well.

Doctor Memory's™
Grammar Graphics & Picture Perfect
Punctuation - Volume I

Designed for students, teachers, and adults, this first in an eight volume series includes fun and unique pictures that "lock in" the application and usage of the fundamental rules of grammar and punctuation. Doctor Memory's™ revolutionary learning methodology makes even grammar and punctuation fun and easy to learn!

Doctor Memory's™
Ready Set Remember The Times Tables

Doctor Memory's™ unique learning methodology is adapted to assist in the memorization of the times tables from 2x2 to 12x12. This book teaches a simple and fun method of seeing numbers tangibly. Each problem is then pictured in a unique way in order to differentiate it from the others.

For Families that Wish to Study the Bible Together

Doctor Memory's™
Bible Memory Made Easy

Doctor Memory's™ unique Learning That Lasts™ methodology is adapted to help students of any age to better understand and remember Bible facts in this eight volume video tape series. Students learn the Books of the Bible, the Ten Commandments, the Fruit of the Spirit, selected Bible verses, Gifts of the Spirit, and much more. Just by watching and listening you will learn and remember many of the important teachings of the Bible!

Doctor Memory's™
Bible Basics

A fun and easy way for the whole family to learn together! Doctor Memory's™ unique Learning That Lasts™ methodology is adapted to help students of any age to better understand and remember Bible facts. Students learn the Books of the Bible, the Ten Commandments, the Fruit of the Spirit, Gifts of the Spirit, and much more as they discover how fun and easy learning can be with this book and two accompanying audio cassettes.

Doctor Memory's™
View-A-Verse™
Bible Verse Learning Program

Doctor Memory's™ unique Learning That Lasts™ methodology has been adapted to help students of all ages memorize Bible verses simply and easily by seeing the verses tangibly on learning cards that can be reviewed much like everyday flash cards. However, since the verses are pictured and associated with common everyday objects, two amazing things will happen. First, the verses are easily learned and memorized. Second, when the commonly used everyday objects are seen in real life, the verses will be automatically remembered bringing the Word of God to mind throughout the day! Learning Bible verses has never been so easy or fun.

Soon to be Released Products for Reading and Writing

Doctor Memory's™
Alphabet Friends™

Doctor Memory's™ unique Learning That Lasts™ methodology is adapted to children's reading and writing in this alphabet and phonetic sound recognition program. Each letter is pictured graphically so as to guarantee the student learns to recognize and write upper and lower case shapes. All possible sounds made by each letter are pictured tangibly, so the student can see and never forget them. This revolutionary product is the first ever published that allows students to actually see all of the sounds tangibly. The student also learns how to read words that include the basic sounds. An interactive computer based training version will be available as well as traditional workbooks with instruction manuals.

Doctor Memory's
See and Know Picture Words™ Reading Program

Doctor Memory's™ unique Learning That Lasts™ methodology is adapted to children's reading in this sight word recognition program.. Two hundred twenty words (220) make up 75% of what students will read through the sixth grade and 50% of all words an adult will read throughout their lifetime. All of these "sight" words are pictured graphically to guarantee the student learns the words permanently. Recognition of all significant sounds made within the English language are also taught, including silent letters, letters that change sounds, and the common consonant sound combinations such as "ch" and "th". After completing this course the student will tangibly see and know every sound in the English language while being able to read and pronounce new words. Doctor Memory's™ Alphabet Friends™ is a pre-requisite to this program which will be available in a computer based training version or a more traditional workbook with accompanying instruction.

Give the gift of Learning That Lasts™
to your family, friends, and colleagues.

Check with your favorite bookstore or place your order
by logging onto our website.

www.doctormemory.com

FOR MAIL ORDERS, PLEASE COMPLETE THIS ORDER FORM:

☐**YES**, I want _____ copies of **Learning How to Learn** at $31.95 each, plus $5.95 shipping and handling for U.S. orders (or $9.70 shipping and handling for foreign orders). Non-U.S. orders must be accompanied by a postal money order in U.S. funds. Please allow 3-4 weeks for delivery within the United States and 6 weeks for delivery elsewhere.

**Call the toll-free phone number noted below
for assistance with completing this order form.**
(Please note: We cannot accept cash, personal checks or C.O.D.'s.)

Check One:

☐Money Order or ☐Cashier's Check (payable to Lucas Educational Systems, Inc.)
☐Visa   ☐Master Card   ☐Discover   ☐American Express

Learning How to Learn @ $31.95 per book   = $_____
Add appropriate shipping charge (as noted above)   = $_____
Add applicable sales tax*   = $_____
TOTAL PAYMENT   = $_____
Include sales tax where required.

Ship to: (please print)
Name_____
Organization_____
Street Address_____
City/State/Zip_____
Phone_____E-Mail_____
Credit Card #_____Exp. Date_____
Signature_____

*For mailing instructions call our
toll free order hot line:*
1-877-479-6463

1-930853-02-5